COLLEGE
WITH A CAUSE

COLLEGE WITH A CAUSE

A HISTORY OF CONCORDIA TEACHERS COLLEGE

BY ALFRED J. FREITAG

CONCORDIA TEACHERS COLLEGE

River Forest, Illinois

PRINTED BY CONCORDIA PUBLISHING HOUSE

SAINT LOUIS, MISSOURI

Foreword

When Alfred Freitag was commissioned to write COLLEGE WITH A CAUSE, Concordia Teachers College said that it considered the publication of a history of the college an important part of its centennial observance.

When a college has been engaged in the single task of teacher education for a century, it needs to assess its performance in relation to the educational movements of that age. It needs also to understand its past so that it may have an awareness of its resources for a fresh and intelligent launching out into the deep of the future. One cannot face the future with confidence unless he understands the past with gratitude.

This publication is made possible and is being sent to the college and university libraries in the United States of America by virtue of a generous grant from the Aid Association for Lutherans, Appleton, Wisconsin. We commend and thank the Aid Association for Lutherans for this act of fraternal benevolence.

We hope that COLLEGE WITH A CAUSE will also become a tribute to The Lutheran Church — Missouri Synod, which has for a century supported this "cause" devotedly and generously. These Lutherans believe that the Lutheran school has a distinctive contribution to make to the society in which it lives and labors.

M. L. KOEHNEKE
President, Concordia Teachers College
River Forest, Illinois

Preface

This history was written to commemorate the first century of Concordia Teachers College in the service of Christian education in The Lutheran Church — Missouri Synod.

The research was done in connection with a dissertation presented to the faculty of the School of Education of the University of Southern California in partial satisfaction of the requirements for the doctor's degree in education. COLLEGE WITH A CAUSE is the first documented history of Concordia Teachers College, River Forest, Ill.

Writing a survey history covering 100 years presents numerous problems of inclusion and exclusion. No doubt some readers will find areas to which more time and space could have been given. There were individuals whose contributions to the college were significant but to whom little space, if any, could be devoted because of limitations of time and space. It was not possible to give adequate attention to the development of nonteaching services and personnel who also have made many contributions to Concordia's growth. The author is well aware of the fact that he has not exhausted all the sources. Possibly in the future certain phases of Concordia's history can be expanded in other studies.

In a century Concordia Teachers College has grown in the service of one cause — training teachers for the church, from very humble beginnings to a school that today graduates more elementary teachers than any other institution of higher learning in Illinois. The college has been blessed by God with capable and dedicated faculties and with gifted administrators who had vision and courage to build for the future.

Acknowledgments

The writer gratefully acknowledges the suggestions and criticisms received from various persons who have been helpful in carrying out this project. Dr. Edward H. LaFranchi, Dr. Robert L. Brackenbury, and Dr. Earl V. Pullias of the School of Education of the University of Southern California, the author's doctoral committee, were especially helpful in guiding the preparation of the dissertation.

The author wishes to acknowledge with thanks the encouragement and help given by President Martin L. Koehneke, who made all college records available and in many other ways made this study possible. Special thanks are also due to Miss Hildegarde Weiss, secretary to President Koehneke, who has served at Concordia since 1942. Her help in making certain archival materials and records available, as well as her assistance in supplying various data, were of great benefit. Dr. Theodore Kuehnert, professor emeritus and former archivist, also gave much help and encouragement, as did also Dr. Wilfred F. Kruse, the registrar, Dr. Albert V. Maurer, Prof. Daniel E. Poellot, Dr. Frank B. Miller, and Dr. Carl L. Waldschmidt, the academic dean.

River Forest and Addison alumni who responded to the author's request for information included Paul I. J. Bachmann (who as a student took many pictures of the 1914 fire), Dr. Herbert D. Bruening, Dr. Arthur W. Gross, Dr. Herbert H. Gross, Walter Hartkopf, William A. Helmkamp, Edward C. Hinz, Joan Kaufmann, Frank Klenner, Barbara (nee Blatt) and Charles Marousek, Edwin T. Pingel, Adolph C. Rosenwinkel, Alwin Roschke, Jacob Schmidt, Henry S. Steinweg, and Henry Waldschmidt.

The friendly interest and help of the Rev. August Suelflow of St. Louis, curator of Concordia Historical Institute, and his staff (especially Mrs. Anna Dorn) aided greatly in discovering new sources of this history. Much good advice and assistance were received from the late Dr. A. C. Stellhorn and from Dr. Carl S. Meyer of Concordia Seminary, St. Louis, Mo. Dr. Elmer Foelber and the Rev. Erich B. Allwardt of Concordia Publishing House, St. Louis, Mo., also gave valuable assistance in editing the manuscript.

Dr. Albert G. Huegli, now vice-president for academic affairs at Valparaiso University, who was the first dean of students at Concordia and the second academic dean, gave some very valuable data and "leads" in a special interview. It was also the author's privilege to have a personal interview with the late Dr. Alfred F. Schmieding, Concordia's first academic dean, who gave valuable insights into the problems of the last 40 years. Thanks are due also to the Rev. Richard H. Raedeke, formerly pastor of St. Paul's Church, Addison, for permitting the author to examine old records of the congregation; also to the Rev. Daniel W. Fuelling, pastor of Zion Church, Bensenville (the original church home of the college), for examination of the old records there and for a tour of Zion Cemetery, where President Lindemann and other Concordia pioneers are buried.

The author is thankful also to Mr. F. H. Schmitt, son of the late Dr. F. H. Schmitt, Concordia's first business manager, for making some of his father's reminiscences available; to Misses Mary and Elfrieda Miller for allowing the use of the late Dr. Albert H. Miller's (Concordia's first registrar) scrapbook, and to Mrs. Paula (nee Beck) Eggers, daughter of the late Dr. Albert Beck (founder of Concordia touring choirs) for granting permission to use her father's memoirs.

One of the major problems encountered was that of distance of the college and other sources from the author's home in California, but here, too, many gave a helping hand. Thanks to Mr. Arnold Johnson, who had the May 30, 1932 *Spectator* duplicated *in toto* for the author. This issue contained a longer undocumented historical sketch of the college. Invaluable assistance was rendered by the author's wife, Doris, in checking and rechecking data, and by members of his office staff at Lutheran High School. Grateful acknowledgment is hereby also made to the Lutheran High School Board of Directors, whose great kindness and understanding made it possible for the author to do this work.

The book is dedicated to all who have served Concordia and to all who have gone out into the teaching ministry from her to build excellence in Christian education. Built on faith in a great mission, Concordia may face its second century with courage and confidence.

Soli Deo gloria!

Contents

PART I

PRELUDE TO A CENTURY

Introduction

The purpose of this study is to provide a documented narrative of factors relating to the origin and development of Concordia Teachers College, River Forest, Ill., from 1864 to 1964. It will examine the objectives of the school to ascertain if there has been a change of thrust from its original aims, and also to note how its teacher education program related to normal school and teacher college development in the United States.

The study will provide some historical source material for students of the history of Lutheran education and of teacher education in general in the United States. It is hoped that it may be useful for administrators, faculty, students, alumni, and others. Special services of the college to the church will be noted. Finally, it will serve as a special memorial in commemoration of the centennial year, celebrated in 1964.

Concordia Teachers College is the first of the Synod's colleges devoted exclusively to teacher training, and historically the fourth of the 16 schools, colleges, and seminaries now operated.by The Lutheran Church — Missouri Synod. Founded in Addison, Ill., in 1864, it was relocated in River Forest, a suburb of Chicago, in 1913.

Most of the records of the first 50 years of the school were lost in a conflagration that destroyed the administration building on Feb. 28, 1914. Data of this period had to be pieced together from many other sources including synodical publications, reports, periodicals, church records, and programs, as well as minutes of the board of control and faculty, letters, newspaper clippings, and reminiscences of alumni.

The archives of the college contained a considerable amount of unclassified material, all of which was examined. More material was found at Concordia Historical Institute, St. Louis, the main archival repository for the Synod. Its quarterly magazine has been very helpful in source material.

Study of the data necessitated a considerable amount of translation since in the earlier years many of the official records were in German, the minutes of the board of control and the faculty even being written in German script. Early publications were also in German. This study will attempt to make these data more accessible.

In a historical study covering a whole century it was necessary to reduce or exclude altogether many details which in themselves are very interesting but are not essential to carry out the major purpose. To include all the biographical data even of the major personalities involved is beyond the scope of this work. The general history of the communities in which the college was situated will not be reported except as it affects the establishment and growth of the college.

The history of Concordia Teachers College, River Forest, Ill., represents a vital portion of the history of The Lutheran Church — Missouri Synod in the development of one of its historic major objectives — providing for the Christian education of its children and youth. From the time it was organized in 1847, the Synod has always felt a great concern and responsibility to establish schools for the preparation and training of pastors and teachers to serve its parishes. This concern for Christian education was a heritage of the Reformation, which stressed the close relationship between religion and education, and specifically between church and school.

In a number of his writings Martin Luther emphasized the establishment of schools, doing his best to convince civil authorities, the public, and the church of the importance of education. Although his primary concern was for the church, he was deeply concerned for the welfare of the state as well; his writings reflect his belief in the necessity for popular education. Painter declares that popular education was the outgrowth of the Reformation.[1]

As the philosopher Horne said: "Following the Reformation there was a great revival of interest in the common schools. When it was judged by Luther and his followers that men must save themselves religiously by exercise of faith and private judgment after the reading and study of the Bible, it was necessary that men must be educated to read, study and think. Without education the new element of individual liberty projected into human society could not have maintained itself." [2]

Arthur M. Ahlschwede, Executive Secretary of the Board for Higher Education, The Lutheran Church — Missouri Synod, pointed out in reference to Luther's concept of popular education: "The thesis that the Bible and the Catechism were to be placed in the hands of every Hans and Lisa had the inevitable corollary of universal education." [3] Of course, what Luther had in mind was Christian education for all.

The Lutheran Church — Missouri Synod has always believed with Luther that only the Christian school could minister adequately to the educational needs of children. Consequently a parish school system has been developed and maintained to carry out the important goals of Christian education.

Lutherans consider the public school necessary and salutary, support it faithfully, and many send their children to it. They recognize, however, that the public school perforce is limited in preparing its children for their major mission in life, since it is not able to teach Christianity, based on the revelation of God in the Bible, as a way of life. [4]

Therefore the Synod has always supported its own system of elementary schools, as well as its own colleges and seminaries. It also has a number of high schools, all of which have been expanding with the needs and growth of the church.

Literature on the History of Teacher Education in America

In writing the history of Concordia Teachers College a general overview of the development of teacher education in America proved to be both interesting and helpful. Although Concordia is primarily a church college with a specific purpose, its development was also affected by the development of education in the cultural milieu of a rapidly growing and expanding country. Several important works were studied to gain the necessary view of this development.

In 1891 John P. Gordy, professor of pedagogy at Ohio University, wrote *Rise and Growth of the Normal School Idea in the United States*. In this treatise he traced the development of teacher training from 1789, when an article appeared in the *Massachusetts Magazine* which called for more thoroughly trained teachers. It was the earliest suggestion of this kind by an American educator that Gordy was able to find. [5] It proposed that institutions prepare young men for "school keeping" and that there be a board of examiners to see if they were qualified after training. [6]

In his introduction Gordy expressed wonder that educators could go along for so many years with the notion that the only preparation required of a teacher is a knowledge of the subjects he undertakes to teach. [7]

Gordy gave a very interesting account of the growing need for trained teachers and the gradual rise of a true teaching profession. He traced the training of teachers in the academies of New York through the first normal schools in Lexington, Mass., and St. Cloud, Minn., and discussed the establishment of chairs of pedagogy at the various colleges, beginning at the University of Iowa in 1873, followed by the University of Michigan in 1879 and of Wisconsin in 1881.

In describing the struggle for recognition of professional teacher training, he concluded:

"To break down the wall of conservation that surrounds our colleges, to secure from them the same respect for the profession of teaching which they give to the professions of law and medicine, would be to effect the most important advances which have ever been made in the history of education or the world." [8]

Jessie M. Pangburn's *The Evolution of the American Teachers College,* a doctoral study of the development of teacher education from 1890 to 1930, was written 90 years after the first state normal school was established.[9]

The author traced factors conditioning changes in teacher preparation, pointing out that it took more than 60 years before any one of the normal schools had advanced its standards sufficiently to be considered a teachers college in the modern sense. The conversion of a large majority of normal schools had taken place since 1920. Within the four decades from 1890 to 1930 the preparatory school for teachers had been changed from one of secondary rank to one of collegiate rank, and a few had added a graduate program.

The normal school and the teachers college are an outgrowth of gradual awareness of the public that there must be some means of preparing teachers to carry out public policies in education.

Among the factors which conditioned gradual change in teacher preparation described by Pangburn are:

1. Local control of public education and the changing needs of society requiring better preparation of pupils.

2. Rising qualifications for teacher certification and accreditation.

3. Centralization of administrative control on all levels including state, county, and local.

4. Inadequate supply of teachers.

5. Expansion of the school systems, due to more wealth and leisure, and compulsory attendance laws.

6. Qualitative changes in curriculum, demanding more and better teacher preparation.

7. Tremendous growth of secondary schools, requiring more and better trained teachers.

8. Rise of accreditation with its emphasis on higher standards.[10]

The emphasis in Pangburn's study is on the adjustments made by 14 representative teachers colleges in respect to the development of curricula and changes in teaching personnel over the 40-year period 1890–1930.

In 1890 the institutions giving teacher preparation were normal schools (state and private), city high schools with teacher training classes (usually a postgraduate year), departments in colleges and universities, and the New York College for the Training of Teachers.

Normal schools admitted students of secondary rank who had completed elementary school. They attempted to give fuller training in elementary subject matter, secondary academic studies, and professional studies including history of education, science of education, methods in elementary subjects, and mental science.[11]

Three aspects of curriculum development were brought out in the development of normal schools to teachers colleges:

1. The expansion of curricular offerings, specialized curricula, elementary and high school, etc.

2. The modification of content.

3. The rise of new curriculum goals, degrees, university recognition of normal school products, accreditation.

Michigan State Normal School at Ypsilanti is said to be the first normal school to become a modern teachers college with a 4-year curriculum in 1903, granting the first degree in 1905. By 1932, 75 percent of all teacher trainees were in teachers colleges.

The National Education Association had a Department of Normal Schools in 1889. In 1902 the North Central Council of Normal School Presidents was formed. This became the American Association of Teachers Colleges, which brought pressure for improvement on all members.

From 1915 on there was an increase in the use of fact-finding studies to help determine standards, policies, and programs for teachers colleges, such as the Commonwealth Study and the Teacher Training Survey of the United States Office of Education.

Gleanings from Various Histories of Education

Several general histories of education were consulted in order to gain understanding of social forces that influenced the development of education in this country, including teacher training, and also to view the total cultural pattern in which Concordia Teachers College was established and in which it developed. Among these were *The School in the American Social Order*, by Edwards and Richey,[12] *The American Teacher*, by Elsbree,[13] *The Story of Education*, by Atkinson and Maleska,[14] and *The Education of Teachers: Consensus and Conflict*, by Hodenfield and Stinnett.[15]

The first normal school was a private institution established by the Rev. Samuel R. Hall in Concord, Vt., in 1823. It was a 3-year school which reviewed elementary subjects and taught some secondary subjects. Opportunity for the observation of teaching was provided, and in the final year a subject called the "Art of Teaching" was introduced. Hall wrote one of the first professional books for teachers in America in 1829, entitled *Lectures on School Keeping*.[16]

Prussia, early in the 19th century, was the first nation to establish a state-controlled system for the training of teachers. Teachers were regarded as public officials; this served to promote professionalism.[17]

By 1825 American educators had become acquainted with the Prussian system of teachers seminaries. Many articles were written by Americans who had traveled and studied in Germany, describing the advantages of the system and recommending it for America. Such articles and many lectures very slowly began to rouse the public out of its apathy, which was still resting on the assumption that teaching required no professional knowledge.[18]

Some states, such as New York in 1834, provided funds for teachers classes in academies to provide teachers for the common schools.

During the 1820s and 1830s more private teachers seminaries were established. It became increasingly apparent that more of them had to be established and supported by the states because the private institutions did not have the resources to provide adequately for the needs of the country for trained teachers.

Massachusetts was the first state to establish normal schools, opening the first one in Lexington on July 3, 1839. The establishment of this school was brought about by the joint efforts of several prominent educators led by Horace Mann, who had persuaded a close friend to contribute $10,000 on a matching basis with the legislature.

Initially there was much opposition which had to be overcome. However, by 1860 there were 12 public normal schools in the United States, six private ones, and one city normal school (in St. Louis). These normal schools were very modest, very little better than secondary schools, and very poorly attended. The Lexington school, which was restricted to girls, opened with three students and one instructor. By the end of the first year the enrollment was 25, and 15 years later it was only 35.

The principal of the Lexington school was Cyrus Peirce. He also taught as many as 17 subjects in a year, besides supervising a model school, serving as demonstration teacher and janitor, and developing professional materials to be taught in the normal school. The program was for one year and included: (1) review of the "Common Branches" (spelling, reading, writing, grammar, and arithmetic), (2) advanced studies such as geometry, algebra, natural, intellectual, and moral philosophy, and natural history as time permitted, (3) the physical, mental, and moral development of children, (4) the science and art of teaching each of the common branches, (5) the art of school government, and (6) practice in teaching and governing a model school.

By the beginning of the 20th century the normal schools had weathered many a storm of opposition.[19] They had become a definite part of the American system of education, training not only elementary but also high school teachers. Gradually it became necessary to lengthen the training period in order to meet demands of accrediting agencies that high school teachers have college degrees, and to raise admission standards.

In 1890, 65 percent of normal school enrollees had entered directly from elementary school, and only about 20 percent had high school diplomas. A normal school training course lasted from one to four years. Rarely, if ever, did a normal school offer more than two years beyond high school.[20] By the turn of the century there was a definite trend on the part of normal schools to become 4-year degree-granting teachers colleges. Colleges and universities were not able to provide enough secondary schoolteachers to meet the ever-growing needs.

In 1908 the Department of Normal Schools of the National Education Association recommended high school graduation as an admission requirement to the normal school. By 1930 this goal had been practically met. In the meantime pressure for extension of the curriculum to include more liberal arts was mounting, and the name "normal school" began to be dropped in favor of "teachers college." In 1920 there were 46 teachers colleges and 137 state normal schools. Eight years later there were 137 teachers colleges and 69 normal schools. By 1933 the number was 146 of the former and 30 of the latter.

The needs of rural schools were especially acute and led to the establishment of a normal training program in many high schools since regular normal schools could not provide enough teachers. Between 1910 and 1925 24 states used this means to supply their rural schools. The number had decreased to seven by 1933, when the normal schools and colleges began to catch up with the demand.

Normal schools had been started by city school systems, beginning in the Civil War years, to help supply the growing urban need for teachers. By 1930–31 80 percent of them had been closed because of the increase in teachers colleges.

In 1880 there had been 114 private and religious normal schools. Of these there were nine teachers colleges and 28 normal schools left by 1934. Elsbree reported in 1939 that, if the trends then apparent should continue, municipal and private teacher preparatory schools would be extinct before long.[21]

The universities and colleges also established departments of education after 1873. Between that date and 1881, Iowa, Michigan, and Wisconsin established professorships in education. By 1892 more than 30 universities had done so. By 1932 there were 593 deans of schools of education or heads of education departments.

In 1908 a canvass of 50 universities disclosed that only 16 of them required practice teaching and 20 did not offer it at all, while 14 offered it as an elective. By 1940 most teachers colleges and colleges of education required it, conducting their own schools.

By 1960 there were 1,133 teacher training institutions in the U. S., including 691 private and 320 public schools and colleges. Public institutions enrolled about two thirds of the students, however, and private institutions about one third.

Between 1950 and 1960 there was a steady changeover from state teachers colleges and normal schools to state colleges or universities. Today there is a definite trend away from the single-purpose colleges and universities. By 1960 all but 10 states required a degree as a minimum for certification of teachers.[22]

Private teacher education in America is 141 years old; state teacher education dates back 125 years. In this relatively short time teaching has become a profession, and although the patterns are still changing, it is certain that there will be further upgrading of teaching standards for higher-quality education.

The history of the teaching profession shows the same pattern of development seen in the development of other professions beginning with apprenticeship, and progressing with higher standards of education.

Notes

1. Franklin V. N. Painter, *Luther on Education* (Philadelphia: The Lutheran Publication Society, 1889. St. Louis: Concordia Publishing House, 1928), p. 82.

2. Herman H. Horne, *The Philosophy of Education* (New York: The Macmillan Company, 1927), p. 153.

3. Arthur M. Ahlschwede, "The Protestant Schools," *Phi Delta Kappan,* XLV (Dec. 1963), 136.

4. Victor C. Krause, ed., *Lutheran Elementary Schools in Action* (St. Louis: Concordia Publishing House, 1963), p. 9.

5. John P. Gordy, *Rise and Growth of the Normal School Idea in the United States,* Circular of Information, 1891, No. 8, Bureau of Education (Washington, D. C., 1891), p. 9.

6. Ibid., p. 10.

7. Ibid., p. 7.

8. Ibid., p. 142.

9. Jessie M. Pangburn, *The Evolution of the American Teachers College* (New York: Bureau of Publications, Teachers College, Columbia University, 1932), p. 1.

10. Ibid., pp. 2—13.

11. Ibid., p. 30.

12. Newton Edwards and Herman G. Richey, *The School in the American Social Order* (Boston: Houghton Mifflin Co., 1947).

13. Willard S. Elsbree, *The American Teacher* (New York: American Book Co., 1939).

14. Carroll Atkinson and Eugene T. Maleska, *The Story of Education* (Philadelphia and New York: Chilton Co., Book Division, 1962).

15. G. K. Hodenfield and Timothy M. Stinnett, *The Education of Teachers: Consensus and Conflict* (Englewood Cliffs, N. J.: Prentice-Hall, Inc., 1961).

16. Edwards and Richey, p. 417.

17. Atkinson and Maleska, p. 351.

18. Elsbree, p. 145.

19. Edwards and Richey, p. 419. Forms of opposition were — the academies, teachers who considered them an unwarranted reflection on themselves, opponents of public schools, and some legislators. In New York, where a normal school had been founded in 1844, apathy of the people and opposition of selfish factions succeeded in closing it in 1849 and a resumption of state aid to academies was begun.

20. Atkinson and Maleska, p. 353.

21. Elsbree, p. 330.

22. Hodenfield and Stinnett, p. 154.

Chapter 1

THE LUTHERAN CHURCH — MISSOURI SYNOD
AND ITS EDUCATIONAL SYSTEM

For a clearer understanding of the origin and development of Concordia Teachers College it will be helpful to examine portions of the history of The Lutheran Church — Missouri Synod and its aims in the establishment of Christian schools for all of its children. The Synod's basic purpose in founding Concordia Teachers College was to provide well-trained teachers for the Christian education and training of its children. In doing so the Synod acted on Luther's principle that schools are necessary for the welfare of both church and state. Its parochial school system developed as a unique feature in the history of education and religion in the United States.

The Missouri Synod was formed by several groups of German immigrants. Most prominent of these was a colony of about 600 Saxons who in 1839 arrived in St. Louis by way of New Orleans under the leadership of Pastor Martin Stephan.[1] They left their homeland and came to America partly for economic reasons and partly because they felt that in Germany they would be unable to maintain their pure confessionalism and transmit it to their children. In Article I of their emigration regulations they affirmed their orthodox confession on the basis of the Scriptures and the symbolical writings of the church as assembled in the Book of Concord of 1580

Contributing to the dissatisfaction of these Saxons with church conditions in Germany was the growth of rationalism (this means the rule of reason and implies the rejection of belief in divine revelation as represented by the Bible). Lutherans in Germany had been restless ever since the Prussian Union had been declared by Frederick William III. The Union was an effort to force Calvinistic and Lutheran churches to unite without having unity in doctrine. The free churches, which had remained independent of the state, registered a protest against the Union.[2]

Shortly after the Saxon group settled in St. Louis and Perry Co., Mo., leadership of the group was assumed by the Rev. Carl Ferdinand Wilhelm Walther, who was to become one of the great leaders in American Lutheranism. Under his leadership the individual congregation was established as the supreme authority in the church, based on democratic principles of operation, and the proper relationship implied in separation of church and state was defined. Both of these concepts were influenced by the ideal of religious liberty in America.

In 1844 Walther began publishing the *Lutheraner*. In this biweekly periodical he expounded the Lutheran confessional views to which the Saxons in America subscribed. The periodical is still published today, together with the *Lutheran Witness*, which is the official voice of The Lutheran Church — Missouri Synod. The *Lutheraner* was a strong contributing factor in uniting some of the scattered groups of Lutherans in the Middle West.

For safeguarding and maintaining the confessional character of the church Walther strongly advocated the establishment of church schools by individual congregations. By this means the educational process was to be kept under the control and supervision of the church. By his publications and his speeches he did all he could to promote Lutheran schools. He believed that if a congregation was not able to have a teacher, then the pastor must by all means teach.

As the *Lutheraner* was circulated, it provoked a considerable amount of correspondence between pastors in other parts of the country and Walther. Gradually the idea developed that it would be advisable to form a new synod which would be confessional in character. After a preliminary meeting and the adoption of a tentative constitution in Fort Wayne in 1846, the pastors of 12 congregations, plus 10 advisory pastors, four lay delegates, and two theological candidates, met in Chicago during the latter part of April and the first part of May 1847 and organized "The German Evangelical Lutheran Synod of Missouri, Ohio, and Other States," now The Lutheran Church — Missouri Synod.

In the constitution adopted during this meeting they recognized the importance of teacher training and the training of children in Lutheran schools. They planned to establish new congregations, each with a Christian school. The constitution expressly stated that some of the Synod's major objectives were to promote parochial schools, found institutions for the training of teachers and pastors, and publish schoolbooks. One of the conditions for membership in the Synod was that a congregation was to provide a Christian education for its children.[3]

Thus the intimate relationship between education and religion was strongly and firmly established and tenaciously adhered to in practice. Although the ideal of one school for each congregation was not achieved, most of the congregations did succeed in establishing schools. No pastor or teacher was allowed to hold office unless he had made a public confession with reference to his doctrinal position. In order that the confessional character of the Missouri Synod might be maintained, it was highly essential to provide for a thorough religious education and indoctrination of the children. Attendance at the parish school was required of all children who were members.

One of the chief difficulties in carrying out the educational program and goals of the Synod from the outset was the lack of teachers who could meet the doctrinal requirements laid down by the congregations. The schools grew very rapidly in size and number, and the need for teachers was both constant and dire. Usually the pastors founded schools and also taught them; but as their congregations and schools grew, they were not able to take care of both pastoral and teaching duties adequately, and the demand for teachers increased.

The first Lutheran school on American soil had been established by Swedish colonists around the year 1640. The Swedes, who settled along the Delaware River, maintained schools for over a century but dropped them when they felt no further need for instruction in the mother tongue. Other Lutheran groups had also established schools almost immediately on their arrival in America. By the turn of the 19th century Lutheran schools had been established by Scandinavians, Germans, and Dutch all along the eastern coast of our country. According to Walter H. Beck there had been more than 400 of these schools.[4]

Other denominations and various civic groups established private schools. However, these schools went into a period of decline from which they never recovered, beginning with the rise of the free, or tax-supported, schools. Although there were many people who tried to stop this trend, it was in vain.

When the leaders of the Missouri Synod met, they freely discussed what they felt was a confessional decline among the churches in the eastern part of the country. They noted that it ran parallel to the decreasing emphasis of these churches on Christian schools. This increased their determination to keep their schools strong. They of course recognized that the developing public schools were very essential for the general welfare of the nation, but they felt these could not adequately serve the requirements of Christian education they had established. It is significant that the 12 parishes which formed the Synod had 14 schools in 1847.[5]

The purpose underlying the founding of Lutheran schools was to establish a dynamic Christian laity, firmly indoctrinated and well trained to exert a wholesome influence at home, in the church, in the state, and in the community.[6]

In the 1963 edition of the *Handbook* of The Lutheran Church — Missouri Synod we find that the constitutional provisions for Christian education have remained constant. Under the objects of the Synod as stated in Article III we note the following paragraphs:

"3. The training of ministers and teachers for service in the Evangelical Lutheran Church."

"6. The furtherance of Christian parochial schools and of a thorough instruction for confirmation."

"7. The supervision of the ministers and teachers of Synod with regard to the performance of their official duties."

Under Article V, "Conditions of Membership," the teachers of parish schools are listed as advisory members of the Synod.[7]

From a small beginning in 1847 The Lutheran Church — Missouri Synod (1963) has grown to 5,832 congregations with 2,683,876 members in North America. The Synod has 1,378 parish schools enrolling 158,050 pupils and taught by 5,919 teachers. Besides this there are 21 community Lutheran high schools with a total enrollment of 10,685 students and teaching personnel of 538, under the supervision and control of individual parishes or associations of parishes.[8]

In carrying out its objective to train teachers and pastors the Synod now has a division of higher education which includes 16 schools and colleges for ministerial or professional education on four levels.

There are 10 high school and junior college combinations (Grades 9–14), one 2-year senior college for preministerial junior college graduates (Grades 15 and 16 only), two seminaries for the training of pastors, and two 4-year teachers colleges. One of the teachers colleges has a 4-year high school connected to it; the other has a fifth-year graduate program leading to the master's degree. The latter is Concordia Teachers College of River Forest, Ill., the subject institution of this study.

Nearly all the junior colleges offered the first two years of teacher training and sent their students to River Forest or to Seward, Nebr., for the last two years. In September 1962 Concordia College of St. Paul, Minn., was granted permission to expand its teacher-training division to four college years — but for women only; men students still had to transfer to one of the teachers colleges. The first 4-year class graduated in 1964.

Early Teacher Training Before the Synod Was Organized

The great need for Lutheran teachers in the expanding program of education was recognized even before the Synod was organized. Shortly after the Saxons settled in Perry County, Mo., a small log-cabin college was founded at Dresden. A notice was inserted in a German newspaper of St. Louis, *Anzeiger des Westens,* on Aug. 13, 1839, in which the founders of the college announced their plan of patterning the course of study after that of the German *Gymnasium.* The subjects included were religion, Latin, Greek, Hebrew, German, French, English, geography, history, mathematics, physics, natural history, elements of philosophy, music, and drawing. Three theological candidates were active in establishing the school — Theodore J. Brohm (father of the third president of Addison), Ottomar Fuerbringer, and Johann Friedrich Buenger. They were also the first teachers.[9] This institution was actually a private school of elementary and beginning secondary level. The founders termed it "an institution of instruction and training."

The school opened on Dec. 9, 1839, and enrolled 10 students ranging in age from 5 to 15. It is difficult to imagine just how the ambitious curriculum they described would be applied to these first pupils.[10] Ottomar Fuerbringer, one of the founders, wrote a letter to Dr. Franz Delitzsch in Germany on Sept. 7, 1839, in which he mentions that they were about to begin a *Gymnasium* which, after it gained in strength, was to be expanded into a university and a theological seminary.[11]

The college struggled quite severely as one after another the instructors were called away to other fields of labor; however, the efforts of local pastors helped to keep it alive. The college was reorganized in 1843 at Altenburg as a seminary for the training of pastors and teachers, although it continued to offer general secondary education. In 1847 it was transferred to the Synod, and in 1849 it was moved to St. Louis. The program here consisted of a *Gymnasium,* which included a high school and college department of 7 years, and a 3-year seminary. Although the college aimed to train both pastors and teachers, it actually trained very few teachers, graduating only three between 1850 and 1861.[12]

C. F. W. Walther was elected by the Synod to be the first president of this college, which later became Concordia Seminary of St. Louis. He held this position until his death in 1887.

To help fill the great continuing needs, a number of teachers were persuaded to come to America from Germany, and a number of laymen were recruited who were privately trained and approved as teachers. Among the latter was C. Eduard Roschke, who had been a tailor by trade.[13] It is interesting to note that this man became so well known as a good teacher that he was placed on the list of candidates for the position of president of Addison in 1864.[14]

Besides the log-cabin seminary in Perry Co., Mo., another seminary had been started before the Synod was organized. It was built in 1846 in Fort Wayne, Ind., under the direction of Pastor Wilhelm Sihler with the financial assistance of Pastor Wilhelm Loehe and other friends in Germany. Its object was to train both pastors and teachers.

The founders of the Synod deemed it essential to acquire full control of all institutions which would train pastors and teachers. Consequently they requested Pastor Loehe to relinquish control of the Fort Wayne seminary to the Synod but to continue to support the institution financially. They further appealed to certain religious leaders in Germany for financial aid for the seminary in Altenburg if the congregations which then owned the seminary would place it under the control and supervision of the Synod.[15] In 1848 these congregations stated their willingness to give the seminary over to the Synod but requested that it be left at Altenburg. However, the Lutherans in St. Louis offered to give two acres of land and $2,000 in cash if the seminary could be moved there.[16] This offer was accepted, and the Altenburg school was closed in December 1849, opening in January 1850 in St. Louis.

Thus, shortly after the new Synod was organized in 1847, it had two institutions which were committed to training pastors and teachers.

The Practical Seminary at Fort Wayne — 1846

Rev. William Loehe of Neuendettelsau, Bavaria, Germany, had interested himself greatly in the spiritual condition of German immigrants in North America. As German immigrants continued to pour into the country, those who were interested in their spiritual welfare were hard pressed to provide enough men to preach to them and to teach their children. Accordingly Loehe and Sihler founded what they called an emergency seminary *(Nothelferseminar)* at Fort Wayne to train pastors and teachers for service as quickly as possible.[17] It opened in October 1846 in temporary quarters with 11 students. Actually this was to be a finishing school for those who had started their training under the direct tutelage of Pastor Loehe or other pastors. In the first 9 years only one of the 89 students was American born.[18]

Between 1846 and 1857 15 teachers were graduated from Fort Wayne. The first was J. Georg Wolf in December 1846, the only graduate at that time. Often there was no waiting for graduation, but students were placed into the field at almost any time during the year when the need presented itself. The Fort Wayne seminary did not have a formal graduation until 1859, when 17 had completed their work.[19]

Pastor Loehe was glad to give the Missouri Synod the deed to the seminary in 1847 with the condition that it always serve the church, that it always remain German, and that it always remain a *Nothelferseminar.*[20]

In 1851 Pastors Friedrich Conrad Dietrich Wyneken and C. F. W. Walther went to Neuendettelsau in Germany to discuss with Loehe the establishment of a separate teachers seminary.[21] The need for such a school was felt at that time to be growing more acute especially since both the Fort Wayne seminary and the St. Louis seminary had graduated very few teachers. Relief for pastors who were teaching school was urgently needed because their work was multiplying so that they were not able to give proper attention to both jobs.

The Milwaukee Private Teachers Seminary

By 1854 the number of parishes in the Synod had increased to 116, yet the number of teachers had increased to only 27.[22] The teachers of the Synod were very anxious to have a teacher-training institution established to meet the growing demand. J. Heinrich Fr. (hereafter referred to as Henry) Bartling of Addison, Ill., was one of the early teachers who interested himself in this matter. In a letter to the St. Louis teachers conference in January 1854 he urged support for the promotion of a teachers seminary.[23]

At times there were enough teachers coming over from Germany to alleviate the shortage, but some congregations had had bad experiences with a few of them because of their rationalistic seminary training. This often led them to expound ideas that were contrary to the doctrinal position of the Synod. It was also true that they were usually too weak in English.[24]

In the fall of 1854 three pastors at Milwaukee, Wis., discussed ways and means of providing more teachers for the church. They were the Rev. Philipp Fleischmann, pastor of St. Stephen's in suburban Walkers Point, the Rev. Friedrich Lochner of Trinity, and the Rev. H. Ludwig Dulitz of St. John's, together with Teacher Christian Diez and Teacher Eckert (first name or initial is not given) of Trinity School. They decided to start a private teachers seminary and give it to the Synod after it was established.[25]

The three local congregations promised to give them help. Accordingly the seminary was started in January 1855 in a building called the Runge House, on Wells, near Fifth Street, with an enrollment of 11.[26]

In July 1855 they published an article in the *Lutheraner* in which they stated that they had recognized the crying need for well-trained Christian teachers. Therefore with the help of their teachers they had determined to begin a private teachers seminary in 1855. Plans for the seminary were brought to the attention of delegates at several District conventions, where the founders received great encouragement and promises of support.[27]

It was reported that there were six enrolled at that time who attended grade school in the morning (since most of them were not yet confirmed). In the afternoon they attended seminary classes for 24 hours a week and studied catechism, German, English, arithmetic, history, geography, drawing, penmanship, piano, violin, and singing. Since they had no dormitory facilities, four students were housed with

Pastors Lochner and Fleischmann. The recommended age for admission was between 15 and 20. The article was signed by Pastors Lochner, Dulitz, and Fleischmann.[28]

The instructors of the school consisted of the three pastors assisted by Teachers Diez and Eckert. The students paid $4.00 a month for board. Appeals were made to the people in the Synod to remember the institution with gifts of money, clothing, and other provisions and especially to pray for its success. A report was made periodically to show the support given and to encourage more of it.

TABLE 1

Typical Report of Contributions to the
Milwaukee Teachers Seminary*

Contributions received from June to December:

A. Cash

From the widowed Mrs. Wichmann at St. Louis		$ 3.00	
Through Rev. Dulitz			
From himself	$5.80		
From Mr. Lindenschmidt	1.00		
From Mr. Boese	.50		
From Mr. Stoll	.50	7.80	
Through Rev. Lochner			
From Mr. Huck	$ 2.00		
From Mr. P——	5.00		
From Mr. E. Eiszfeldt	5.00		
From Mr. W. Friese	1.00		
From Mr. ——g	9.25		
From Mr. Ludwig Wergin	10.00		
Collected at the jubilee service	6.91	39.16	
Through Rev. Schwan in Cleveland			
From Miss Louise Kohlenberger	$ 1.00		
From Miss Elizabeth Woelfert	1.00	2.00	
Through Rev. Hattstaedt from his town congr.		8.00	
Through Rev. Geyer			
Collected at the wedding of Mr. W. Krueger	$ 2.47		
From Mr. Christian Koepsell	2.00		
From Mr. David Volkmann	1.00		
From Mr. Gottlieb Mueller	1.00		
From Mr. Friedrich Brendemuehl	1.00	7.47	
Through Rev. Selle collected by his			
congregation at the jubilee service		6.00	

Through Rev. Trautman
    From his congregation $ 2.22
    From himself   2.78   5.00

Through Rev. Lemke
    From his congregation $ 3.00
    From Mr. Schoenamsgruber   1.00   4.00

From Teacher Luecke in Sheboygan   2.05
Through Rev. Keyl in Baltimore   9.40
Through Rev. Guenther collected at the
    wedding of Mr. Franz Manthei   2.50
From Mr. Milbrath in Town 8   .12½
Through Rev. Brauer
    Collected at the harvest thanksgiving day $27.50
    Collected at the baptism at W. Precht's   2.50   30.00

Through Teacher Riedel from the congregation
    at Frankenmuth   22.00

           Total $148.50½

B. Items received

One violin from Rev. Lemke
58 lbs. of rye flour from a member of Rev. Guenther's
    congregation in Town 8
One blackboard from two members here
One small stove from J. P—— here
One sack of rye flour, about 98 lbs., from Mr. Eilers
    in Freistatt
One pig from Mr. Eilers in Freistatt
From numerous young ladies of Trinity Congregation to be
    distributed at Christmas: shirts, undershirts,
    underpants, socks, handkerchiefs, pillowcases, bed-
    sheets — half a dozen of each.
From a number of women for the same purpose: eight silk
    neck scarves and one-half dozen shirts.

    For this increasing assistance we give God thanks, and to the donors we say, "God bless you!"

Milwaukee, Dec. 29, 1855   *F. Lochner*, Pastor

* Published in Der Lutheraner, XII (Jan. 15, 1856), 87.

The seminary remained in Milwaukee for nearly three years. During that time four graduates went into the service of the church. "Graduation" meant simply that they were considered ready to go out to assume the duties of teaching. The four graduates are listed here:

1855 — Franz Bodemer, who was 24 at the time he graduated and served the church 31 years.

1856 — There were two graduates the second year: Louis S. Deffner, 30, who served 36 years, and Peter Nickel, 20, who served 20 years.

1857 — Harold Mueller (age unknown), who taught 21 years.[29]

When President Wyneken of the Synod circulated a list of the issues that would be discussed in the synodical convention to be held in Fort Wayne in October 1857, one of the prime issues was the synodical sponsorship of the Milwaukee teachers seminary and its possible relocation.

It was reported that the experiences of Pastors Lochner, Dulitz, and Fleischmann had led them to the conclusion that Milwaukee would not be a suitable place for the continued location of the seminary. It was suggested by Dr. Sihler, pastor of St. Paul's, Fort Wayne, that since Prof. Fr. August Craemer needed instructional help in the Fort Wayne seminary at this time, it would be a good idea to call another professor who could fill this need and also be the director of the teachers seminary in case the two institutions would be united. Against this view the Chicago teachers conference petitioned the Synod to locate the teachers seminary in Addison, stating their feelings that it would be better to keep the teachers seminary as a separate institution. At this time the Chicago teachers conference consisted of six teachers, three of whom were teachers of the Addison congregation — Henry Bartling, J. Nicolaus G. Kirchner, and H. Riebling. The others were E. Theodore Buenger and Georg H. Fischer of Chicago and Peter Nickel of Crete, Ill. The congregation at Addison through its pastor, the Rev. Adolph Gustav Gottlieb Francke, and its delegate, Mr. F. Fiene, expressed its willingness to have the institution located at Addison and offered the help of the congregation in locating it there.

The Synod gave careful consideration to the entire problem, including the petitions of the Chicago teachers conference and Zion Congregation, Addison. However, they were convinced by the contention of Dr. Sihler and his congregation that the teachers seminary should be united with the pastors seminary in Fort Wayne and that a professor should be called who would also lead the teachers seminary division.[30] The dedication of the new English Academy in Fort Wayne during this convention helped provide needed building space and also opportunity to study the English language. More will be said about this academy later.

The Synod adopted this plan and immediately called the Rev. Philipp Fleischmann of the Milwaukee teachers seminary to be the professor at the Fort Wayne seminary and *Direktor* of the teachers seminary. Actually this meant that the original purpose to prepare pastors and teachers together was again being established.

This action in 1857 put the Synod into a special teacher training program for the first time. Although it was not a separate institution at the time, it was a separate department, thus paving the way for the founding of the Addison seminary in 1864.

The Fort Wayne Teachers Seminary

Fleischmann arrived in Fort Wayne on Nov. 10, 1857, with four students: J. Riebling, A. Bellin, E. A. Eggers, and another named Schoenefeld.[31]

Dr. Sihler was selected as *Praeses der Anstalt* of the combined institution. He was regarded as a capable teacher and gave instruction in the seminary from time to time. Teacher J. G. Kunz, who was also organist at St. Paul's, gave instruction in music, assisted by the Rev. J. Paul Kalb and another teacher, E. Stegner.[32]

In the spring of 1858 the combined seminary had an enrollment of about 50 students — 20 in the preparatory department, 12 in the normal, and 18 in the theological department.[33] The following year the total went to 75, including 24 in the teachers seminary.[34] Most of the records bearing on the history of the teachers seminary during this period were destroyed in the fire of the administration building at River Forest in 1914.

Direktor Fleischmann announced in 1862 that students 14 to 17 years old were especially desirable in the seminary since he felt that this was the best age for learning English and music. Applicants should be well recommended, particularly for their spiritual under-standing and conduct. They should also have the gifts necessary for teaching, be inclined to learn music, have some knowledge of English, read fluently, write dictation without too many errors, and be able to handle arithmetic through the study of fractions.[35]

Conditions at Fort Wayne were very primitive. Many who came were very poorly prepared for college studies. Very few could speak English. English was taught by Dr. Sihler, who had learned it in Germany. A student who had attended public school in Washington, D. C., also gave private lessons in English. Moreover, the continuing need for teachers was so great that the boys were urged, often with hardly a bare minimum of attainment, to supply the urgent need.

Many of the students were very poor and found it difficult to raise even the $13 a year required for board. Some were supported by their congregations. The farmers around Fort Wayne contributed many farm products toward the support of the seminary, and there was a large vegetable garden near the seminary which was cared for by the boys. Ladies societies of neighboring congregations knit clothing for the students and performed other services for the school. All of these activities helped to keep the costs down.

In the earliest days of the Synod a great need was seen to do more work in English. As early as 1852 the Synod, meeting in Fort Wayne, had voted to sell certain lots which had been donated to it and give the proceeds to the Fort Wayne seminary to raise the educational standards in respect to the English language. Prominent English citizens had voiced a desire to have an English college at Fort Wayne. A committee was appointed to proceed with plans. Many comments were made to the effect that the children would become English in spite of all efforts that might be made to keep them German — that English people can also be true Lutherans.[36] In 1854 the Synod considered the matter important enough to permit a small amount to be borrowed for the purpose after a general collection had been taken. The congregations at Fort Wayne pledged $7,000 for a new building to house the seminary as well as the English Academy. The new building was dedicated Oct. 26 at the close of the synodical sessions of 1857. This is one of the factors that brought the teachers seminary here from Milwaukee. Actually it saved the cost of erecting another building. It was emphasized that the new English Academy would give teacher-training students an opportunity to participate in various courses and especially to receive a thorough instruction in English. Mr. A. Sutermeister, who had formerly taught in an English mathematical school in Boston, was the first professor of the English Academy, which opened Nov. 16. The curriculum is rather interesting, for all the instruction was in English, except religion, which was taught in German.[37] The English Academy was closed by 1860 because of lack of money and students.

At the beginning of the Civil War the Synod had two theological seminaries. The one at St. Louis was known as the "theoretical" seminary. The purpose of a "theoretical" seminary was to establish and maintain the ideal of the learned ministry, of a clergy that was theologically educated in considerable depth. The training course at this institution was therefore longer than that of a "practical" seminary such as the one in Fort Wayne. The main function of the "practical" seminary was to train men as quickly as possible to take over pastoral duties among the German immigrants. That is why it was called a *Nothelferseminar*, a "seminary for emergency helpers." The graduates, generally speaking, had little if any college or university training. They were equipped primarily as practical men to carry out the various duties of the ministry.

The outbreak of the Civil War brought about an important change which had a profound effect on the teachers seminary in Fort Wayne. The Synod deemed it wise, because of war contingencies, to combine both seminaries into one institution to be located in St. Louis, and to combine the preparatory college, or *Gymnasium*, of the St. Louis school with the Fort Wayne preparatory college. This resolution was carried out in 1861. The teacher training department was forced to move out since there was no longer sufficient room for the combined institutions in the Fort Wayne seminary buildings. Accordingly the teacher division was moved to the second story and attic of Simon's Bookstore in downtown Fort Wayne. The accommodations here included a classroom, a music room, and sleeping room for about half of the student body. The other half was quartered in a nearby flat.[38] In 1861 the enrollment grew to 36. The Rev. Chr. August Thom. Selle of Rock Island, Ill., was called to be the second professor of the seminary. Selle was one of those who helped to organize the Synod in 1847 in First St. Paul's Church, Chicago, where he was pastor. The classes taught by him were singing, piano, English, theory of music, arithmetic, geography, and Bible history.[39]

During that year the students still paid only $13 for the entire year of instruction, including board and room. A number of the students received free meals on Sunday from local families who also took care of their laundry gratis. (These were called *Waschleute* or "benefactors.") A number of the students had their meals with the Fleischmanns. The congregations in the vicinity donated most of the food, fuel, and other things to the seminary and to Fleischmann; this helped to keep the board and room fees low. According to one report, a student paper was circulated at that time under the name of *Augensalbe* (Eye Salve). The editor was C. F. Keller, the copyist was A. Bellin, and the caricaturist was G. Steuber.[40]

After a year the seminary was forced to move again. This time quarters were found in an abandoned tavern about two miles out of the city on the Piqua Road. The building had sufficient accommodations to house the families of the professors, the kitchen personnel, and the seminary students. However, dormitory space was provided by partitioning an old barn. This barn also housed the seminary horse and several cows, and it was promptly named "Adam's Cow Barn" by the students. Even under continued adverse conditions the school enjoyed a good reputation, and its enrollment steadily increased. It graduated 10 students in 1862, seven in 1863, and 11 in 1864.

It had become increasingly apparent to the entire Synod that the school had to have a permanent home. This problem was considered in several conventions. The Lutherans of Chicago had repeatedly asked that the seminary be removed to that locality. It was also recalled that in 1857, when the Synod had taken over the private teachers seminary from Milwaukee, Zion Congregation at Addison had been eager to have it established there. In 1863 the congregation urgently renewed the invitation and offered to donate 20 acres and a considerable sum of money if the seminary would be located there. Other sites also had been suggested. One of these was in the area now known as Lincoln Park in Chicago, which could have been obtained at that time at a very reasonable price. However, the Synod decided to accept the offer of Zion Congregation with thanks.

Thus a new chapter was to be written in the history of teacher education in The Lutheran Church — Missouri Synod. It was the beginning of a century of teacher education in a separate institution.

How the Teachers Seminary Came to Addison

Zion Lutheran Church of Addison (now in Bensenville), Ill., was founded in 1838 and has a very interesting history of its own. This congregation had always had a great interest in Christian education, having started a school at the church in 1840, which was taught by the pastor, the Rev. F. A. Hoffmann. When it became a hardship on the parents in outlying areas of the parish to transport their children to the school, district schools began to be organized. At one time the congregation had eight different school districts, formed between 1849 and 1885. Over the years these districts gradually became independent and built churches, forming new congregations. All of them still have Christian schools at this writing.

On Jan. 14, 1849, 20 men, heads of families, members of the congregation who lived in and around the village of Addison, formulated and signed a document, organizing a society (*Schulgemeinde,* literally, "school congregation") for the purpose of operating English and German schools. This was called the West District *(Westbezirk)* School. The first teacher of the new school, Henry Bartling, was formally installed into office by the pastor of the congregation, the Rev. Ernst August Brauer, who himself had taught school after Pastor Hoffmann had left.[41] Zion Congregation joined the Missouri Synod in March 1856, and in 1857 the Rev. A. G. G. Francke, who was to be very instrumental in locating the teachers seminary in Addison, became pastor of the congregation.[42]

With this interest in schools, one can readily see why the congregation would take a great interest in the teacher supply. Later on the congregation was also active in establishing a Lutheran orphanage in the area, which for a number of years was closely connected with the Addison seminary in various ways.

In 1861 a theological student named George Seitz was sent to the school of the West District in the village of Addison from the Fort Wayne teachers seminary as a supply teacher. One evening in Teacher Bartling's home, Seitz informed those gathered there that he had received a letter from Fort Wayne stating that Fleischmann and Selle had often considered the advisability of relocating the seminary at Addison. According to the story told by Pastor T. Johannes Grosse, who wrote the 50th-anniversary history of the Addison congregation, one of the members present said, "I know what is missing or needed to get the seminary here. It is money I sold several head of cattle and gave the money from this for the building of the church. However, I still have a young horse. I will sell it and give the proceeds to the seminary." Another member offered to sell pigs and donate the proceeds. Finally they asked Teacher Bartling's son to get paper, ink, and pen to write the following: "If the seminary comes to Addison, then I promise for the seminary the sum of ...." This paper was then circulated and sums of one hundred to two hundred dollars were pledged. Teacher Bartling was astounded at this turn of events. Finally he remarked, "Do you know what you did today? I believe you have brought the seminary here." [43]

This development was reported to Pastor Francke, and it was decided to send word of it to the two professors with a student, George Bartling, who was returning to the Fort Wayne seminary. Fleischmann and Selle discussed it with Wyneken, the President of Synod, but he felt that not too much would come of it.

Both professors came to survey the area. Since Zion Congregation wanted the seminary close to its church, they felt at first that it would be a good idea to use the old church building for that purpose. Together they visited all the congregations in the vicinity and later changed their minds completely. They now felt that the school must be located near the West District school in the village of Addison so that the students would have the opportunity to teach the children. It is interesting to note that Teacher Bartling objected most strenuously to this, feeling that it would not be in the best interest of the pupils of his school. No doubt this contributed to the fact that practice teaching was not permitted until 1878 and then only for four 30-minute periods a year per student. After the professors had returned to Fort Wayne, they wrote back, stating that their thinking had again changed and that the seminary would undoubtedly remain in Fort Wayne.[44]

In 1862 Pastor Francke received a letter informing him that although church leaders in Fort Wayne were definitely against the removal of the seminary, leaders in St. Louis were heartily in favor of it, and there was a good chance that it would actually be moved. On May 2, 1862, the congregation instructed its delegate, Mr. W. Precht, to propose to the Western District of the Synod, in convention in Crete, Ill., that a memorial be sent to the Delegate Synod favoring the removal of the seminary to Addison. The Western District approved this and prepared the memorial, stating the following reasons:

1. The congregation would provide the property free of charge. Moreover, they would, with the help of neighboring congregations, raise an additional amount for some, if not all, of the expenses.

2. The removal would be of great benefit to the congregations of the Chicago area. This would give them an institution which would be a challenge to their Christian charity. Moreover, the seminary would become a center for various church festivals and celebrations, thus becoming a focal point for the entire area.

3. The relocation would make it possible for the Fort Wayne

congregations to concentrate their efforts on one institution instead of two.

4. The congregations of the Chicago conference would support the teachers seminary by providing foodstuffs as donations to help reduce the cost to the students.

5. The Addison area was very desirable geographically and physically.[45]

The Synod met in Fort Wayne Oct. 14–24, 1863. The synodical floor committee which reported on the overture added other considerations as follows:

1. It stressed the hope that the seminary would be placed near the school of the West District of the Addison congregation (in the village of Addison). It pointed out further that there, even more than in Fort Wayne, there would be a good opportunity to observe teaching and at times to participate in the teaching under the supervision of an experienced teacher.

2. The proximity of a larger city would offer too much attraction to young people so that they might be diverted from their major purpose by chasing after amusements and wasting their time. But the location in Addison would be more secluded. (This is probably the major reason why they turned down a location in the Lincoln Park area of Chicago.)

3. The seminary at Addison would become a center for all types of church festivals and also a central meeting place for various teachers conferences.[46]

Synod unanimously decided on the relocation from Fort Wayne to Addison, appointing Pastor Francke as *Praeses der Anstalt*. It was also resolved that a building be erected at once so that the teachers seminary could begin in its new quarters on Sept. 1, 1864. The building committee was to consist of Pastor Francke as chairman, Pastor Friedrich Wilhelm Richmann of Schaumburg, Ill., and Teacher Bartling, Mr. F. Krage, Sr., and Mr. F. Graue of the Addison congregation.[47]

This committee had the immediate problem of obtaining the necessary land. The Synod had specified that this be near the school and not near the church as the congregation had wished. On Nov. 14, 1863, the West District school society sold the Synod six acres of land for $10. Later an additional 14 acres was secured.

True to its word, the entire congregation donated cash for the new seminary in the amount of $3,128.00, despite the fact that they had just dedicated a new church on Dec. 4, 1862. Members (of the West District particularly) hauled the building material for the first building, which was to house 60 students and two professors. Some of the farmers even paid their hired men to help them, many of them devoting as much as two whole weeks to the project. The Synod in 1864 expressed its hearty thanks to the committee and especially to Teacher Bartling and members of the Addison church, who hauled loads over roads that were at times well nigh impassable and during a period when farm work was very pressing. Special mention was made of the tireless work and devotion of the 70-year-old "Father" Krage.[48]

Through June 1864 the Fort Wayne teachers seminary was still in operation in the tavern on the Piqua Road.

The constant demand for teachers was getting to be a serious problem. Congregations were not willing to wait until students had graduated. In 1863 *Direktor* Fleischmann reported that although 16 men had passed their examination the year before, 12 others had since then been sent into the field because of the great emergency. As a result the enrollment was down to 19 from the previous figure of 40. Only four of the 19 were more mature students. He complained in the *Lutheraner* that the school's educational aims were being undermined and pleaded that congregations send more students.[49]

The rapidity with which new congregations were being established demanded more and more time of the pastors, and it became increasingly difficult to reach the ideal of a school for every church.

Two other developments at this time are worthy of note. One is that efforts were made at some in-service training for teachers by the formation of teachers conferences beginning as early as 1856. Second, a resolution of the Eastern District was presented as a memorial to the general Synod, suggesting that a school committee be established for the purpose of supervising the schools, determining the needs, and actively promoting improvement of the schools. They suggested further that this committee could list candidates for the proposed teachers seminary and recommend teachers to congregations. Finally, the committee should be responsible to publish a supplement in the *Lutheraner* which would keep teachers in touch with what was being done in educational methods both in this country and in Germany.[50]

The system of German schools was rather universally admired, also by many leaders of public education in the United States. No action was taken by the Synod in its 1857 convention.

In view of the great and continuing teacher shortage and of the training facilities that were to be built in Addison, Professor Selle announced in 1863 that Pastor Friedrich Brunn of Steeden, Germany, was ready to send a number of teachers and students to America provided the congregations paid the traveling expenses. However, Selle emphasized particularly the need for American boys because of their better acquaintance with American conditions and knowledge of English.[51]

In July 1864 Selle repeated the plea for American students, stating that there ought to be at least 20 graduates a year since they were then receiving approximately 30 calls annually. (*Direktor* Fleischmann had resigned early in 1864 because of eye trouble but agreed to serve to the end of the school year, after which he took a call as pastor to Soest and later to Kendallville, Ind.[52]) The announcement said further that there would be 19 students transferring from Fort Wayne to Addison and that the school year would begin Sept. 1 even if the building should not be finished. Professor Selle's address would be Addison, Du Page Co., Ill., after July 8.[53]

Four pastors and one teacher were nominated as candidates for the position of president of the new school at Addison: Pastors Johann C. W. Lindemann, Friedrich Lochner (one of the founders of the private seminary in Milwaukee), Friedrich W. Foehlinger, and Wolfgang S. Stubnatzi and Teacher C. Eduard Roschke. Lindemann was elected by the electoral board as the first president of Addison.[54]

The Lutheran Teacher

The aim of the church in teacher education was to establish a Christ-centered program of education and training for its parish schools. Its curriculum was generally in advance of the normal-school program then in existence.

Besides being well qualified in the schoolroom, the Lutheran teacher was expected to be proficient in music, including choir conducting, piano, organ, and violin, so that he could teach music to the schoolchildren and lead congregational singing in church services. The violin was often the only instrument available to teach and lead singing. Violin was compulsory for all until 1905, when the Synod voted to make it an elective but kept piano and organ on the required list.

The duties of the Lutheran teacher gradually expanded into other areas of service to the church, including youth work, working with part-time agencies of Christian education such as the Sunday school, Saturday school, and vacation Bible school and the training of lay teachers for them. He also serves other functions in the ministry of the church as conditions and needs require.

The office of a Lutheran called male teacher is part of the ministry of the church and is so recognized by the government of the United States, which classifies him as a minister of the Gospel and a minister of religion.

Background of the System of Higher Education Of The Lutheran Church — Missouri Synod

Historically the program of higher education was greatly influenced by the German *Gymnasium* in both structure and philosophy. The pattern of the *Gymnasium* was stamped more deeply into the synodical system by the fact that most of the teachers in these schools were themselves trained in the system. Classicism pervaded all curricula.[55]

The peculiar inflexible form of the *Gymnasium* program, with reference to school program, teaching methods, and personal development of students, also left its mark on Missouri Synod schools by making teaching too mechanical and learning too often an exercise in obedience.

Signs of breaking away from the *Gymnasium* at Concordia Teachers College came in 1908, when a sixth year was added and an American-style high school and junior college program was begun. In 1920 the Synod officially abandoned the *Gymnasium* idea, adopting American high school and junior college classification for all its preparatory schools. In the 1920 *Proceedings* the Synod said there should be 4-year classical high schools and 2-year classical junior colleges. More English was to be taught and more subjects in English. Accreditation was to be sought, and class loads were to be modified.[56] The *Gymnasium* had 30–32 class periods for six years. The American high school had 25–30 hours per week, the junior college 15–18 hours. Further progress came in the 1930s, when the third and fourth college years were added, and in 1950, when the high school department was dropped. Concordia Teachers College was the first senior college in the Synod.

Administration of the Synod's colleges also followed the German pattern for many years. It consisted of a *Direktor* (or president, which term we shall use throughout this work) and a *Lehrer-Collegium* (faculty). The president was merely *primus inter pares* (the first among equals), whose authority was never commensurate with his responsibilities.

Besides this, the president often had a full load of classes to teach. He had hardly any voice in selection of personnel or in establishing policy. The institutions suffered for lack of coordination and planning.

The local boards had hardly any power, as even trivial matters all had to be referred to higher synodical authority.[57] Before 1908 the Synod itself decided everything, even matters referring to operation of the physical plant. By 1914 regulations were established by the Synod for a local board of control consisting of the president, one pastor, and three laymen. This gave the local board a few more privileges, mainly regarding supervision of the physical plant.[58]

A Board of Directors of the Synod was set up in 1917, which was to have considerable control over all its schools, including educational, financial, and personnel policies.[59] For 30 years it functioned mainly through a "Committee on Higher Education."

In 1938 a Board for Higher Education was established as a separate entity with complete control of all colleges and seminaries except in matters of capital investments, which remained with the Board of Directors.[60] In 1945 the Rev. Martin J. Neeb was installed as the first Executive Secretary for this new board.[61]

A radical change in administrative policy was adopted by the Synod in 1947. This centralized the broad policy-making responsibility for its institutions in the Board for Higher Education but gave the local administration (board of control and president) a great amount of freedom in three important ways:

1) In the preparation and administration of its own budget.

2) In the selection of personnel by the local board only on recommendation of the president, thus finally doing away with the ancient system whereby electors who had no connection with the school chose its professors. The board of electors was not abolished, but it would act only on a list of candidates approved by the president and the local board.

3) The president was given power in accord with the unit concept of control, which placed all departments of the school under his jurisdiction. He now had full responsibility for all phases of the school's operation, both educational policy and business management. For the first time he was the school's responsible head and executive officer of the board and no longer merely *primus inter pares.*[62]

Summary

The Lutheran Church — Missouri Synod always attached great importance to its educational institutions because of a strong desire to preserve the Lutheran teaching. One of its biggest problems was that of maintaining the ratio of one school for each congregation. The shortage of teachers was so great that in the earlier years of the Synod most pastors also had to teach. As the church grew, constantly redoubling its efforts to reach the thousands upon thousands of German immigrants who entered our country toward the middle of the 19th century, it was simply impossible to find enough manpower to serve them all and to provide Christian education for their children. It is estimated that a half million German immigrants entered our country between 1830 and 1850 alone.

Teacher training began with the Perry County school (1839) and the emergency theological seminary at Fort Wayne (1846). Both were taken over by the Synod when it was formed in 1847. A private teachers seminary founded in Milwaukee (1855) is the historic seed from which Concordia Teachers College finally emerged. In 1857 this was given over to the Synod and combined with the Fort Wayne theological seminary.

When the Fort Wayne theological seminary was combined with the one at St. Louis, the Fort Wayne campus was turned into a preparatory school only, of the German *Gymnasium* type. Since there was no longer room for the teachers seminary on the same campus, it was moved into other quarters.

In 1863 the Synod decided to move the school to Addison, Ill. When *Direktor* Fleischmann resigned to reenter the parish ministry, the Rev. J. C. W. Lindemann of Cleveland, Ohio, was elected as the first president of the separate teachers seminary.

A description of the office of the Lutheran teacher served to clarify the needs of the students at Addison and River Forest.

Finally, the background of the Missouri Synod's system of higher education showed the developing pattern of administrative control.

Notes

1. William H. T. Dau, ed., *Ebenezer: Reviews of the Work of the Missouri Synod During Three Quarters of a Century* (St. Louis: Concordia Publishing House, 1922), p. 7.

2. Carl S. Meyer, *A Brief Historical Sketch of The Lutheran Church — Missouri Synod* (St. Louis: Concordia Publishing House, 1963), p. 6.

3. *Die Verfassung der deutschen evangelisch-lutherischen Synode von Missouri, Ohio und andern Staaten — 1846* in *Der Lutheraner,* III (Sept. 5, 1846) 2—6, reprint. This first constitution was drawn up in a meeting in Fort Wayne in 1846. It was to be considered by congregations until its adoption and the formation of the Synod in 1847.

4. Walter H. Beck, *Lutheran Elementary Schools in the United States: A History of the Development of Parochial Schools and Synodical Educational Policies and Programs* (St. Louis: Concordia Publishing House, 1939), p. 47.

5. August C. Stellhorn, *Schools of The Lutheran Church — Missouri Synod* (St. Louis: Concordia Publishing House, 1963), pp. 66, 67.

6. Ibid., p. 67.

7. *Handbook of The Lutheran Church — Missouri Synod,* 1963 edition.

8. *1963 Statistical Yearbook of The Lutheran Church — Missouri Synod* (Saint Louis: Concordia Publishing House, 1964), pp. 176, 196, 197, 221. Community Lutheran high schools are operated by associations of parishes not directly under the control of the Synod as distinguished from those secondary schools directly attached to the Synod-operated junior colleges.

9. Dau, pp. 229, 230.

10. Theodore Buenger, *"Die Gründung der ersten Lehranstalt,"* Der Lutheraner, XCV (Feb. 14, 1939), 52.

11. Ibid.

12. Stellhorn, p. 138.

13. Ibid., p. 129.

14. *Der Lutheraner,* XX (Feb. 15, April 15, 1864), 95, 126, 127.

15. Dau, p. 105.

16. Ibid., pp. 231, 232.

17. H. C. Gaertner, "A Brief Historical Sketch of Concordia Teachers College, River Forest, Ill.," *Lutheran School Journal,* LXVII (May 1932), 387.

18. Stellhorn, p. 130.

19. Gaertner, p. 387.

20. Dau, pp. 162, 163.

21. *Der Lutheraner,* XI (Jan. 30, 1855), 93.

22. Stellhorn, p. 131.

23. Ibid., pp. 131, 132.

24. Gaertner, p. 386.

25. From historical document taken from cornerstone at Addison as it was razed in 1924. See *Lutheran School Journal,* LX (Feb. 1925), 44—48.

26. *Lutheran School Journal,* LXVII (May 1932), 389.

27. The Synod had divided into four Districts in 1854.

28. *Der Lutheraner,* XI (July 3, 1855), 180.

29. Stellhorn, p. 133.
30. *Synodal-Bericht*, 1857, p. 54.
31. *Evangelisch-Lutherisches Schulblatt*, IV (July 1869), 321.
32. *Lutheran School Journal*, LXVII (May 1932), 390.
33. Ibid.
34. Ibid.
35. *Der Lutheraner*, XVIII (March 19, 1862), 126.
36. Dau, p. 428.
37. *Der Lutheraner*, XIV (Nov. 17, 1857), 51, 53.
38. *Lutheran School Journal*, LXVII (May 1932), 391.
39. *Der Lutheraner*, LIV (Oct. 4, 1898), 177.
40. *Lutheran School Journal*, LXVII (May 1932), 392.
41. Daniel E. Poellot, "A Century of Christian Education: The History of the Evangelical Lutheran School of St. Paul, Addison, Ill., 1849—1949." Booklet: Addison, Illinois, August 1949, pp. 7—10.
42. *125th Anniversary of Zion Lutheran Church, Bensenville, Illinois*, ed. Daniel W. Fuelling (1963), p. 7.
43. T. Johannes Grosse, *Geschichte der Deutschen evang.-lutherischen Gemeinde* (Chicago: Franz Gindele Printing Co., 1888), p. 69.
44. Ibid., p. 70.
45. Ibid., pp. 70, 71.
46. Ibid., p. 71.
47. *Synodal-Bericht*, 1863, pp. 73—81. These pages give complete details of all matters pertaining to the plans for the new seminary.
48. *Synodal-Bericht*, 1864, p. 4.
49. *Der Lutheraner*, XIX (May 15, 1863), 149, 150.
50. *Zweiter Bericht des Oestlichen Distrikts* (Second Report of the Eastern District), 1856, p. 27.
51. *Der Lutheraner*, XX (Dec. 15, 1863), 61, 62.
52. Ibid. (Feb. 15, 1864), 95.
53. Ibid. (July 15, 1864), 174, 175.
54. Ibid. (April 15, June 1, 1864), 126, 127, 151.
55. Thomas Coates, "The Making of a Minister" (mimeographed book, undated conference essay published about 1954), p. 23.
56. *Proceedings*, 1920, pp. 14—16.
57. Coates, p. 80.
58. *Synodal-Bericht*, 1914, pp. 114, 115.
59. *Synodal-Bericht*, 1917, p. 90.
60. *Proceedings*, 1938, pp. 41—43.
61. *Lutheran Witness*, LXIV (Nov. 20, 1945), 394.
62. *Proceedings*, 1947, pp. 745, 746.

PART II

THE ADDISON SEMINARY, 1864—1913

President J. C. W. Lindemann, 1827—1879

Johann Christoph Wilhelm Lindemann was born in Goettingen, Germany, on January 6, 1827. He came from a distinguished family, having descended from Johann Lindemann of Eisenach, grandfather to the great Reformer Dr. Martin Luther. His home life was not very religious; however, his stepmother did teach him to pray. Although he had an aptitude for drawing, the family was not able to afford even a Gymnasium education for him, so he was apprenticed to an uncle to learn the trade of cabinetmaking.

In 1846 Lindemann went to Leipzig, where he became interested in religion and joined a Roman Catholic church, determining to become a Catholic missionary to Africa. His parents and his home pastor dissuaded him, however, and he left the Catholic church. Continued study of the Bible made him more deeply interested in Lutheran doctrines, and Lindemann resolved to become a Lutheran teacher.

He was tutored for six months by a teacher who gave him an opportunity to practice-teach in a local school, following which he studied for six months in the preparatory department of the Hanover Teachers Seminary. He volunteered to accept a call to Baltimore, Maryland, arriving there on July 6, 1848. Lindemann married a Mrs. Dieterle, a widow with three children. Twins were born to them in 1851, one of whom died, and the other later became Prof. Friedrich Lindemann of Addison, who enjoyed a successful career as a teacher.

In 1852 Lindemann followed the advice of several friends and entered the practical seminary in Fort Wayne to study theology, and in 1853 he became assistant pastor to the synodical President, Rev. H. C. Schwan of Zion Church in Cleveland, Ohio. Within a short time he became pastor of a new congregation (Trinity) on the west side of Cleveland, serving here till 1864, when he was called to become the first president of Concordia Teachers College, then known as the Evangelical Lutheran Teachers Seminary, in Addison, Illinois.

President Lindemann was a profound scholar and a prolific writer, both capable and efficient. In 1865 he became the first editor of Evangelisch-Lutherisches Schulblatt, a professional educational journal known today as Lutheran Education, writing most of the first 10 volumes himself. His textbook on pedagogy (Schulpraxis) and German Grammar (Deutsche Grammatik) were used for many years. His deep insights and zeal for learning and Christian teaching gave the new college a sense of urgency in service that has remained throughout its history. President Lindemann died suddenly at 52 years of age on January 15, 1879, having attained a position of high honor and the love and respect of his church.

Chapter 2

J. C. W. LINDEMANN'S ADMINISTRATION 1864—1879

The new seminary was to be completed by September 1864 — in only 11 months. The committee was hard pressed although it went into action immediately to handle details concerning the site, building plans, wartime shortages, finances, and general supervision of the project.

The building plans were drawn by the Rev. Martin Stephan, whose father had been leader of the Saxon immigration of 1839. He was voted $35 by the Synod in 1864 "as a token of appreciation." [1] He had also designed the first Concordia Seminary building in St. Louis when he was a student there in 1849. [2]

The plans provided for a central building with three stories and basement, with a two-story addition and basement attached to either side. The initial plant would have a capacity of 60 students.

The center section with one of the smaller additions was to be complete by Sept. 1. Specifications of the Synod included one large and one small classroom, six study rooms to accommodate 10 boys each, two music rooms, a hospital room, a dining hall, a dormitory, a washroom, living quarters for the steward, and the necessary house-keeping accommodations. Specifications for the professors' dwellings were also given. [3]

In April 1864 Pastor Richmann issued a call for cash to be paid on pledges and also for additional pledges. Total subscriptions from 59 congregations in 17 states were $11,629. The Addison congregation had donated the land and had pledged a total of $3,128 to head the list of givers. [4] At this time pledges were still $5,000 to $6,000 short of the needs, estimated at $16,000. The contract had been let and work was underway. It was hoped to have the building under roof by May. [5]

Throughout construction members of the Addison congregation were zealous and faithful in providing transportation for building materials. The nearest rail terminus was Elmhurst, 4 miles from Addison. Several of the farmers even hired help in addition to giving their own services. Members of the Schaumburg and Rodenberg congregations also gave a great deal of assistance. A special "Assistance Committee" organized in Zion Congregation included H. Buchholz, F. Meier, F. Fiene, Mr. Heidemann (first name or initial not given), and Christian Heidemann.[6]

The cornerstone was laid June 15, 1864, by Pastor Francke as *Praeses der Anstalt*.[7] Pastor Richmann conducted the service, and Professor Selle preached the festival sermon.

Included in the cornerstone were the Book of Concord of 1580, Dietrich's Small Catechism, the Constitution of the Synod, the *Synodical Proceedings (Synodal-Bericht)* of 1863, the *Lutheraner* of April 15, 1864, and a special handwritten document giving the history of the school from the beginning of the Synod through the Milwaukee and Fort Wayne teachers seminaries to June 15. On the edge of this document a note in another handwriting states that Pastor Heinrich Schmidt of Elk Grove, Ill., had also given a brief address.[8]

During July 1864 Professor Selle and his family moved to Addison. They found the building program months behind schedule because of wartime shortages of labor and material. Lindemann, the new president, did not arrive till the end of August.

In the meantime quarters had to be found since the school was scheduled to open in September. A vacant tavern, a two-story building, was rented.

The first student body numbered 43 boys and men of all ages, 18 of whom had been at Fort Wayne. Some were new recruits from Germany, sent over by Pastor Brunn of Steeden. One student was married, and his wife worked in the kitchen under the supervision of the steward. The rest were older men (35 to 40 years of age) and young boys. There were Civil War veterans — some of them amputees, several teachers from Germany, and a former public school teacher. It was a real challenge to President Lindemann and Professor Selle to form class units out of a group such as this. Special English classes had to be established for those who had come from Germany.[9] The enrollment gradually built up to 55 during the first year.

Most of the students had had very meager academic preparation. The problem of the seminary was to prepare them as adequately and as quickly as possible to meet the urgent demand for teachers in the Lutheran schools. The curriculum included Bible, Bible history, Catechism, memory work, the Augsburg Confession, Luther's Large Catechism, music, violin, piano, organ, and singing. Training in lesson planning and teaching was generally included in each subject. Oral and written examinations were the final graduation requirements. In 1864 the Synod designated the President of the Western District (Rev. Johann Friedrich Buenger), the *Praeses der Anstalt* (Pastor Francke), and the two professors (Lindemann and Selle) to be the official examiners.[10] Calls for the graduates were assigned by the faculty. At the end of June 1865 12 graduates were sent out to teach. One, Friedrich M. F. Leutner, had been sent out some months prior to this to take a position in Cleveland.[11]

Living conditions were severe during that first autumn. The old tavern was in a poor state of repair, with wide cracks in the walls and broken windows.[12] It had two stories, the first of which provided quarters for the steward, "Father" Heinrich Gehrke and his family, plus kitchen, bakery, and dining room. Gehrke had been teacher of the North District School of Zion Congregation from 1858 to 1864. The second floor had a large room used as a classroom and several smaller ones used as bedrooms. A number of students slept in Professor Selle's attic. According to Daniel Fechtmann, one of the students, the bedrooms could have passed as "open-air" sleeping quarters.[13]

The weather was mild until the end of November, when severe winter weather suddenly set in. One night it was so cold that students were forced to put on all the clothes they could and march in the room all night to keep from freezing. Efforts to start a fire proved futile. It was impossible to attempt instruction. Adverse wind conditions caused heating stoves to smoke, and meals could not be prepared because the cookstove could not function properly. Some students became ill. Since these conditions were growing worse, President Lindemann sent all the boys to their benefactors *(Waschleute)* in the community two weeks before Christmas.[14]

On Dec. 28, 1864, the new building was finally dedicated as the first home of the seminary destined to become Concordia Teachers College. A beautiful mild day brought large numbers out for the occasion. Classes were begun in the new building on Jan. 2, 1865.[15] At last now they could have instruction uninterruptedly. Much work still needed to be done to clean up the premises, but students helped in this project.

Custodial work was handled by students, and all took turns in sawing and splitting wood for the many stoves used to heat the seminary.

The cost to the student for the entire year was $20.00. This was made possible by generous donations of the farmers of Addison and environs who gave meat, potatoes, flour, and other produce gladly, in recognition of their responsibility for the seminary, in which they took great pride. They also served as *Waschleute* (or benefactors), doing the laundry for the students and giving them Sunday dinners and suppers.[16] The benefactor system, continued well into the River Forest period, was very popular among the students, who looked forward to the fine Sunday meals they usually received.

During the first year a chorus was organized which sang twice during the second semester — at Rodenberg and Schaumburg. They had to walk there on Saturday, stay overnight, and walk back Sunday night, tired and dusty.

Food was not in great variety, but there was usually sufficient. Meat was used as it came in, for there was no means of preserving it for long. Butter was a luxury. At 10:00 in the morning students could have a thick piece of bread sprinkled with salt. Because of Civil War conditions, imitation coffee was used, which was made by boiling roasted grains. It was dubbed "Lincoln coffee" by the students.[17]

Fechtmann says in his reminiscences: "Of the various happenings in the country such as the end of the Civil War, or the assassination of President Lincoln, we heard very little. There were no newspapers in the seminary. Only when a student returned from a visit to Chicago did we hear of the latest news events." [18]

The teaching staff included President Lindemann, Professor Selle, and a student assistant, Wilhelm F. Hoffmann, who was retained as a music instructor for a year after he graduated in 1865.

Johann Christoph Wilhelm Lindemann's formal training above the secondary school was one year and six months, but he had been an avid reader and a tireless student and worker, so that by his own efforts he attained knowledge of great breadth and depth.[19] Besides this he was regarded as a very devout and compassionate man, sincerely interested in Christian education and Christian training as an important means of building the church. He had been a teacher in St. Paul's Lutheran School, Baltimore, Md., in 1852 entered the Fort Wayne seminary to study theology, and in 1853 became the organizer, pastor, and teacher of Trinity Church and School in Cleveland, Ohio.[20]

Christian August Thomas Selle was called to the teachers seminary department in Fort Wayne in 1861. He had very little education, none at all beyond the elementary grades in Germany. Yet he studied privately, and according to some reports, almost constantly, receiving some guidance in his earlier years from Dr. Sihler of Fort Wayne. He had served as a pastor in Columbiana Co., Ohio, St. Paul's Church, Chicago, where the Synod was organized, Crete, Ill., and Rock Island, Ill.[21]

Both Lindemann and Selle were known and respected for their scholarship and teaching ability although most of their colleagues, the leaders in Synod, were university trained. By their teaching and writing they were to have a profound effect on Christian education in the latter half of the 19th century.

An interesting insight regarding President Lindemann and his capacity and willingness to work can be noted in the origin of the *Evangelisch-Lutherisches Schulblatt*, one of the oldest educational journals in America (probably the oldest in continuous publication), which will celebrate a century of Christian educational journalism in 1965. It has been published by the Addison and River Forest faculties since 1865.

In 1864, while the construction of the new seminary was underway, the Western District Teachers Conference of the Synod resolved to publish a journal on education. The Western District at that time had 53 teachers and included the states of Illinois, Missouri, Iowa, Tennessee, Texas, Louisiana, Kansas, and California.

Lindemann was prevailed upon to become editor of *Evangelisch-Lutherisches Schulblatt* (Evangelical Lutheran school paper, or journal). It was to be a monthly publication in the interest of education and training. The first issue appeared in September 1865 as a 32-page German magazine. The subscription cost was $2 a year.[22] For 99 years it has been an in-service professional training instrument for Lutheran teachers.

In his Preface to the first issue Lindemann lauded the teachers for establishing a journal to assist them in professional growth. He called attention to the forces of evil, which try to confuse educational needs by denouncing religious training in the schools, disregarding man's need to prepare for the life hereafter, and emphasizing only human values.

Lindemann declared that the journal would be entirely in harmony with the two petitions of the Lord's Prayer, "Hallowed be Thy name, Thy kingdom come." Primary attention would be given to the parish school and everything pertaining to it, the teacher, congregation, curriculum, teaching methods, pupils, and discipline. However, attention would also be given to the home and home training which supports or thwarts the Christian school. Further, it would include news of higher education, gleanings of all kinds from other publications, and biographies of good and bad teachers. Its benefits would be not only to teachers, but pastors and parents were also to profit by it.

For four years Lindemann remained sole editor of this publication, preparing a manuscript of 32 pages each month without secretarial help, writing almost the entire contents himself. Besides this he had to lead the new seminary in the development of its curriculum and counsel a growing student body as well as teach a full load of classes. One can see how he gained a reputation as an indefatigable worker, zealously dedicated to the large tasks of the church.

In 1869, by request of the Teachers' Conference, Synod made the *Schulblatt* (as it was commonly known) its official educational publication.[23] Sponsorship was to begin with the January 1870 issue. Lindemann was to continue as editor-in-chief assisted by Professors Selle and Karl Brauer. It became the responsibility of the Addison faculty. In 1921 it became officially bilingual, and its name was changed to *Lutheran School Journal;* since 1947 it is called *Lutheran Education*. The first English article appeared in 1879 and the last German article in February 1935, completing the changeover in languages.[24]

During the school year 1865–66 the enrollment went up to 58, and 14 graduated in June 1866. At the end of this school year Wilhelm F. Hoffmann, who had been assisting in music, accepted a call to Trinity School, Milwaukee. In the fall convention of the Synod a professor of music was authorized.[25] Teacher Karl Brauer of Baltimore accepted the position, arriving on Dec. 27, 1866.

Brauer had come to America from Germany in 1850 and served schools in Philadelphia, St. Louis, Cleveland, and Baltimore. A capable musician who was well known in the Synod, he issued a *Choralbuch* (Chorale Book) in 1888 which was used by Lutheran churches for many years. He was the first full-time professor of music in the Synod, serving till 1897.

By 1868 the 5-year curriculum was firmly established. In Table 2 the teaching schedule for the year 1869 is shown for each of the three professors. By 1875 President Lindemann's schedule had been reduced to 17 periods.[26]

TABLE 2

THE 1869 CLASS SCHEDULE OF THE ADDISON SEMINARY*

C. A. T. SELLE

Subject	Periods per week
Bible History	2
Symbolic writings	1
Geography	2
English language	9
Piano	13
	—
Total	27

KARL BRAUER

Singing	5
Violin	5
Piano	15
Organ	7
Theory of Music	1
	—
Total	33

PRESIDENT J. C. W. LINDEMANN

Catechism	2
Isagogics	1
Memory work	2
School Administration	1
Practical Catechetics	2
German	6
Arithmetic	4
History	1
Nature Study	1
Penmanship	4
Drawing	2
	—
Total	26

* J. C. W. Lindemann, "Das Schullehrer-Seminar in Addison," *Evangelisch-Lutherisches Schulblatt,* IV (July 1869), 335.

President Lindemann and Professor Selle had been faced with problems of admission since the seminary opened in 1864. During the first year the ages of the students had a range of 14–33. The range of attainment was just as wide.

What kind of boys were suitable for admission to the teachers seminary? In view of the great shortage of teachers which was being held before the church, it is not strange that this should be asked. Would it be possible to maintain high standards in the midst of urgent efforts to recruit teachers?

In considering these and other questions that were being asked, Lindemann was concerned not only for the welfare of the seminary but also for the whole church. To establish minimum entrance requirements he asked, "What is required of a teacher?" In answer to this question he listed the following in *Schulblatt* in August 1868:

1. Christian character.

2. Good working knowledge of German and English.

3. Skills — including the ability to read and write well in both German and English, good ability in calculation, ability to sing well, and do well in piano, organ, and violin.

4. The Scriptural standard: "Apt to teach." [27]
He felt that the foregoing would give *pastors* and *teachers* guidelines in writing their letters of reference for applicants.

Boys should be between the ages of 16 and 18 and have completed the seventh or eighth grade, besides being confirmed members of the church. There should be no extremes, such as great intelligence and no or little piety, or great piety with low ability.[28]

Lindemann continued his appeal for quality students, despite pressures which were being brought to hasten the preparation of teachers even at the expense of lowering standards.

In an article written for the *Lutheraner* in 1871 entitled *"Our Teacher Shortage,"* Lindemann wrote: "It isn't going to help to fight against the use of state schools by our people if our teachers cannot prove that they can do better than the state schools." He stated further that there must be no adherence to the old rule which pertained in Europe, and which some German immigrants had carried with them to America: "Since the boy is not good enough to become a cobbler, let him be a teacher." Pursuing the thought he continued: "It is shocking to behold the sort of individual sometimes sent to us with the expectation that we should make teachers out of them." He stated further that personal piety alone did not qualify a person to teach: "Piety is not enough, else all good Christians should be good teachers." [29]

Lindemann went on to list 10 characteristics of a good teacher. They included being a pious Christian; having the ability to tell stories, to communicate with others intelligently and forcefully, to answer questions and explain, to comprehend rapidly; a good memory (a faithful memory is more important than a fast one); an ear for music; a fine sense of order; an attitude of perseverance; and a natural sense of composure and patience.

In conclusion Lindemann pleaded: "Please spare us from older people who still have to learn their ABCs after they get to the seminary, who at the age of 20 or 25 do not know what one is supposed to have learned in the humblest village schools." [30]

With increases in enrollment the Synod resolved in 1866 to erect the north wing of the seminary and authorized $10,000 for this purpose, thus making accommodations for 30 more students.[31] The new wing was erected between March and October 1868 and dedicated Nov. 5, with the Rev. Henry Wunder of Chicago and President Lindemann as speakers.

A fourth professor was greatly needed to help with the constantly growing student body, but the Synod declined to vote the additional help in 1869. Despite this Dr. Herman Duemling was called to this position in 1870 from Milwaukee under rather unusual circumstances. The Lutheran high school in Milwaukee in which he had been teaching was closing. Dr. Duemling had an offer to teach in the New York City schools, but he expressed his preference to serve the Missouri Synod. Consequently a resolution was offered in the Northern District convention meeting in Adrian, Mich., to make Duemling a professor at Addison, the District to pay his salary and housing until 1872, when the Synod could act.[32] They hoped that the other Districts would help out in the meantime. The Addison board of control accepted, and Synod approved the appointment in 1872.[33] Dr. Duemling served till he was called to the Fort Wayne college in 1874, becoming the first to leave the Addison faculty. He was replaced by Teacher Clemens E. Haentzschel of Emmanuel Lutheran School, Fort Wayne. Haentzschel was a Union Army veteran who had fought in a number of famous battles, notably Chancellorsville and Gettysburg.

CONCORDIA TEACHERS COLLEGE

7400 Augusta Street

RIVER FOREST, ILLINOIS

Dear Librarian:

The enclosed copy of <u>College With a Cause</u> is being sent to all college and university libraries in the United States as a sequel to the 100th anniversary of Concordia Teachers College, River Forest, Illinois.

This courtesy is made possible by a grant received from the Aid Association for Lutherans, Appleton, Wisconsin.

In a never ending search to be of service to the field of higher education, the author, Alfred J. Freitag, has told the story of Concordia, illustrating the uniqueness of this denominational school which has never altered fundamentally its purpose of teacher education in 100 years of preparing men and women for the Lutheran teaching profession.

Concordia is a four year college with graduate school certified by the North Central Association and by NCATE (National Council of Accreditation for Teacher Education).

Cordially yours,

David T. Stein

David T. Stein
Acting Director of Field Services

February, 1965

DTS/me

Enclosure

Probably the first regular minutes of the Board of Control *(Auf-sichts-Behoerde)* were recorded on Nov. 29, 1874, for the first resolution of that meeting states that, beginning on that date, the board would have all its resolutions recorded in the form of regular minutes. Mr. H. Oehlerking was elected secretary.

It was reported in this meeting that the overcrowded conditions in the buildings (110 students in housing for 80) had been brought to the attention of the Synod in its last delegate convention, held in Fort Wayne Oct. 14–23 of the same year. The Synod had concurred in the need and authorized $10,000 for the construction of the three-story south wing, the building to be erected during the following summer. President Lindemann was to prepare circulars with an appeal for funds and to submit the plans and the design of the new building.[34]

The Synod purchased 12 additional acres for the seminary and accepted the donation of three additional acres. A house on this property was to be made over into a hospital for the seminary. The maximum campus area was completed by 1890, when seven more acres were purchased.

On Oct. 12, 1875, the south wing was dedicated.[35] It provided a new dining hall and custodian's quarters, a large lecture hall seating 400 which was also used for devotions later, a dormitory, and several smaller rooms. The enrollment in 1875–76 was 132.

In the convention of 1874 the Synod had also voted to establish a fifth professorship, which was filled by the Rev. T. Johannes Grosse of Chicago. He was installed on Oct. 12, 1875, the day the south wing was dedicated.[36] He served four years till 1879, then went back into the ministry.

An interesting development occurred as the Synod observed its 25th anniversary during the convention in St. Louis in May 1872. In one of the committee rooms it was mentioned by someone that it would help the new teachers college in Addison if an orphanage were established there so the children could be enrolled in a practice school.

A newspaper erroneously printed a report that it had been decided to establish such an institution in Addison. This report was published by other newspapers, but no one took the reports seriously. However, within a month after the convention, a check for $24.25 was received by Zion from a neighboring congregation marked "For the Addison Orphanage." As other donations also started coming, the congregation regarded it as a sign from the Lord to enter this work. Finally the Evangelical Lutheran Orphan Asylum Association of Northern Illinois was founded June 27, 1873, by 13 congregations. Pastor Francke and several others had secured 54 acres of ground west of the seminary, of which 15 acres were sold to the Synod in 1874. This acreage was now turned over to the new association, of which Pastor Francke was the first president, Professor Selle the vice-president. Dedication was held Oct. 28, 1874. One of the reasons for founding this association was to give the seminary students an opportunity for practice teaching.[37]

Gradually an annual festival was organized which became one of the social highlights of the year for the seminary students and faculty, as well as for all congregations in the vicinity and Chicago. The festival was usually held on a Sunday in September, with special offerings in both morning and afternoon services. Children's choirs and the seminary chorus and band supplied music for the occasion. The first festival was attended by about 5,000 people.

One of the main reasons advanced in 1863 for moving the seminary to Addison had been the proximity of the Lutheran school taught by Teacher Henry Bartling. It was hoped that here the student teachers would have an opportunity to observe actual classroom instruction and to participate in formal teaching under the supervision of an experienced teacher. For the first 14 years the only practice teaching available consisted of teaching the lowest classes in the seminary.

As the great need for practice-teaching was felt more and more, repeated discussions were held with the Addison congregation without success.

The school district had misgivings about such a program, fearing it might be detrimental to the welfare of the children. However, the seminary faculty had asked for only four half-hour training periods a week (in Catechism, Bible history, mathematics, and English) and had stated that they would not make any changes in the schedule or school regulations. They also promised not to interfere with the discipline of the school, which was the regular teacher's duty. The teacher was to be present during all instruction by students. Under these terms the agreement was made on Feb. 23, 1878, with the West District school for practice-teaching and observation on an experimental basis only till the end of the school year.

When the Synod met in St. Louis in May 1878, the delegates were elated over the report of the plans that had been made for practice teaching and requested that this arrangement might be continued. On Aug. 25, 1878, the West District voted to continue the arrangement, reserving the right to change or drop it at any time.[38]

Transportation to Addison had always presented a problem. The nearest railroad station was at Elmhurst, 4 miles away. Students had to walk the 4 miles carrying their hand luggage. Heavier items were brought to the seminary by horse-drawn wagon. When special celebrations were held, at least the women and children had to be provided transportation from Elmhurst by a wagon train.

The problem was not solved until 1893, when a railroad spur to Addison was built. Numerous efforts had been made over the years to induce the Illinois Central Railroad to build such a line. After the annual Orphan Festival was established, these efforts were greatly increased. The company agreed to do so if the right-of-way would be purchased for them. In 1891 the Addison Railroad Company was formed of those who contributed to the spur line, including the Addison Village residents, the Synod (on behalf of the seminary), and the congregations in the Orphan Asylum Association.[39] The railroad was a boon to the students as well as to all visitors to the seminary.

During the convention of the Synod in St. Louis in 1878 a lengthy discussion was held concerning the need for more English instruction in the teachers seminary. President Lindemann was one of the leaders who urged favorable consideration for more English instruction. The question was raised whether the two-year seminary course was long enough to train the graduates in all subjects and especially in English. It was pointed out that some schools which needed English teachers were forced to close because there were none qualified. A strong plea was made to add another year to the seminary and to add another professorship in English.[40]

The Synod declined these recommendations (probably for financial reasons) and referred them to the Addison board for further study. Professor Selle was to continue to teach English in the meantime. The library allocation was raised from $30 to $50 for the year, and an appropriation of $50 was voted to increase physical-education facilities.[41]

On Jan. 15, 1879, President Lindemann suddenly died of a heart attack at the age of 52 years, 9 days. His death was a blow to the seminary and to the entire church. Twelve days before this his good friend, Pastor Francke, had died. Lindemann had completed a biography of Francke only a few hours prior to his own death.[42] He was the only president to die in office in the school's first century.

Church leaders from seven states traveled in bitter-cold weather under the most primitive conditions to be present for the funeral on Jan. 20, including Dr. Walther, president of Concordia Seminary, St. Louis.

Lindemann's body lay in state in the largest lecture room of the seminary. A brief address was given here by Illinois District President Henry Wunder. This was followed by a service in Zion Church in which the President of the Synod, Heinrich C. Schwan of Cleveland (under whom Lindemann had begun his ministry), preached. Students and alumni were pallbearers, and the seminary chorus sang several selections. Lindemann's grave can still be seen in Zion Cemetery.[43]

During his 15-year administration the school had grown from 43 to 122 students, and 279 had graduated.

Less than three years before his death we read in the minutes of the Board: "Since President Lindemann as a result of constant over-exertion is suffering from a lingering illness, it was resolved to inform the President of the Synod, Professor Walther, of this situation. Pastor Francke was delegated to do this." [44] The minutes continued: "As soon as President Lindemann has again sufficiently recovered to be able to travel, he shall be given leave of absence." [45] His ailment was described as a nervous illness.

Lindemann's contributions to Christian education were many and far-reaching. By his students, he was regarded as a very fine teacher and a firm, kind, and fair disciplinarian. His aims for the seminary were to educate and train Lutheran teachers so that their personalities would reflect their Christian objectives and be exemplary in the lives of their pupils. His personal concern for the students was shown in his care for their physical well-being. He often nursed sick students himself, having taken one into his own study for that purpose just two weeks before he died.[46]

Lindemann's activities show his great ability as a writer and historian. His book on principles of teaching, *Amerikanisch-Lutherische Schul-Praxis* (American Lutheran School Practice), served as a textbook in the seminary for a number of years, well into the 20th century. He completed the Preface in 1878, about two months before his death. The book was published posthumously in 1879. The introduction dealt with the Christian school as an institution and the office of the Lutheran teacher. He discussed school management and discipline, instruction (general methods and specific subject methods), and school training (the teacher, the pupil, goals, means, and the activity involved in training). In the appendix he gave examples of right and wrong practices.[47]

Other works included an arithmetic for German elementary schools in America, *Deutsche Grammatik* (German grammar), *Katechismus Milch* (Catechism Milk), and *Dr. Martin Luther als Erzieher der Jugend* (Dr. Martin Luther as a Trainer of the Youth).

From 1872 till his death he was editor of the *Amerikanischer Kalender fuer deutsche Lutheraner,* now known as the *Lutheran Annual.* He often published articles in the *Lutheraner.* He also wrote fiction stories for a German family magazine called *Abendschule* (Evening School). At times he used a pen name, J. C. Wilhelm.[48]

His greatest literary contributions came during his editorship of the *Evangelisch-Lutherisches Schulblatt.* Here he revealed his broad knowledge of education and history, as well as religion. Some of the titles are (translated) "Luther as the Reformer of the German Educational System" (Vol. I); "The History of Schools in America" (Vol. IV); "Johann Heinrich Pestalozzi" (Vol. V); "The Educational Activity of Women in Christendom" (Vol. VI. He concluded that it was not detrimental to use women in teaching, contrary to the views expressed by some church leaders. It is interesting to note that this was 65 years before coeducation was introduced at Concordia.)

Lindemann's leadership established the school firmly on the course outlined by the Synod to train capable Christian teachers to serve the growing church.

Summary

In this chapter we have considered the founding of the school physically and academically in line with its spiritual aims from 1864 to the death of President Lindemann in 1879. The first student body and some of the beginning experiences were reported, as was the curriculum and the growth of the faculty. The beginning of the Lutheran professional educational journal (now known as *Lutheran Education*) was reviewed. The establishment of the Addison Lutheran Orphans' Home helped to solve a transportation problem for the students since it aided in focusing attention on the need for a railroad to Addison. The annual orphan festival became one of the social highlights of the year for the seminary students. Practice teaching was begun in the West District school of Zion Church in 1878 by special arrangement with the District. The untimely passing of the school's first president was a shock not only to the seminary but also to the entire church. His ability as an educator and writer had been widely acclaimed.

Notes

1. *Synodal-Bericht,* 1864, p. 4.
2. *Concordia Historical Institute Quarterly,* XIV (Oct. 1941), 82.
3. *Synodal-Bericht,* 1863, pp. 78—81.
4. Henry Bartling, account sheets showing a note register beginning April 2, 1864. Names are repeated numerous times, indicating that as farmers sold animals or grain, they would bring small amounts to assist in the great need for cash. St. Louis: Concordia Historical Institute, File C 130102.
5. *Der Lutheraner,* XX (April 15, 1864), 125, 126.
6. From a historical document and a listing of other contents of the cornerstone printed in *Lutheran School Journal,* LX (Feb. 1925), 44—48. It came to light when the seminary buildings were razed in September and October 1924, when a number of alumni interested themselves in establishing a memorial to their alma mater. Professor Edward W. A. Koehler of River Forest was present when the box was opened, and he described the contents as being in a very crumbling condition. Painstakingly, as he puts it, he on Dec. 31, 1924, copied the document word for word "for the benefit of dear posterity."
7. Ibid., p. 47.
8. Ibid., p. 48.
9. Daniel Fechtmann letter to 50th-anniversary committee of Concordia Teachers College, May 1, 1914. Fechtmann, a member of the Addison student body in 1864—65, came from Germany as a special student *(Hospitant)* and was sent out to teach in 1865. He was one of Pastor Brunn's recruits.
10. *Synodal-Bericht,* 1864, p. 5.
11. Fechtmann letter, p. 9.
12. *Der Lutheraner,* XXI (March 15, 1865), 105—107.
13. Fechtmann letter, pp. 5, 6.
14. Ibid., p. 7.
15. *Der Lutheraner,* XXI (March 15, 1865), 105—107.
16. Fechtmann letter, p. 8.
17. Ibid., p. 9.
18. Ibid., p. 10.
19. August C. Stellhorn, *Schools of The Lutheran Church — Missouri Synod* (St. Louis: Concordia Publishing House, 1963), p. 144.
20. Theodore J. C. Kuehnert, "J. C. W. Lindemann: Pioneer Lutheran Educator," *Lutheran Education,* XCIX (Jan. 1964), 194—202.
21. *Evangelisch-Lutherisches Schulblatt,* XXIV (Sept. 1889), 284.
22. Ibid., I (Sept. 1865).
23. *Synodal-Bericht,* 1869, pp. 35, 98.
24. *Lutheran School Journal,* LXX (Feb. 1935), 241—244.
25. *Synodal-Bericht,* 1866, pp. 83, 84.
26. *Katalog der Lehranstalten der deutschen evangelisch-lutherischen Synode von Missouri, Ohio u. a. St.,* 1875—76, pp. 20, 21.
27. *Evangelisch-Lutherisches Schulblatt,* III (Aug. 1868), 360—369.
28. Ibid.

29. *Der Lutheraner,* XXVII (May 15, 1871), 137, 138.

30. Ibid., p. 139.

31. *Lutheran School Journal,* LXVII (May 1932), 395.

32. *Verhandlungen des Noerdlichen Distrikts,* 1870, p. 56.

33. *Synodal-Bericht,* 1872, p. 98.

34. Minutes, Board of Control, Nov. 29, 1874.

35. *Der Lutheraner,* XXXII (Jan. 15, 1876), 9.

36. *Synodal-Bericht,* 1874, pp. 45, 46.

37. Ross D. Scherer, "The Evangelical Lutheran Orphan Home (Addison, Illinois) 1873—1940" (unpublished master's thesis, University of Chicago, 1947), p. 81.

38. T. Johannes Grosse, *Geschichte der Deutschen evang.-lutherischen Gemeinde* (Chicago: Franz Gindele Printing Co., 1888), pp. 72, 73.

39. Scherer, pp. 6—9.

40. *Synodal-Bericht,* 1878, pp. 23—29.

41. Ibid.

42. August C. Stellhorn, *Concordia Historical Institute Quarterly,* XIV (Oct. 1941), 83.

43. Ibid., p. 90.

44. Minutes, Board of Control, April 10, 1876.

45. Ibid.

46. Stellhorn, *CHIQ,* XIV (Oct. 1941), 83.

47. J. C. W. Lindemann, *Amerikanisch Lutherische Schul-Praxis* (St. Louis: Concordia Publishing House, 1879).

48. A. C. Stellhorn, *CHIQ,* XIV (Oct. 1941), 83.

President Eugen A. W. Krauss, 1851—1924

Eugen Adolf Wilhelm Krauss was born June 4, 1851, at Noerdlingen, Bavaria. He was a student at the Augsburg Gymnasium, and studied theology at Erlangen and Leipzig 1869 to 1873. He severed his connection with the state church and joined the Missouri Synod. In 1874 he became a pastor at Cedarburg, Wisconsin, returning to Germany the following year to serve a congregation at Sperlingshof, Baden. Upon the death of J. C. W. Lindemann, he was called to be the second president of Addison, assuming that office in 1880. He was to be the youngest president (age 29) to serve the school during the first century.

In 1905 President Krauss was called to Concordia Seminary, St. Louis, as professor of church history and propaedeutics. He was widely known as a scholar, writer, speaker, and lecturer on many subjects, with a profound knowledge of church history. He was given the degree of Doctor of Theology by Northwestern College, Watertown, Wisconsin. He died October 9, 1924.

Dr. Krauss married *Juliana Philippina Ottilie Wille* of
Freistadt, Wisconsin, on August 29, 1875, just prior to
his departure for Germany. Two daughters were born to them
but both died before they returned to America in 1880. Back
in America they adopted a nephew, W. A. Dobberfuhl, as a son
(he became a professor at Concordia College, St. Paul, Minnesota).
They also had an adopted daughter.

Chapter 3

E. A. W. KRAUSS'S ADMINISTRATION 1880—1905

The death of two such important leaders as President Lindemann and Pastor Francke was a serious loss. The seminary suffered a third loss in 1879 when Professor Grosse accepted a call which had been extended to him a second time to fill the vacancy at Zion caused by Francke's death. He had been named acting president after Lindemann's death. In accepting the call he agreed to serve as assistant instructor at the seminary and temporarily as *Praeses der Anstalt* until a new president could be called.[1] Professor Selle was appointed acting president after Pastor Grosse left in spring, serving in this capacity until March 15, 1880, when the second President was installed.[2]

To fill the vacancy caused when Professor Grosse left, Professor Theodore Brohm of Northwestern College (a Wisconsin Synod school), Watertown, Wis., was called. One of his duties was to supply the need for more English instruction. He was installed in September 1879.

A sixth professorship was established in 1879 in a rather unusual way to fill the urgent need for another professor in music. Ordinarily the Synod created all professorships in a regular convention, but since there would be no convention until 1881, the President of the Synod requested permission of the various Districts, which was granted. Professor John Merkel was appointed in 1879 to fill the position temporarily. He served till 1881, when Ernest Homann, a Lutheran teacher from Chicago, was called to replace him. Homann was known as a very proficient pianist.

In November 1879 Eugen Adolph Wilhelm Krauss of Sperlingshof, Baden, Germany, was called to become the second president of the seminary in Addison, and on March 15, 1880, he was installed.[3]

When the Synod met in Fort Wayne in 1881, the actions of the board were ratified, including the sixth professorship. However, a major policy change in administration was inaugurated when the Synod combined the offices of *Praeses der Anstalt* and *Direktor* (president) into one position, ending the peculiar dual headship that had existed for many years.[4] Immediately after Krauss became president, it began to be more and more evident in the catalogs of the teachers seminary that the president handled all business affairs pertaining to the institution.

The convention also resolved to pay Mrs. Lindemann $200 per annum as a pension. A new organ and piano were authorized to keep up with the needs of the growing enrollment — 125 in 1880–81, of whom 16 were graduating in June. Two professors' homes were to be turned into dormitories, and three new dwellings were to be built (one for the sixth professor).

During the 1881 convention President Krauss was requested to draw up minimum entrance requirements for the seminary. Such a statement was long overdue to solve an aggravating problem which had beset the seminary from its beginning: the degree of preparation of its entering students. The constant aim of the seminary was to raise graduation requirements, which was not feasible unless entrance standards were raised also.

Five years earlier, President Lindemann had written in the *Lutheraner:* "It simply cannot go on any longer that large numbers of boys and young men are sent to us who often lack not only the most common knowledge but must also begin their first piano lessons here. . . . We must establish preparatory schools in various parts of the country, without cost to the Synod, and give the students an entrance examination, also in piano. . . . Only in this way can our seminary fulfill its purpose in the future, and our training of future teachers be a success." [5]

He described the type of student who should come: He should be a Christian, of good ability, healthy, a graduate of a Lutheran school, and have a definite aim to make Lutheran teaching his life's calling.[6]

President Krauss proposed minimum admission requirements which the Synod adopted. The entering student in the lowest class of the preparatory school should know at least the following:

I. Bible History.

The applicant should be familiar with the following Bible stories: The Creation, the Fall of Man, the Deluge, the patriarchs, the principal facts concerning the life of Christ, the pericopes taken from the four gospels and the Book of Acts, and the Last Judgment.

II. The Catechism.

Luther's Small Catechism up to the Christian Questions should be memorized.

III. German.

The applicant should be able to read selections from the German Second Reader fluently and intelligibly. In German grammar he should at least be able to recognize nouns, adjectives, and verbs; decline nouns together with adjective modifiers; conjugate a verb in the indicative mode, active and passive voice. If in regard to an easy and simple sentence the questions are asked: "Of whom is something asserted?" or: "What is asserted?" he should be able to give the correct answer, even though he does not know the technical terms subject and predicate.

IV. English.

The applicant should be able to read the contents of a First Reader without difficulty, to understand its vocabulary, and to write it correctly. This requirement pertains to pupils coming from our schools.

The same requirement holds good with regard to the spelling of the vocabulary in a German First Reader.

V. Arithmetic.

In Arithmetic the entrant should not only be able to perform the four fundamental processes with denominate numbers mechanically, but should also be capable to solve practical problems.

VI. Music.

The entrant should be able to sing alone and correctly such melodies as are being sung in his church nearly every Sunday.

Besides these requirements the applicant should be able to write a fairly regular hand.[7]

Special entrance examinations were begun in 1881. In 1882 graduates had to pass both an oral and a written examination. In its convention in 1890 Synod asked the faculty to set up new standards of achievement in line with the new curriculum. Table 3 illustrates a typical public examination schedule used during these years.

TABLE 3

PROGRAM OF PUBLIC EXAMINATIONS
AT THE TEACHERS SEMINARY
ADDISON, ILLINOIS
*June 29–30, 1880**

TUESDAY

(Examinations for the general student body)

8:00—8:35	Catechism	(Krauss)
8:35—9:00	English	(Selle)
9:00—9:25	Arithmetic	(Haentzschel)
9:25—10:00	Piano	(Merkel)

Recess of 10 minutes

10:10—10:35	German	(Haentzschel)
10:35—11:00	Geography	(Selle)
11:00—11:25	Nature Study	(Brohm)

Recess of 10 minutes

11:35—11:50	Violin	(Brauer)
11:50—12:20	History	(Krauss)
12:20—1:00	Singing	(Brauer)

WEDNESDAY

(Examinations of the graduates)

8:00—8:35	Symbolical Books	(Selle)
8:35—9:00	Isagogics	(Grosse)
9:00—9:25	Bible Stories	(Krauss)
	(Demonstration)	

Recess of 10 minutes

9:35—10:00	English	(Brohm)
10:00—10:30	Catechism (Dem.)	(Krauss)
10:30—10:45	Geography (Dem.)	(Selle)

Recess of 10 minutes

10:55—11:10	Arithmetic (Dem.)	(Haentzschel)
11:10—11:35	School Management	
	Hist. of Education	(Krauss)
11:35—12:15	Organ	(Brauer)

(The end)

During the current school year 125 students were enrolled, including 42 in the seminary and 83 in the preparatory school. Today and tomorrow 21 graduates will be examined. Of the remaining students, six have been advised to seek a life's calling other than that of a Christian teacher.

* Translated by the author from an original copy found in the archives at River Forest.

On Sept. 24, 1881, Professor Brohm's father, Pastor Theodore Julius Brohm, died and was buried in Zion Cemetery. He had been living with his son in Addison and had assisted in teaching at the seminary since 1879. One of the original Saxon immigrants, he was one of three theological candidates who built the log-cabin college in Perry County, Mo., in 1839.[8]

Pastor Grosse, who had continued to assist in teaching since 1879, was forced to give up this activity in 1883. With the increase in enrollment to 161 in 1883—84, the Synod added a seventh professorship,[9] and Johann Leonhard Backhaus, an 1864 graduate of the Fort Wayne seminary and a Lutheran teacher at St. Matthew's, Chicago, was called to fill the position, serving until 1915.[10]

The Synod of 1884 approved the proposal of the seminary faculty to establish a special curriculum for the preparation of German immigrant teachers so they could help out in the perennial shortage. This group was known as "Division B." Because of a surplus of teachers in Germany, some of them, including several with experience, wanted to come to America to serve in Lutheran schools, applying for admission to the Addison seminary. They were generally deficient in English, music, and Lutheran doctrine. It was not feasible to place them in one of the regular seminary classes, because English in these classes was too difficult. The seminary faculty and board established a two-year preparatory course to overcome their deficiencies. It was reported that there were eight in the program in 1884.[11]

Although a number of teachers were served in this way, Division "B" was discontinued in 1888. Apparently it was not a successful experiment, for in 1889 President Krauss wrote an article in which he told "The Tragic History of a German Teacher Who Tried to Be Admitted to the Seminary in Addison." He ended the article with the words: "German teachers, stay in Germany." [12]

Another important step taken by the Synod in 1884 was the resolution to erect a new building to relieve the overcrowded conditions. For this and for building two more professors' dwellings a total of $26,000 was appropriated. An appropriation of $500 was allowed to construct a plank sidewalk from the seminary to the church, but in 1887 it was reported that the village of Addison had paid $300 of this.[13]

The building, dedicated Sept. 20, 1885, had four large classrooms, a faculty room, two dormitories, a large assembly hall, and several smaller rooms used for a library and museum.[14] Although this building stood for more than 40 years, it was always called "the new building" *(der Neubau)*.[15] During the same year the enrollment reached 240, highest since the school was founded in 1864.

Drainage problems and the pressure of increasing enrollment made it impossible to continue dining and hospital facilities in the basement of the South Wing; therefore the "Commons" building was erected. The new building provided an adequate kitchen, dining hall, proper living quarters for the steward, his family, and his helpers, as well as hospital rooms, a cellar, and a food preparation room. Built at a cost of about $14,000, it was dedicated Oct. 21, 1886.[16]

Another urgent need was fulfilled when in the summer of 1895 a gymnasium was built. It was primarily a physical-education building containing various kinds of physical-culture apparatus, not a gymnasium in the modern sense. Since the Synod did not take an official interest in providing gymnasiums for its colleges, a circular was sent to the teachers and pastors of the Synod asking them to make personal contributions, also to announce it to their congregations and societies. By this means they gathered sufficient funds ($1,800) to erect the building, which was dedicated Nov. 13, 1895.[17]

In order to improve the standards of the seminary, several curricular changes were made (1880–83) after President Krauss arrived. Physical education *(Turnen)*, introduced after Easter 1881, consisted of *Geraetschaftsturnen* (working out with equipment such as Indian clubs, or dumbbells) and *Freiturnen* ("free" gymnastics such as calisthenics). It was required of all students two periods each week. *Stenographie,* a form of shorthand, was introduced and taught by President Krauss.[18]

Geography was introduced in the college classes, and chemistry was begun although it was still included in nature study at this time. In the preparatory classes (the lower three classes) geography and penmanship, organ, violin, piano, and music theory were added. Practice teaching *(Praktische Uebung)* was conducted, the graduating class using the parish school classes and the first-year college class using the lowest preparatory class as pupils. The graduating class spent an hour a week practice teaching Bible history, Catechism, arithmetic, and geography; the other class taught Bible history and Catechism. Student costs were $55 a year, including firewood, plus $3.00 for the sick fund.[19]

In 1887 a special report indicated that year after year the demand for graduates had been 40% to 50% greater than the supply. In the previous year there had been a slight improvement with 52 positions and 42 graduates. It was reported to the 1890 Synod that a Mr. Barkhoff of Salem, Ohio, had built an organ in the chapel *(aula)* and donated $1,294.54 of the $4,194.54 cost.[20]

The 25th anniversary of the seminary was celebrated by the Northwestern Teachers Conference, which met at Addison in July 1889. The festival sermon was given by Pastor Lochner, one of the founders of the private teachers seminary in Milwaukee, basing his sermon on 2 Kings 6:1-3. Professor Selle gave the welcoming address, and Henry Bartling sketched the 25-year financial picture.[21]

By 1892—93 the 5-year curriculum included the following:

1. Catechism of Martin Luther according to Conrad Dietrich's explanation. The techniques of catechization (regarded as one of the very best methods of instruction).

2. Bible — Bible history, isagogics, Bible study and reading.

3. The symbolical books of the church, including the Augsburg Confession.

4. Education, including discipline, methods, and training.

5. German.

6. English.

7. Arithmetic, including elements of geometry and algebra.

8. History, including world history, American history, and Reformation history.

9. Geography.

10. Nature study and science.

11. Penmanship.

12. Drawing.

13. Practical studies and practice teaching included catechization, Bible history, arithmetic, and geography in the Addison West District school, which now had three rooms.

14. Music, singing, piano, organ, violin, and theory.[22]

In 1893 a series of steps leading to a teaching colloquy were developed.[23]

It is interesting to note that beginning about 1881—82 there was a gradual transition from German to English in all branches except religion.[24] By the early 1890s this transition was nearly complete.

The Synod acquired its sixth school in St. Paul, Minn., in 1893 (the fifth having been opened in Milwaukee in 1887).[25] It was established as a *Progymnasium,* a preparatory school sending its teacher training graduates to Addison for the seminary years. This program was discontinued in 1908. In 1894 a second teachers seminary was opened in Seward, Nebr. It was designed to serve only the preparatory classes, which were sent on to Addison to finish their seminary training. In 1905 Seward began to add the two seminary years, graduating its first class in 1907, thus becoming a full-fledged sister seminary to Addison.[26]

In 1894 the Addison seminary enrolled 251 students, the record enrollment in its 49-year history. Between 1895 and 1902 the enrollment averaged slightly under 200 again, and by 1905 it was 242.

Recognizing the need to improve living conditions of the school plant and to reduce the fire hazard, the Synod added steam heating to the seminary buildings in 1896, and so ended 32 years of wood chopping and coal carrying by students.[27]

One of the greatest needs of the seminary which had been expressed over a number of years was to have its own training school. The four half-hours of practice teaching per week allowed by arrangement with the West District school since 1878 were woefully inadequate. Nor did using the lower preparatory classes give an adequate substitute for a real school situation. Finally in 1896, despite much opposition, the Synod authorized the establishment of a training school which would give opportunity for practice teaching under guidance and supervision of the professors.[28]

This school was to be established in connection with the Lutheran orphanage, which was near the seminary. The orphanage board drew up the regulations by which the first four grades were sent to the schools,[29] which was opened after Easter 1898 in one of the seminary lecture rooms.[30] After one year the enrollment included 54 orphans and two professors' children.

Professor Backhaus was director of the training school and supervised in the mornings; Professor F. Rechlin, who assisted him, supervised in the afternoons. Each member of the graduating class spent four weeks in the training school, either teaching or observing, and during this time had no regular classes at the seminary.

The Synod in 1902 received the report that a separate training school building had been dedicated on Dec. 8, 1901. The building, containing one schoolroom 27×40 feet with a 13-foot ceiling and a 5-foot hall, was considered quite advanced because it was equipped with single desks for the pupils. The enrollment from 1899 to 1902 varied between 53 and 60 students.

A special presentation by the Fort Wayne Pastors and Teachers Conference pointed out that education in America had made great strides forward in upgrading the standards which necessitated higher requirements for teachers and teacher training schools. They raised questions regarding the adequacy of the training program in the seminary and expressed concern that general preparation in the common branches of study outside of religion was not receiving sufficient attention.

Further questions were posed: Do we have enough faculty members? Do we have enough equipment? Is the curriculum complete enough? The great importance of the parish school to the welfare of the congregation was urgently stressed.

They pointed to the need for two more professorships and a visitation program making it possible for professors to visit Lutheran schools to ascertain the actual needs in the field. Such a visitation program should be extended to include other teacher training institutions, training schools, grammar schools, and colleges, both public and private, to learn about methods, equipment, and curriculum and to share this practical knowledge with Addison graduates.

Attention was called to the great need for extending the course of study to six years instead of five, which had been the pattern since 1864 and had been copied from the teachers seminaries and *Gymnasia* in Germany.

They felt that Latin should be included in the seminary curriculum and at least a reading ability in French. The lack of proper equipment for science and the poor library facilities were emphasized.

A seven-member committee was appointed to report on the foregoing items in 1905. The Addison faculty was urged to keep informed on what was going on in education in the various states.[31] This encouragement was repeated in Detroit in 1905.[32] Such critical self-examination betokened good health and strength for the future of the Lutheran schools.

When the Louisiana Purchase Exposition was planned for 1904

by the city of St. Louis, which was and is the established center of
the Synod, the Addison faculty recommended that the Synod participate by presenting an exhibit of its schools. This the Synod resolved to do.[33]

The exhibit was "to serve as a testimony of God's goodness and
grace in having given to the Synod the great treasure of parochial
schools, to offer evidence to opponents of parochial schools and to the
entire world that the schools of the Synod were not exclusively religious schools or German schools, but that they embraced all the
studies of the public school curriculum, and to encourage the Lutheran Christians and congregations gratefully to continue their noble
efforts in behalf of congregational schools, the precious treasure of
the Lutheran Church."

Only 261 schools and 460 teachers in 27 states participated, representing about one tenth of all schools in the Synod. The high schools
and colleges of the Synod also had exhibits. The Addison seminary
exhibited classwork and examination papers covering all the curricular
offerings in English, German, history, geography, physiology, chemistry, zoology, botany, arithmetic, catechetical exercises, penmanship,
drawing, and harmony.[34]

The Addison faculty was appointed as a central committee to organize the exhibit. It appointed an executive committee including
Professors Friedrich Koenig, chairman, G. C. Albert Kaeppel, secretary, and Friedrich Rechlin. The results were highly successful, ful-
filling the goals of the Synod. More than 14,000 people registered.

William T. Harris, the United States Commissioner of Education,
wrote to an Addison professor, "I have twice visited your exhibit at
the Louisiana Purchase Exposition with increased admiration." [35] Dr.
R. Tombo of Columbia University also praised the Lutheran schools,
heartily concurring in the judges' decision awarding a gold medal to
the Missouri Synod parish schools.[36] This medal is still in the Concordia Teachers College archives.

During President Krauss's 25-year administration there were numerous changes in the faculty. In 1881 Teacher Ernest Homann was
called to the sixth professorship, and in 1884 Teacher J. L. Backhaus
was called to the seventh. Professor Haentzschel died in 1890 and
was succeeded by the Rev. Friedrich Koenig, who served until 1909.
When the venerable Professor Selle retired in 1893 (he died in 1898),
the Rev. Friedrich Lindemann, son of the first president, was called

to replace him. An eighth professorship was authorized in 1893, to which Friedrich Rechlin was called. In 1897 the last of the "founding faculty," Professor Karl Brauer, retired, and Teacher G. C. Albert Kaeppel of Trinity Church, St. Louis, was called to replace him.

When the Synod met in 1905, it rejected the proposals to add a sixth year to the seminary and to introduce Latin in the curriculum. However, provision was made for a ninth professor, and all faculty members were encouraged to visit schools and colleges, both public and private.

Violin was no longer to be required of all students but was to be an elective. A suggestion by Professor Koenig to separate the preparatory classes from the seminary and locate them toward the eastern part of the country was not accepted.[37]

The Addison congregation was requested by the Synod to establish a new congregation in the village to serve the seminary as a church home.[38]

In the fall of 1905 President Krauss accepted a call to Concordia Seminary, St. Louis, having completed 25 years of service to the Addison school. Until his death in 1924 he served there as professor of church history and propaedeutics.

President Krauss could look back on the achievements that had been made during his administration with some satisfaction. He had built up a reputation as an excellent scholar, lecturer, and instructor, as well as an authority in church history and the Confessions. The enrollment of the school had nearly doubled from 122 to 226. The faculty of six had expanded to nine. The graduates now totaled 1,176 as compared with 279 when Krauss arrived. The largest number ever to graduate from Addison was 56 in 1899. This record was equaled in 1905 but not surpassed till 1922 at River Forest. He had seen the campus grow to its ultimate size.

Curricular offerings had been considerably enriched during Krauss's administration, and requirements for admission and graduation had been raised. However, the teacher-training program was probably one of the most important developments during his tenure when a training school was finally established in a separate building on the seminary campus.

As chief editor of the Schulblatt, 1889—94 and 1902—04, he showed himself a capable writer and a zealous promoter of Christian parish schools of highest standards. It is interesting to note that he was opposed to the kindergarten movement, which had been developing in the United States since 1856, when it was started by a student of Friedrich Froebel, Mrs. Carl Schurz, in Watertown, Wis.[39] Later he admitted that a kindergarten could in some circumstances be both necessary and desirable.

Summary

During President Krauss's tenure the teachers seminary was "growing up." The curriculum was enriched and a full-fledged practice teaching program established in a separate training school. A classroom building, a commons building, and a gymnasium had been added to the campus. The seminary had shown interest in self-examination and improvement to carry out its goals.

Notes

1. *Synodal-Bericht*, 1881, pp. 53—55.
2. *Der Lutheraner*, XXXVI (May 15, 1880), 78.
3. *Lutheran School Journal*, LXVII (May 1932), 397.
4. *Synodal-Bericht*, 1881, p. 55.
5. *Der Lutheraner*, XXXII (Jan. 15, 1876), 11.
6. Ibid. (Aug. 1, 1876), 118.
7. *Synodal-Bericht*, 1881, p. 56, trans. Henry C. Gaertner, *Lutheran School Journal*, LXVII (May 1932), 399, 400.
8. *Der Lutheraner*, XXXVII (Dec. 15, 1881), 188—190.
9. *Synodal-Bericht*, 1884, pp. 41, 46.
10. *Der Lutheraner*, LXXV (June 17, 1919), 191.
11. *Synodal-Bericht*, 1884, pp. 42, 43.
12. *Evangelisch-Lutherisches Schulblatt*, XXIV (Nov.—Dec. 1889), 357—360.
13. *Synodal-Bericht*, 1884, p. 47; 1887, p. 34.
14. *Der Lutheraner*, XLI (Jan. 1, March 15, Sept. 15, 1885), 3, 47, 139.
15. Henry C. Gaertner, "A Brief Historical Sketch of Concordia Teachers College, River Forest, Illinois," *Lutheran School Journal*, LXVII (May 1932), 398.
16. *Evangelisch-Lutherisches Schulblatt*, XXIV (Jan. 1889), 28. This is the only building of the old campus which is still standing. It is being used as a storage building for the Village of Addison.
17. *Lutheran School Journal*, LXVII (May 1932), 400—402.
18. *Katalog der Lehranstalten der deutschen evang.-lutherischen Synode von Missouri, Ohio und anderen Staaten*, 1881—82, p. 18.
19. *Katalog* . . . , 1882—83, pp. 15, 19.
20. *Synodal-Bericht*, 1890, p. 41.
21. *Evangelisch-Lutherisches Schulblatt*, XXIV (Sept. 1889), 257—274.
22. *Katalog* . . . , 1892—93, p. 23.
23. *Synodal-Bericht*, 1893, pp. 64, 65.
24. *Katalog* . . . , 1881—82, pp. 14—20.
25. *Der Lutheraner*, XLVI (Aug. 1, 1893), 127.
26. Herman O. A. Keinath, "Historical Sketch of Concordia Teachers College, Seward, Nebraska," *Lutheran School Journal*, LXX (Dec. 1934), 145—152.
27. *Synodal-Bericht*, 1899, pp. 44, 45.
28. *Synodal-Bericht*, 1896, p. 123.
29. *Evangelisch-Lutherisches Schulblatt*, XXXII (June 1897), 186—188.
30. *Synodal-Bericht*, 1899, p. 44.
31. *Synodal-Bericht*, 1902, pp. 44—47.
32. *Synodal-Bericht*, 1905, p. 36.
33. *Synodal-Bericht*, 1902, p. 124.
34. Frederick Lindemann, *Exhibit of Parochial Schools in Connection with the German Ev. Luth. Synod of Missouri, Ohio, and Other States, at the Louisiana Purchase Exposition, 1904.* (16 pages)
35. *Synodal-Bericht*, 1905, pp. 167—173.

36. *Evangelisch-Lutherisches Schulblatt*, XL (Feb. 1905), 63, 64.
37. *Synodal-Bericht*, 1905, p. 36.
38. Ibid., p. 37.
39. *Evangelisch-Lutherisches Schulblatt*, XIX (March 1884), 37—40, footnotes.

President Theodore Brohm, 1846—1926

Theodore Brohm was born April 10, 1846, in New York City,
the son of Theodore Julius Brohm, one of the founders of
Concordia College, Altenburg, Missouri. His education for the
ministry included studies in Concordia College in St. Louis and
Fort Wayne (as the St. Louis college was moved there in 1861).
He graduated from Concordia Seminary in St. Louis in 1866
and went on to postgraduate studies in New York University.
In 1869 he became pastor at Immanuel Lutheran Church, East
Boston, Massachusetts, serving until 1871, when he accepted a call
as a professor to Northwestern College in Watertown, Wisconsin.

Prof. Brohm was called to the Addison seminary in 1879, where
he served until 1905 as a professor of English and other subjects,
acting president till 1906, and president till he retired in 1913.
He moved to Oakland, California, where his son Theodore
Brohm, Jr., was president of California Concordia College,
a synodical preparatory school for pastors. Here he served as

instructor until 1925. In 1921 he was awarded the degree of Doctor of Divinity by Concordia Seminary. He died April 27, 1926.

Dr. Brohm was married to Lucia Schaller, daughter of Prof. Gottlieb Schaller, in 1870, and 11 children were born to them. His wife died in 1906.

Chapter 4

THEODORE BROHM'S ADMINISTRATION 1905—1913

Professor Theodore Brohm was the only faculty member to become president of the seminary in its first century. Having been appointed acting president in 1905, when President Krauss accepted a call to Concordia Seminary, St. Louis, he was elected permanently to the position and was installed March 30, 1906, as the third president.

The ninth professorship, authorized by the Synod in 1905, was filled by Teacher Albert H. Miller of Danbury, Conn., graduate of Addison in 1889. Ferdinand H. Schmitt, alumnus of 1901, was appointed assistant professor to take some of President Brohm's teaching duties. He was called permanently in 1906. Other staff changes were also made during Brohm's 8-year administration. Professor Lindemann died of a heart attack Dec. 13, 1907, at age 57. The vacancy was filled when the Rev. Edward W. A. Koehler of Knoxville, Tenn., was installed Jan. 15, 1909. Professor Koenig accepted a call into the parish ministry in May 1909. His successor, the Rev. Charles William Gustav Eifrig of Ottawa, Ont., Canada, was installed Oct. 6, 1909. Then in 1911 Professor Homann retired, and the Rev. Prof. Martin Lochner of Immanuel Lutheran College, Greensboro, N. C., was called to his position and installed Nov. 21, 1912.[1]

In 1907 the new St. Paul's Lutheran Church of Addison was completed and dedicated. This congregation had been founded following a request of the Synod made to Zion Church in 1905. On July 10, 1906, Zion Congregation released a nucleus of 45 voting members, who organized St. Paul's Congregation, Addison, in the so-called "West School District." [2] The Rev. Adolf Pfotenhauer of Lemont, Ill., was called to be the first pastor in 1906.

One of the purposes of the new congregation was to provide a parish home for the seminary students and faculty, their first since

1893. From 1864 to 1893 the students had had to travel the 2½ miles to Zion Church on foot. The rigors of this arrangement had led to the establishment of services in the college chapel in 1893 by permission of Zion Congregation. Pastor Grosse conducted them every other Sunday, alternating with Professors Selle, Krauss, Brohm, and Koenig.[3]

Since the seminary was to be served by St. Paul's Congregation, the Synod had given permission for its member congregations to be circularized for contributions, and some financial assistance was received.[4]

In the formation of the new parish there was again evidence of Zion Congregation's willingness to work and sacrifice for the seminary, still true to promises made in 1863. The presence of the college had been mutually beneficial to both over the years. The professors had given much assistance to the congregation, and the congregation had done a great deal to support the seminary.[5]

When the Synod met in Fort Wayne in 1908, many of the questions about curriculum and the need for a sixth year, which had been asked since the turn of the century, were still being discussed. The greatest problem, however, was the need for improving the substandard living conditions at Addison which clamored for solution.

The Synod approved the request to install a sanitation system including a large septic tank, sewers, and toilets for $7,000. In response to a plea by the Addison Board for a dormitory, living rooms, lecture rooms, laboratories, and a library, the Synod voted $30,000 for a new building, although, according to one report, somewhat reluctantly.[6] Undoubtedly the original plant at Addison was in very bad condition, and drastic changes and improvement would be required to keep it in service. The alternative of moving the school entirely or in part had also been suggested on several occasions, and this touched off many a debate over the advisability of moving to a new site rather than investing more money in Addison.

The question of separating the preparatory department from the seminary was again discussed. A suggestion was made to have both Seward and Addison become preparatory schools only, which would send students to a seminary to be established at Springfield, Ill. This could be accomplished by closing the "practical" seminary which had been located there since its separation from St. Louis in 1874–75. Other suggestions were heard which proposed to relocate the entire institution in a larger educational center. Spirited discussions of these problems were frequent throughout the Synod.

A very important step forward was made in 1908, when a sixth year was added to the seminary, making it a 4-year high school and a 2-year junior college. It automatically established high school graduation as the entrance requirement for the college normal department. The high school was patterned after the American high school, and the two college years were gradually set up to conform to the state normal schools.[7] It is interesting to recall that in 1908 the Department of Normal Schools of the National Education Association recommended high school graduation as the minimum normal school entrance requirement.

In 1908 the Synod established a new board called the General Board of Control of the Colleges of the Evangelical Lutheran Synod of Missouri, Ohio, and Other States. It was to consist of three men and have general oversight over the plans and financial needs of the various institutions, including major repairs. Local boards were to present all their needs to this general board, which would make all requests to Synod. One of the duties of the new board was to visit the various campuses and become personally acquainted with the needs of each. Congregations were told to consult with this group if they wished to establish a new institution.[8]

The new building for which the Synod had authorized $30,000 in 1908 could not be built because the funds were not forthcoming. Thus the problem of inadequate facilities continued. The needs of the seminary became more acute, and further study of the needs indicated that $30,000 was not nearly enough to combat the growing inadequacy of the plant.

The proponents of moving to a new location had been very active since 1908. Pastors and prominent laymen in and around Chicago wanted to have the school moved there, including the high school and the college, or the college alone, leaving the high school classes at Addison. Among them were the Rev. Paul Sauer, Rev. William C. Kohn (then President of the Northern Illinois District), City Alderman A. W. Beilfuss, Theodore Lamprecht, and Paul Schulze. They urged the Chicago pastoral conference to promote the transfer of the seminary. The conference agreed, and by December 1910 they had promised to aid in collecting money for a building site which could be donated to the Synod in 1911. Pastor Sauer of St. John's, Chicago, collected the first $1,000 donation for it on Dec. 26, 1910.[9]

This group now formed an organization to give active and systematic support and direction to the project. After a preliminary meeting of interested individuals held Jan. 12, 1911, in Mr. G. Tatge's office in Chicago, the official organization of the Lutheran Education Society took place. By 1914 its membership had grown to more than 900, including most of the prominent Lutherans of the area.

According to its constitution, the purpose of the society was to "promote higher education among the members of the Evangelical Lutheran Synod of Missouri, Ohio and Other States living in Chicago and vicinity; to assist financially or otherwise for specific purposes of the Teachers Seminary, now to be transferred from Addison, Illinois, to Chicago or one of its suburbs . . . to foster the educational spirit in the Lutheran Church generally and bring about a clearer understanding of the needs of our church and its institutions." [10]

Since the synodical convention would meet in St. Louis in May, the society had to move quickly. On March 31, 1912, the Rev. Ferdinand Sievers addressed a letter to all congregations in the area in which he disclosed that $20,000 had been definitely pledged and much more was anticipated. Pastors and teachers conferences were informed on April 10 that a tract of land comprising at least 20 acres would be offered to the Synod as a gift by May, for the purpose of relocating the Addison teachers seminary in the Chicago vicinity.[11]

Reasons advanced for the move included the following: students will come in contact with a large number of fellow Lutherans in various stations of life; students will benefit from the many cultural opportunities in Chicago (museums, libraries, art centers, lectures, and concerts); instructors will be in a better position to improve themselves by further schooling. Also, the old plant was a fire hazard, and the Village of Addison had little to offer in the way of fire protection.

The leadership of the move was provided to a large degree by Pastor Sauer. He was encouraged by District President Kohn, ex-officio member of the board of control for the Addison seminary. On Feb. 11, 1911, he wrote to Pastor Sauer, "Work hard on your problem. . . . All eyes are looking to you. It is the greatest thing for our college in the Century. You *will* succeed and the church will thank you." [12]

On Feb. 16, 1911, Kohn again wrote as follows: "The faculty in Addison is unanimously opposed to the Chicago plan (to move the

seminary) and in favor of building up the campus at Addison." [13]
Pastor Sauer received word from Fort Wayne on April 22 that the
feeling there was against moving the seminary only (without the
preparatory department) and that they had tabled the idea of moving the entire institution. The teachers in the Fort Wayne area opposed it.[14] The opposition of the Addison faculty was quite influential,
and this undoubtedly caused the final vote to be very close.[15] The
Lutheran Education Society kept working, however, and had more
than $50,000 subscribed by convention time as well as a site for the
college in River Forest.

The Addison board of control came to St. Louis with a request for
$105,000 for a new dormitory to house 200 and a new classroom build-
ing. This sum would also allow sufficient funds to remodel the old
buildings completely so that they would include a library and reading
room, auditorium, laboratories, and music rooms.[16]

The Lutheran Education Society now proposed that the seminary
alone be moved to Chicago or one of its suburbs, leaving the high
school in Addison. They stated that the majority of Christian people
in that vicinity were ready to present a good-sized plot of ground to
the Synod for this purpose and that the pastoral and teachers conferences were fully in accord with this plan.[17]

After considerable debate the Synod resolved by written vote to
move the entire institution to Chicago. The vote was by a small majority, 216 for and 206 against.[18] This action took place on May 17,
1911. The Lutheran Education Society was asked to give their land
donation for the entire school. The Northern Illinois District was asked
to contribute the $30,000 they had pledged for a new building in Addi-
son, and the Synod itself voted $100,000 for the new plant.[19]

The Addison board was authorized to dispose of the old property
and use the proceeds towards the new buildings. The wish was expressed that the old plant not be sold to anyone of a different faith.
After thanking the Lutheran Education Society the convention unanimously passed a resolution requesting everyone to work shoulder to
shoulder to carry out the resolutions of the Synod.

However, the opposition to the move was not satisfied. At least
one attempt was made to force a reconsideration of the problem.
A 4-page circular was drawn up by Dr. E. W. Marquardt, Mr. F. Rittmueller, who had been a delegate to the 1911 synodical convention
in St. Louis, and Mr. Louis Leeseberg, a member of the Addison

board of control, which was distributed at all Chicago church doors after the transfer had been voted.[20]

They claimed that the delegates had been misled by false reports and that all should hear the "other side of the story." They felt that the reports had neither fairly presented the strong points of the Addison location nor the weaknesses of the River Forest site.

The new property was described as being over a mile north of the nearest Chicago Northwestern railroad station. It was a flat, low piece of ground which had two drainage canals. Both treeless and shrubless, it was bounded on the north and south by cornfields, on the west by grassland (one mile west along the Des Plaines River was a forest) with Oak Park, another suburb, to the east.[21]

They agreed that there were no saloons in River Forest or in Oak Park, but they pointed out that Forest Park to the south had at least 25, six of which were only about seven blocks from the south border of the new site. There was a large amusement park about 2 miles south (it was rumored that it might move to River Forest). They were convinced that these things would tempt the students and harm their studies.

Moreover, they felt that the fire danger, held to be so great at Addison, would still be present in River Forest and the protection no better. The installation of steam heat had reduced the fire danger in Addison sufficiently, they felt. Arguments were advanced regarding the septic tank system newly installed in Addison, versus the sewer disposal system of the city, which might contaminate drinking water sources. They asserted that the drinking water was of better quality in Addison, which was also high and dry compared with the swampy River Forest land. Concern was expressed over the future buildings that might be built in River Forest, and the peaceful village was pictured as a place conducive to the best study.

A considerable point was made that St. Paul's Church in Addison, which had been built in 1907, largely at the request of the college and the Synod, would now be half empty. Now again the students would have to walk 2 or 2½ miles as they did from 1864 to 1893 before services were started at the seminary, because all the nearer churches were full. They proposed to have all money collected for the new buildings impounded until the next convention, which was to be held in Chicago, so that people would have a chance to see both places and reconsider the entire matter.[22]

Protesting letters and cards which were received by Pastor Sauer, who led the promotional planning to move the seminary, indicated the stronger emotions that were engendered by the move. One correspondent wrote: "Come out and see the new College site at River Forest at once. The imaginary sewers failed to take away the water. The site is certainly out of sight, as it is under water. It would be more appropriate to build a natatorium there." Another wrote: "How do you enjoy reading the circular concerning the Addison College? I think the best thing to do in Forest Park is to start an ice business and River Forest a skating rink." There were others who felt the move was a serious mistake, but there were many more who approved the move strongly. All protests were to no avail. Through the efforts of C. H. Zuttermeister, Theodore Lamprecht, and others the land was secured by Sept. 30, 1911, and by June 10, 1912, the congregations of the Northern Illinois District were informed that the deed had been given over to the Board of Directors of the Synod. Total cost of the nine different parcels that had to be secured was $53,500.[23]

The site consisted of about 40 acres in the northeast corner of River Forest, then a town of 1,200. The land had been a cornfield, and most of it had been a swamp. The tract was nearly square, running 1,259 feet on Monroe Avenue (the west boundary) and Bonnie Brae Avenue (east) and 1,257 feet on Division Street (north) and Augusta Street (south). Only Augusta Street was paved. There was nothing to indicate that River Forest was destined to become one of the wealthiest suburbs of Chicago. Property values began to rise almost immediately, and in 15 years one lot near the college was sold for $13,000. The campus would have yielded 110 lots of that size.

Ground was broken for the new buildings on Nov. 12, 1912. The cornerstone was laid Dec. 15, with more than 8,000 people attending. President Theodore Brohm of the Addison seminary officially opened the festivities and greeted the people, who were addressed in German by the Rev. Adolf Pfotenhauer and in English by the Rev. Jacob W. Miller of Fort Wayne, Second Vice-President of the Synod. Special music was supplied by the Addison Seminary Chorus of 75 voices directed by Professor Kaeppel and a massed mixed choir of 400 voices directed by Teacher Max O. Frieser of St. Luke's Church, Chicago.

Accompaniment for congregational singing was furnished by a brass choir from Aurora, Ill., directed by Teacher Emil C. Hoffmann. The Rev. Theodore Kohn, secretary of the board of control, placed

the following items in the copper box designed for the cornerstone
(most of these are in German):

The Book of Concord

Catechism

Hymnal

German Reader (New series I–III)

German Language Books (I–III)

English Language Books (I–IV)

English Readers (I–V)

Standard American Arithmetic (I–V)

Synodical *Handbook*

Synodal-Bericht, 1911

Katalog der Anstalten, 1911–12
(Catalog of Schools)

History of the Seminary
(*Alma-Mater,* Jan. 1912)

House rules and class schedules

Graduation programs of 1910 and
1911 plus many pictures

A report of the transfer of the Seminary

Constitution of the Lutheran Education Society

The following German newspapers:

*Westen; Concordia; Sonntagspost
und Presse*

Das Schulblatt, Dec. 1912

Der Lutheraner, 1 Oct. 1912

Lutheran Witness, Dec. 5, 1912

Stadtmissionar, Dec. 1912

Program of the day

Lists of Names:

Synodical officers and Board of
Directors

Northern Illinois District Officers

Professors and students of Addison

Addison Board of Control

Electors of the Seminary

House steward

Building committee

The architect — John Ahlschlager
and Son

The contractors

The Officers of the Lutheran Education Society

The President of the U. S., William Howard Taft

The Governor of Illinois, Charles
Deneen

The President of River Forest
Village, J. E. Adams

Pastor Kohn then locked the box and handed it to President
W. C. Kohn, of the Northern Illinois District, who officiated at laying the stone. The cornerstone had been donated by T. C. Diener,
who also had the contract for the stonework.[24]

Consideration was given to the name of the new school. The
faculty on April 16, 1913, suggested the name "Lutheran Normal College of the German Evangelical Lutheran Church." [25] In the May 20,
1913, faculty meeting a resolution was sent to the Board of Control
requesting that the school not be incorporated under the name "Concordia College." [26] However, the name Concordia Teachers College
was selected, and the charter, which was issued by Illinois Secretary
of State Louis G. Stevenson on April 28, 1915, was vested in "Concordia Teachers College, a legally organized Corporation." [27]

President Brohm had announced his intention of retiring early in 1913 after 34 years of service to the seminary. His administration of 8 years was the shortest during the first century, but they were years of profound and significant change for the second half century. The close of his administration on June 12, 1913, marked the end of 49 years of separate teacher training in the Missouri Synod, as well as the final closing of the Addison seminary itself.

A farewell banquet for President Brohm was held in the dining hall of the seminary on June 12, 1913, sponsored and prepared jointly by the students, the faculty, and the faculty families. The hall was beautifully decorated for the occasion. Many tributes were paid recognizing his long and faithful services.[28] Among his gifts was a photograph album showing interior and exterior scenes of Addison.[29]

The *Schlussfeier* (closing celebration), which was always a very special occasion at the Addison seminary, had a special significance in 1913. For several years previously these graduation programs had been held in Orchestra Hall in Chicago. However, a number of historical events of vital importance to the seminary were converging on June 13, 1913, which made it appropriate that they meet in Addison at this time and place.

The graduation program of the 24-member class of 1913 was the last one for the Addison seminary as well as the last one for President Brohm. However, it also included the installation of W. C. Kohn as the fourth president of the institution and the first president of Concordia Teachers College in River Forest.[30]

As the visitors and officials arrived at the Addison railway station on June 13, they were serenaded by the seminary band, which was directed by William Bertram, a member of the graduating class. They were greeted further by a welcoming committee consisting of Professors Miller, Schmitt, and Lochner. Led by the band, the entire gathering marched to the seminary dining hall for lunch.

The graduation began promptly at 12 o'clock. The first part included presentations by various members of the Class of 1913, including an organ selection by Paul W. Gugel, an English address by Frank B. Miller, and the farewell address in German by Adolph C. Rosenwinkel. A response was given by student Alwin R. Roschke, and the four upper classes sang a number. President Brohm addressed the class briefly, earnestly admonishing them to faithfulness, and gave out diplomas to the following: William Bertram, R. M. Beyerlein,

E. E. Bickel, H. M. Bleck, A. W. Buescher, Theodore Fruend, E. Glawe, P. W. Gugel, Hans Hansen, M. Hesemann, E. C. Hinz, A. Koch, A. M. Kummer, Theodore Meves, Frank B. Miller, E. G. Mossner, J. Neukuckatz, Arthur Nickel, P. H. Peters, A. Reiss, A. M. Richter, A. C. Rosenwinkel, Gustav Scheiderer, and E. Simantel. He also announced the places to which the graduates had been assigned.[31]

President Kohn was installed immediately after the distribution of the diplomas. Northern Illinois District President Frederick H. Brunn, who had succeeded Kohn in that office when the latter accepted the presidency of the seminary, gave a special address for the installation. In his sermon he reviewed the duties of the president as follows:

The president was to be the official representative of the institution to the Synod and its boards and to all who had business with the school. This would also necessitate handling correspondence and all notices. He was to be the inspector of the entire institution and its personnel. In that capacity he was to supervise all the classes of all the professors by visiting them from time to time to see that the schedules and course of study were being carried out and that all regulations were obeyed. His supervision further encompassed the work of the steward, the cleanliness and orderliness of the school, and oversight of student expenses. He was to be a "house father" to watch diligently over the souls of his students and be the chief religion teacher. Finally, he was to observe the students at work and at play and be responsible for their Christian training.[32]

Secretary Theodore Kohn of the board of control installed his brother in a brief ritual. The new president then addressed the people paying special tribute to his predecessor, Theodore Brohm. Then he spoke to them about the progress in River Forest. He announced that a very generous gift had been received for the new music building which was being built, although it had not been included in Synod's appropriation in the 1911 convention. Funds were being solicited from people with means. This gift of $15,000 had been solicited by Mr. G. A. Fleischer, a very active member of the Lutheran Education Society, who invited President Kohn to go with him to meet the donor, Mr. Henry Schoellkopf, owner of a grocery and delicatessen.[33]

Summary

As he left Addison to go into retirement in Oakland, Calif., in 1913, President Brohm could look back on 34 years of faithful service to the seminary. In his 8-year administration two very important issues were decided. The issue of curricular improvement was met when the sixth year was added in 1908, the first such change since the school was founded in 1864. This was a major step forward to keep pace with the better normal school development in America and the first step away from the German *Gymnasium* curriculum pattern which had been in use in all of Synods' schools. The faculty had increased to nine, and in 1911–12 a special physical education instructor had been engaged, H. B. Camann of Chicago, who came on Saturdays. The enrollment gradually decreased from 226 in 1905 to 168 in 1913 because the college at Seward, Nebr., had added the seminary years. The total number of graduates since 1865 was 1,484. The Village of Addison had a population of 149 at this time.

The second major problem was also solved, that of relocating the school. Although it may not have been entirely to everyone's satisfaction at first, the ranks were closing behind the relocation, and a new phase of service for the school was beginning.

Notes

1. *Lutheran School Journal*, LXVII (May 1932), 402, 406.

2. *100th Anniversary: Zion Evangelical Lutheran Church, 1838—1938* (Church-ville, Ill.), p. 13.

3. Ibid.

4. Robert Schlesselman, ed., "Rejoice in the Lord," golden anniversary booklet of St. Paul's Evangelical Lutheran Church, Addison, Ill., 1956.

5. Daniel E. Poellot, "A Century of Christian Education." History of the Evangelical Lutheran School of St. Paul, Addison, Ill., 1849—1949. Booklet: Addison, Ill., Aug. 1949), p. 27.

6. *Lutheran School Journal*, LXVII (May 1932), 404.

7. Ibid., p. 403.

8. *Synodal-Bericht*, 1908, pp. 61—63.

9. *Northern Illinois District Messenger*, VIII (May 1932), 4.

10. Ibid.

11. Ibid.

12. W. C. Kohn postal card to Paul Sauer, Feb. 11, 1911.

13. W. C. Kohn postal card to Paul Sauer, Feb. 16, 1911.

14. M. Luecke postal card to Paul Sauer, April 22, 1911.

15. M. Luecke letter to Paul Sauer, May 6, 1911.

16. *Synodal-Bericht*, 1911, p. 49.

17. Ibid., p. 52.

18. J. Kastner postal card to Paul Sauer, May 17, 1911.

19. *Synodal-Bericht*, 1911, p. 52.

20. Dr. E. W. Marquardt, F. Rittmüller, Louis Leeseberg, *"An die Brüder der Evangelisch-Lutherischen Synode von Missouri, Ohio, und anderen Staaten"* (To the Brethren of the Evangelical Lutheran Synod of Missouri, Ohio, and Other States). A 4-page circular.

21. Ibid.

22. Ibid.

23. Henry W. Horst, "Important Facts and Figures." Reports of two surveys evaluating the property at River Forest for the Synod in 1918 and 1932. It includes the charter of the college and the deeds as well, also a record of all buildings and additions up to and including 1932. (Unpublished, bound in one book, unpaginated.)

24. *Stadtmissionar*, Dec. 15, 1912. Account of the celebration of the cornerstone laying of the new teachers seminary in River Forest. Clipping in the Theodore Kohn scrapbook in the archives at Concordia Teachers College, River Forest, Ill.

25. Faculty minutes, April 16, 1913.

26. Faculty minutes, May 20, 1913.

27. Henry W. Horst. The charter is one of the documents in this book.

28. Clipping from *Concordia,* a magazine current at that time. Undated. In the Theodore Kohn scrapbook in the Concordia Teachers College archives in River Forest.

29. This photograph album is now in the River Forest archives.

30. Theodore Kohn scrapbook.

31. Ibid.

32. Ibid.

33. Ibid.

Chapter 5

VIGNETTES OF ADDISON SEMINARY LIFE

No history of the college could be complete without giving consideration to the student, his characteristics, attitudes, living conditions, and
activities. The Addison seminary enrolled only male students throughout its 49-year history, a practice which was continued in River Forest
another 26 years.

The constant shortage of teachers kept up a steady pressure to
lower the graduation and admission standards of the seminary. On
the other hand, the desire of the administration and faculty to keep
standards high gradually had a stabilizing influence on the student
body.

In September 1864 the first student body consisted of 43 students,
to which 12 more were added as the year went on, their ages varying
from 14 to 30. Eighteen of these were transferred from Fort Wayne.
Ten others came from Germany, sent by Pastor Brunn of Steeden in
Nassau, who had opened a preparatory school in that city in 1861.
It is estimated that his school furnished the Missouri Synod about
250 men.[1] These students were called *"Brunnsche Sendlinge"* (Brunn's
sendlings) and represented various degrees of preparation.

Apparently the situation was not much different in 1867, for a member of that graduating class wrote in 1932: "We were a motley crew.
Some young boys from our own circles, young men, some of native
growth, some more or less acclimated, others just landed on America's
shores. There was a considerable number of *Brunnsche Sendlinge*
varying in age from eighteen to forty. No less varied were the trades
and professions they had followed in Germany. Two or three had
been teachers, four had their pedagogical studies interrupted by reason of military service in the Prusso-Austrian War, just ended. Our

Union Army of the Civil War was represented by three men, one minus a leg, another an arm. In a class by himself was a native who had taught in a public school." [2] Thirty-two were born in Germany, Holland, or Switzerland. [3]

In his reminiscences written for the fiftieth-anniversary celebration of Concordia Teachers College, William Henry Bewie identified the three Civil War veterans as students named Engelbrecht, who had lost a leg at Shiloh, and Schmalzried, who lost an arm in the wilderness (he refers to them as being "rather incomplete"), and himself. [4] During his days many men around 30 years of age enrolled in Addison. He says: "On the day of opening (1866) we had a very impressive sermon by Professor Selle, after which the President read to us the 'Rules and Regulations' of the institute. These sounded somewhat different than the 'Articles of War' which had been read to me five years before. The object of both were the same, to govern the conduct of those concerned. I immediately proceeded to put myself in compliance by handing to the President my rather formidable looking six-shooter, prized as a memento." [5]

A considerable number of students during the beginning years of the seminary were not only older but also quite well educated, and in many cases they did not even need additional instruction in music. The chief need of these students was in doctrine, and probably next in importance was English. Graduation was practically an individual matter for such students, who were placed into the field as soon as they were judged to be ready.

From an Early Brochure

About the turn of the century President Krauss published a brochure of the seminary giving information to prospective students. He stated the purpose of the Synod in establishing the seminary: "to provide well-prepared and God-fearing teachers for the church." Enrollees must be members of the Lutheran Church, at least 14 years old, have the necessary spiritual and intellectual gifts, diligent, faithful, and obedient. They must have a positive and reliable evaluation of their pastors and teachers. [6] Certification of graduation from a good parish school gave admission to the lowest class. Higher placement could be achieved by examination. [7]

Three trains from Chicago daily furnished the transportation to Addison, requiring an hour or more to make the run. Students were warned not to come without written permission. All were urged to bring as little luggage as possible.

Students were to bring a pillow and two each of pillowcases, bedsheets, towels, and quilts and have identification on them. Mattresses could be purchased for $2.00, featherbeds being permitted only if the need for them could be shown. From 1864 to 1883 the students had filled their own straw ticks each year. In 1883 the college steward made the mattresses which were sold to students. Washbasins, oil lamps, chairs, and textbooks could be purchased at the seminary or in Addison stores. First-year students were advised to wait a year before they purchased a violin so that they might have the assistance of the instructor and avoid buying a poor instrument. Violin was required of all students until 1905.[8]

Students under 18 had to give their personal funds to one of the professors for safekeeping and keep account of it under his supervision. This service was not available for older students except by special request of the parents.[9]

Many boys were very poor. President Krauss made it clear that poverty should not keep an otherwise qualified student from coming. He felt that their congregations and their relatives should be encouraged to help and that the parents or anyone else who sent students should make it clear in advance how much assistance would be needed.

Two report cards a year were sent to the parents, who were reminded that enrolling their sons included a promise of obedience to rules and regulations. Parents were urged to pray for the seminary, its faculty and students.

Costs

When the seminary opened in 1864, the cost to the students was $20 for the entire year. This amount was gradually increased to $55 by 1885, and to $70 by 1909, when the sixth year was added. It was understood that the Synod itself was underwriting a portion of the costs, and the rule was established that students who quit the seminary voluntarily were to reimburse the Synod $40 for each year of attendance.[10]

Cost to the student, not including personal needs, at the beginning of the 20th century was $65 a year, payable quarterly, besides $2.00 for the sick fund, $1.00 as a guarantee fund, and 50 cents for desk rental. All money was to be sent to the faculty treasurer, Professor

Backhaus.[11] Besides these fees, the cost of laundry averaged $10 to $12 per year.

The entire cost for one student including board ($55) in 1883–84 was $92.29. This included all personal expenses. It is interesting to note items listed such as the following: [12]

haircut	$ .10	collection for baseball club	$ .05
lamp chimney	.11	collection for party	.05
collection for student treasury	.25	eatables for night watch	.35
collection for library	.10	village road tax	1.50

Students paid their fees to a faculty treasurer who together with the president directed the purchasing of food and supplies by the steward. It is not clear who had charge of this function when the seminary opened in 1864. Presumably it was Professor Selle, who moved with the seminary from Fort Wayne. Probably the second was Professor Haentzschel, who won the admiration of the students by not only feeding the students and meeting all other expenses on the fee of $55 per year but also saved enough out of it to treat all students to a picnic in Turner Park at the end of 1883–84.[13] He was succeeded by Professor Backhaus, who served till 1913.

Student Life

Initially the seminary was divided into a 3-year preparatory department (the students were called *Praeparanden*) and a 2-year seminary department (the students were called *Seminaristen*). The lowest preparatory class was called the "fifth class" and so on up to the graduating class, called the "first class" after the German *Gymnasium* system. After 1908 the sixth year was added, and "sixth class" was the name used for the high school freshmen. A member of either of the two lowest classes was called "fox" *(Fuchs)*. They were placed under the supervision of the upper classmen, to whom they were expected to be obedient. They had to sweep and dust the room, carry coal and ashes (prior to 1896), fill the lamps, and carry in a fresh bucket of water for drinking. The study rooms were called "living rooms" and housed from four to six students as a rule. However, two large living rooms, which had formerly been classrooms, housed around 20 students each and were known as the "Union Stockyards" and the "Pacific Stockyards." [14]

Each of the rooms was placed in charge of a member of the graduating class selected by the faculty and known as the "room buck."

He made rules and regulations regarding duties and conduct. The "foxes" had to handle all sorts of menial chores, including cleaning the room and running errands for the "ruling element" (upper classmen).[15] There were occasional indignities and hazing.[16] Discriminatory and ignominious treatment of lower classes he had seen still angered Markworth after more than 50 years.[17]

Daily Program

During the early years of the seminary the students were called forth to the day's activity by a 5-o'clock bell (5:30 in winter months); they had to hurry through morning ablutions and be ready for chapel a half hour later. The washroom under the north wing could be reached only by going outside — an unpleasant experience on rainy days or in the snow, sleet, and cold of winter. The students had to carry their washbasin, soap, towel, and comb with them to the wash room, pump water into the wash pan out of a rain-water cistern, return to finish dressing, and be in the chapel seat for roll call. The chapel room was called the *aula,* the same term that was used in German schools and universities to designate the assembly hall. The devotions were conducted by the president.[18]

Chapel was followed by breakfast, after which there was a one-hour study period till 8:00, when classes began. At 10:00 the "room buck" procured a slice of bread for each room-mate for a "second breakfast." [19] Dinner was served at noon, and afternoon classes began at 1:00. The students enjoyed free hours from 4:00 to 6:00, when the large seminary bell rang for supper. Prescribed study periods were held between 7:00 and 9:30, at which time roll call and devotions were held again in the *aula.* All were to be in bed at 10:00, when lights were put out.[20] The president or one of the professors came to inspect during study hours and after students were in bed. During the 1890s the day started an hour later, eliminating the morning study hour.[21] Saturdays lessons were held from 7:00 to noon.

The Campus

In 1913 the seminary property consisted of a triangular plot of ground of 27 acres, beginning at the corner of Lake Street and Army Trail Road in Addison. The first 5 acres (the apex of the triangle) was an attractive park which also included two tennis courts built and maintained by individual classes. Behind this park the various buildings were arranged, including the original "Main" building with its two wings, a separate lecture building, dining hall, training school, and other outbuildings. There were five dormitories and 22 study rooms, or "living rooms," as they were called. The buildings were not conveniently arranged. There was an endless confusion of narrow halls, doors, and stairs which made the whole plant impractical. One of the important lacks was clothes closets. Students had to keep clothes in their trunks or hang them on hooks on the wall and cover them. In describing the new modern plant at River Forest in contrast to the Addison seminary, Hermann Zagel, an Addison graduate of 1882, defined "modern" as meaning entrance halls, stairways, and corridors wide enough so one could not only pass people but actually move a trunk, desk, bed, or even a piano without risking one's limbs or breaking out plaster in the walls. Also, it meant no more running around from building to building in all kinds of weather, no more running from pump to pump for water in order to find one that isn't dry, no more overcrowded study and dormitory rooms. He pointed out that students had to go from building to building 25 to 30 times a day in all kinds of weather, moving after every 40 minutes.[22]

Zagel declared that the buildings had never been up to modern standards even in the time they were built. The students felt the inconveniences and great lack of comforts. There was no central heating and no heat in the dormitories or washrooms. The fire hazards due to kerosene lamps were always serious, for all lamps were filled from cans kept in the study rooms. Until the 1880s there was no fire escape on the buildings, and moreover, all doors opened into the rooms instead of the corridors. The halls were incredibly narrow, the main entrance hall being merely 4 feet in width. Each building had but one stairway, very steep and narrow. Fire extinguishers were added about 1881. At this time there was no fire engine even in the village.

The installation of steam heat in 1896 put an end to woodchopping and coal carrying as well as to the night watches, which had been a part of college life for 32 years. Night watch was an all-night duty assigned to two upper-class boys who kept the 35 study room stoves going during the long winter nights. They received a coffee cake and coffee from the steward and a kerosene lantern, working from after chapel till 5:00 a.m. and being excused from classes the next day.[23]

Final improvements were added to the Addison seminary in 1908 with the installation of septic tanks and modern plumbing, including fountains, showers, and toilets. Electricity was never installed.

Care of the Sick

We have seen that President Lindemann had nursed a sick student in his own home just a short while before he died. It was not out of the ordinary for the college presidents to "doctor" sick students. A doctor was retained in the village to come on call, but the students did the nursing, serving in 8-hour shifts and going into the sickroom only as needed since they were not required to stay. The sickroom was very cold in winter.[24]

Food Services

In 1882 the breakfast and supper consisted of bread, thin coffee, and "dubious" butter. The latter was so called because of its color and the fact that it was a mixture of rancid and good butter. On Sundays coffee cake was substituted for bread. The potatoes were often taken to the study rooms for frying later, although this was against the rule. The students would often go to Weber's or Treichler's stores in Addison to buy gingersnaps and "whitewash" cakes in order to supplement their seminary diet.[25] Gradually the quality improved, and only fresh butter was used. Syrup was added to the diet during. the 1890s, which was renamed *Schmier* by the students.[26] There was always an ample supply, and the bread was of the very finest quality according to all reports. Snacks of bread were provided at nine and four o'clock.[27]

Kniepenburg

The students' name for Addison was *Kniepenburg* or more usually *Kniepen*. According to Wegener, the name originated among the farmers from farther west who brought their produce to Chicago, a two-day trip each way. Since Addison had a tavern, they stayed there overnight. Some of these farmers felt they were overcharged by the tavern keeper. They would warn the others in their Low German dialect: *"Passt up. Hier dod se die kniepen"* (Be careful, here they pinch you). This explanation was given to Wegener by Mrs. T. J. Grosse, wife of the former professor and pastor of Zion Church.[28]

The Orphan Festival Brings a Train to Addison

For nearly 30 years the only railway station for Addison was the Northwestern at Elmhurst, 4 miles away. In 1893 the Illinois Central Railroad built a branch to Addison, much to the relief of the students, and the Addison "dummy" train became a byword to them.

The first trains were run on the Sunday morning of the annual orphan festival in September 1893 on a track that had been finished just that morning. Sixty-five cars in five sections were needed to transport the huge crowds from Chicago. As they returned in the afternoon, a Burlington train, which used the Illinois Central tracks to enter Chicago, ran into the last section of the Orphan Home Special, killing seven or more and injuring many.

The orphan festival was considered one of the highlights of the school year. Held during the first part of September, it brought together thousands of Lutherans by special trains, the number reaching as high as 20,000–30,000.[29] The day opened with three divine services held on various parts of the grounds, and stands in various places served food and refreshments.

Seminary students served as guides, showing the visitors the seminary buildings. Since the visitors also included girls, the day was regarded with great interest by the seminarians, to whom all associations with girls, even by mail, was strictly forbidden. A. C. Rosenwinkel writes: "Of course the girls wanted to see the gymnasium, try out the dumbbells, Indian clubs, wands, climbing ropes, climbing poles, etc. Very exciting and interesting! Most boys had an eye for feminine beauty coupled with a searching appraisal of the contents of the large (or sometimes small) lunch basket carried by the father or mother or sometimes by young ladies unaccompanied by parents. It was a disappointing experience to have shown a charming girl about the "Sem" and then end up with a very frugal or poorly-prepared lunch from the young lady's basket. The boys generally admitted that often they had to make a very difficult choice between a pretty girl with an anemic looking lunch basket and a not so charming young lady with a very large and very well-stocked lunch basket."[30]

Student Government

Throughout the Addison period the seminary students had very little voice in the government. The direction of the affairs was controlled by the faculty and the board of control. Student privileges were few and restricted.[31] Martin J. Roschke writes: "With the exception of the long-established *Hausordnung* [house rules] we have no code of written rules and regulations to guide us. We have 'unwritten law' only, and that, usually is the customary mode of procedure. These customs have continued year in and year out through innumerable generations of college life. In many respects, the control of the Faculty, but principally of the President, is indirect."[32]

The highest honor that could be given a student was that of being selected as the chairman of the student body (known as *Seminarbock* or "sem-buck" or at times "seminary elder"). The selection was made only from the graduating class. A vice "sem-buck" was selected by the faculty for each wing, and a "room-buck" over each room. All of these were selected from the two upper classes only.

By 1905 the faculty appointed an executive committee of five, including the chairman (seminary elder), charging them with the responsibility of maintaining order and cleanliness in the buildings. The chairman was regarded as the go-between from faculty to student body (referred to as the "coetus") and vice-versa. The secretary was the one officer elected by the students. Each class had its own elected officers. Meetings of the student body are described by Roschke: "German is the official language in regular meetings, but in special meetings, pertaining usually to athletics, English is permitted, because the vernacular would prove unwieldy. . . . The protocols are subject to the examination of the President, who vetos all measures not conducive to the welfare of the institution."[33]

Athletics — Physical Education and Recreation

No official attention was given to this area of student life in Addison with the exception of a small amount of gymnastics which was introduced about 1880 or 1881. In 1895 the building of the gymnasium gave more opportunity for gymnastics. At no time in the Addison period was there even a coach or athletic director on the faculty. By 1908 there was a special instructor in gymnastics, a Mr. Camann who came from Chicago on Saturday mornings to instruct and lead all classes.[34]

In the earliest days of the seminary the students had to saw and split wood for the numerous stoves all fall and winter, besides keeping the wood supply for the cook stoves. In spring and fall they made hay on the campus. Activities connected with the rather extensive vegetable garden, such as harvesting and carrying potatoes, gave a good deal of exercise. Zagel reports that the main recreation was taking walks.[35] Addison students walked 2½ miles to church and back each Sunday and sometimes did this also on Saturday to announce for Communion. On Saturdays they walked distances varying from less than a mile to 13 miles to their *Waschleute* (benefactors), who did their laundry and often gave them Sunday meals. When the distances were greater, the students were usually kept overnight on Saturdays.

Gradually an interest developed in sports activities among the boys, baseball being the first sport to be introduced. John G. O. Sebald writes of the sports during his student years, 1890–95 as follows: "These were not organized as they are today. There were no baseball games with outside clubs. The spring of the year was looked forward to on account of its baseball season. In the noon hour a little warming up could be done between the Middle and North Buildings. After lessons from four to six o'clock there was ball practice on the field providing two of the teams were not crossing bats. The only exercise during the winter was to walk to *Kniepenburg* and back. Dumbbell and Indian club exercises were indulged in occasionally by the very few who possessed them. A walk to our *Waschleute* on Saturday (mine lived seven miles north of the college) proved healthful exercise also. We stayed with them on Saturday night, rode to church with them on Sunday morning and walked back to college. . . . Football was unheard of, and tennis was considered a 'sissy game.' There was very much talk during our time of building a gym for the boys at Addison, but the depression of those years must have been even greater than that of today [1932]." [36]

Baseball was a forbidden activity in 1871, but by 1876 it had become a recognized sport, although it was not encouraged. According to the student paper, *The Spectator*, the first intercollegiate game was played with Elmhurst College sometime between 1876 and 1880, and occasional games were played with Wheaton College and Elmhurst between 1880 and 1895.[37]

The main interest in baseball was intramural, and teams representing each building were pitted against one another. By 1884 the students had organized a baseball club to which each member contributed a small amount which was used for equipment. By 1912 the baseball club had 100 members who contributed ten cents each month, for which the club furnished balls, bats, and gloves. The club was divided into three leagues of two or three teams each. The official seminary team was formed of the best players and was called the "Regulars." All games were played at home since the faculty would not permit the team to go away to play. The club manager and an assistant scheduled all league games during noon hours and after classes and also all interscholastic games usually on Saturday afternoons. In 1912 the Regulars played eight games.[38]

After the baseball season closed for the winter, the students played indoor baseball — outdoors. Each class organized its own club. The interclass games were very competitive, and class rivalry was at a high pitch.

A basketball club was organized in much the same way as the baseball club. It was introduced in 1907 by a few students who played on the baseball diamond at first. The club numbered 40 members within a short time. After repeated requests they received faculty permission to use the gymnasium. By 1912 112 of the total enrollment of 149 were members of the basketball club. Late in the 1910 to 1911 basketball season the club received permission to play outside teams on the home floor but not more than one game in two weeks. By June 1912 they had not lost a game.

Tennis, the only other sport which became established at Addison, was started about the same time as basketball. Participation was limited because there were but two courts, one belonging to the "Tennis Club 12" and the other to the high school juniors who formed the "Tennis Club 14". Since these were class clubs, restricted to 20 members of the class, only club members could use the courts, which were made of cinders and had very primitive backstops. When the class graduated, the club "shares" were sold to others.[39]

Other recreational activities including reading, outings, excursions to Chicago, walks along Salt Creek, and entertainment programs they themselves prepared. A chess club was formed, but card playing was strictly forbidden. One of the important social events was the banquet for the graduating class.

Music

Although instruction in music was always an important part of the curriculum due to the need of the church for teachers of music, organists, and choral directors, music also became an important source of extracurricular activity in the Fort Wayne days, but even more so in Addison. Since the school was founded every graduate had to be capable in organ, piano, vocal music, and violin. The latter was dropped as a requirement in 1905.

Even in the first year, 1864–65, the seminary chorus went out to sing in Rodenberg and Schaumburg, walking both ways. This chorus was called on many times over the years for special music at church. In 1866 a small choir was organized just before Christmas. On New Year's Eve they went caroling at the homes of residents, who gave them donations of money for the household fund. By 1912 the student body was divided into three choruses of two classes each.

In the autumn of 1911 a vocal club of 18 members was organized under the name Euphonia Glee Club. Its purpose was "to stimulate a musical interest . . . for entertainment and recreation." A faculty member conducted one of two weekly meetings and a student the second. The predecessor of the Euphonia Glee Club had been the Schubert Chorus.[40] Over the years there had been many special choruses, quartets, and glee clubs. Popular music of the day (1912) was known as "ragtime," and a group was organized to render it which was called "The Ragtime Gang." [41] The various groups performed at the two annual student entertainments, together with the band and orchestra.

Instrumental music was begun in the Fort Wayne days, but it continued with varying degrees of emphasis throughout the history of the college. In 1884 President Krauss was director of the 19-member band, which rehearsed three days each week from five to six o'clock in the afternoon. The next director was student A. Paesler, regarded as a fine leader and an excellent cornetist. He trained the next student leader, Karl Haase, to follow him as a cornetist and leader from 1888 to 1891. Haase later became professor of music at the Seward seminary.[42] After this time the band program struggled to exist and was often dropped. However, by 1912 there were 17 members in the band which played for the cornerstone laying at River Forest. This band had a constitution which was adopted in 1907. There was also a seminary orchestra of 20 members. Both organizations took part in the annual student entertainments held in the gymnasium. The orchestra had given financially successful programs at La Grange and Aurora.[43]

Some individual graduates also became proficient at the organ, piano, violin, or in some phase of vocal music. One of them, Edward

Rechlin (son of Professor Rechlin), became nationally known as a concert organist. Others became professors of music in other colleges of the Synod.

Throughout the 49-year period of the Addison seminary there was no electricity in the institution either for light or for power for the organs. Accordingly each upper-class student had an underclassman (*Fuchs,* or fox) assigned to him to pump the organ for his practice period. These pumpers were called *Windfuchs* (wind-fox). Pumping was considered a most disagreeable task and very hard work, and the "foxes" were sometimes very difficult to find when pumping time came around. Only the upper-class boys had organ lessons. Both in organ and in piano the students had four practice periods per week.

Library Developments

From 1864 till 1908 very little had been done to provide library facilities for the students. In 1869 President Lindemann announced that there was a small collection of literature in the seminary library which was made available twice each week to the students.[44]

In 1886 Professor Brohm told the students he had bought some English books for $8.50 and that he would welcome suggestions for spending the balance of $16. Seven students were appointed to make recommendations.

That collection remained small and the use of it even smaller according to the account of a member of the class of 1889, Oscar F. Rusch, who had been appointed librarian. As a senior he did not know where the library was. He was directed to a cupboard in Organ Room IV, where he found a confusion of old books and periodicals on three or four shelves. The new student librarian met with President Krauss and pleaded for a room for the library. Being successful in obtaining a very small and dingy room, he reported on the conditions of the holdings and lack of equipment to the student body, which voted funds to equip the room, rebind damaged books, and provide for more rapid growth in books and periodicals. The library became very popular during that year.[45]

The faculty library was very well equipped by comparison, and students had repeatedly requested permission to use it — at least for the upper classes. Nothing came of these requests for some years; however, by 1912 the college classes could check out books from the faculty library, or "General Library," as it was called then. They were allowed two periods per week in this room.[46]

The student library remained in a deplorable condition until 1908, when Professor Koenig successfully contacted friends for gifts totalling $1,500 to buy library shelving and furniture. The faculty proposed to establish a "book concern" (bookstore) so that its profits could be used to purchase library books and equipment. Professor Koehler was appointed manager of this enterprise, which was on the second floor of the south wing and opened in September 1909. The beginning of this enterprise was very slow. By April 1911 the book concern could give librarian F. H. Schmitt $15 for books. However, by February 1929 the total profits given to the library amounted to $8,535.85.[47]

By the end of the Addison period the student library checked out books on three days a week. More important, however, was that the need for improvement in this area had been firmly established.

Grades, Graduation, and Miscellany

Most evaluations of their days and training by alumni of Addison emphasize their belief that despite all the deficiencies of the physical plant and campus, their professors were generally men of faith, integrity, and vision who were well aware of the cause of Christian education they were serving. Their students were regularly reminded of their high calling and urged on to do their best work.[48]

Many of the graduates were filled with zeal for their work. A graduate of 1901, Carl Marquardt, wrote in 1956 that he had been instrumental in encouraging seventy-five boys to enter the ministry of teaching or preaching in the church.[49]

Examinations for graduation were public and tested students in Catechism, German, English, and theory of music. In 1903 report card marks were based on 10 points as follows: 1 — excellent; 2 — very good; 3 — nearly very good; 4 — good; 5 — nearly good; 6 — satisfactory; 7 — nearly satisfactory; 8 — hardly satisfactory; 9 — poor; 10 — bad. The diplomas, or certificates of graduation, also included evaluation of the student in three levels of achievement: 1 — "the necessary requirements prescribed"; 2 — "the most necessary requirements prescribed"; or 3 — "the indispensably necessary requirements prescribed." [50]

In 1907 the grading system was changed to percentages. The

passing grade was 70%. This remained in effect as long as the college remained in Addison.[51] .

Only one reference has been found regarding a student newspaper. It was published on Sept. 12, 1881, bearing the name *The Seminary Observer* and numbered Book I, Volume I. It consisted of a composition book with the news items written in longhand. It was edited by Andrew G. Frinke assisted by Carl C. J. Rupprecht and Fred A. Doepke. The stories bore titles such as "A Night's Lone Hour," "Football Meetings," "Notice of President Garfield's Death," and "Sparks." One paper was prepared each month and passed from room to room.[52]

The colors of the college, maroon and gold, are said to have been selected by the student body of 1907—08, who adopted the colors of the Class of 1908, which claimed to be the first class to receive diplomas in the present sense of the term.[53]

Corresponding with girls was strictly forbidden, and boys were often forced to open suspicious-looking or smelling letters for censoring. Student "mailmen" often delivered such letters intact, despite the rule. Four out of five daughters of one of the local teachers married Addison graduates, despite the fact that visiting local girls was frowned upon. Card playing was strictly forbidden.[54]

In closing the story of student life we refer to a statement made by Professor Ernst Henry Engelbrecht, a graduate of 1891, who wrote about many of the hardships the students had to endure even in life at Addison. He wrote in 1932: "Let no one get from this the impression that we felt we were not well treated and were dissatisfied with our lot. We were just as happy and just as healthy as the students are today. We did not miss bathrooms with hot and cold running water nor all the modern conveniences which our students have today . . . because most of us had never had them. We came from the country and the small towns, and those of us who had lived in the cities were not from the homes of the rich. Heat or cold did not matter much to us. We walked two miles to church on Sunday in all kinds of weather, often through mud . . . so deep that it was difficult to walk at all. On Saturday some of us walked ten to twelve miles to our benefactors. . . . We lived through it all and came out ready to tackle real jobs." [55]

Summary

In this chapter an attempt has been made to present a survey of various facets of student life in the Addison seminary in order to gain an insight into the development of the school and of student activities and services from their point of view. Despite the hardships and inconveniences they endured, the Addison graduates seem to have kept the vision of the cause they were to serve.

Notes

1. "Brunn, Friedrich," *Lutheran Cyclopedia* (St. Louis: Concordia Publishing House, 1954), p. 144.

2. *The Spectator*, VII (May 30, 1932), 5. The author of the letter in this issue of the River Forest student paper is not given.

3. *Evangelisch-Lutherisches Schulblatt*, II (Oct. 1866), 47, 48.

4. William Henry Bewie (no title given to the 10-page account of his life in Addison; document is in the archives of Concordia Teachers College, River Forest), pp. 1, 2.

5. Ibid., p. 2.

6. E. A. W. Krauss, *Auskunft ueber das deutsche, evangelisch-lutherische Schullehrer-Seminar zu Addison, Illinois* (Information on the German Evangelical Lutheran Teachers Seminary at Addison, Illinois, undated brochure of information, published about 1900), p. 1.

7. Ibid., p. 6.

8. Ibid., p. 4.

9. Ibid., p. 5.

10. Ibid., p. 6.

11. Ibid., p. 4.

12. "Complete record of one year's expense at Addison, 1884." This is an unsigned record found in the archives in River Forest.

13. William Wegener, "Reminiscences of Old Addison," *Concordia Historical Institute Quarterly*, XIX (Jan. 1947), 168.

14. Jacob Schmidt letter to the author, March 9, 1962. Schmidt graduated from Addison in 1891.

15. Karl A. Markworth, autobiography in *Fifty-Fifth Anniversary Reunion of the Addison Seminary Class of 1901*, mimeographed book of autobiographies, published in 1956.

16. Albert H. Beck, unpublished autobiography, August 1960.

17. Markworth, autobiography.

18. Wegener, p. 166.

19. Ibid.

20. Ibid.

21. Theo. J. C. Kuehnert, "Reminiscences," in a letter to the author, Dec. 3, 1963. Dr. Kuehnert was a graduate of Addison in 1903. He has served on the faculty at River Forest since 1927.

22. Hermann H. Zagel, *Aus Frühlingstagen* (Erie, Pa.: The Erie Printing Company, 1923), p. 156.

23. Wegener, p. 168.

24. E. H. Engelbrecht, "Reminiscences," *The Spectator*, VII (May 30, 1932), 25.

25. Zagel, p. 175.

26. Kuehnert, p. 3.

27. Martin J. Roschke, "Addison Seminary Organism," *Alma Mater*, II (Jan. 1912), 137.

28. Wegener, p. 161.

29. Beck, p. 18.

30. Adolph C. Rosenwinkel (alumnus of 1913), "Notes and Reminiscences on the Addison Teachers Seminary 1908—1913."

31. Roschke, p. 135.

32. Ibid.

33. Ibid., p. 136.

34. August C. Stellhorn, "Recollections of Addison," letter to the author, April 1963, p. 7.

35. Zagel, p. 207.

36. John G. O. Sebald letter to Prof. Albert Miller, March 14, 1932.

37. *The Spectator,* VII (May 30, 1932), 22.

38. *The Blue and Gold* — Class Annual of Addison Class of 1912, p. 37. This was the first annual published. The proceeds were designated for the new seminary at River Forest.

39. Roschke, p. 139.

40. Ibid., p. 137.

41. *The Blue and Gold,* p. 25.

42. *The Spectator,* VII (May 30, 1932), 19.

43. Roschke, p. 138.

44. *Evangelisch-Lutherisches Schulblatt,* IV (July 1869), 341.

45. *The Spectator,* VII (May 30, 1932), 20.

46. Roschke, p. 138.

47. *The Spectator,* IV (Jan. 22, 1929), 4.

48. Frank B. Miller letter to the author, Jan. 1964. Dr. Miller is a 1913 graduate of Addison.

49. Carl R. Marquardt, autobiography in *Fifty-Fifth Anniversary Reunion of Addison Seminary Class of 1901,* mimeographed book of autobiographies, published in 1956.

50. Kuehnert letter.

51. *The Spectator,* IX (Jan. 25, 1934), 7.

52. Ibid., III (May 9, 1928), 8. Professor Schmieding and a student, Erwin W. Boeker, had attended a Lutheran teachers conference at Mount Olive, Ill., where the latter made a special presentation regarding the school paper, *The Spectator.* Teacher Frinke, then of Collinsville, Ill., told Professor Schmieding that he had been editor of a student paper at Addison, and the following day he showed this relic to him.

53. Stellhorn letter, p. 14.

54. William A. Helmkamp, "Reminiscences from the middle of Concordia's (River Forest) Century." Unpublished list of memoirs of Addison. Helmkamp graduated from River Forest in 1915.

55. Engelbrecht, p. 25.

PART III

RIVER FOREST, 1913—1964

President William C. Kohn, 1865—1943

William C. Kohn was born in Germany June 2, 1865. After attending the elementary school in his native country he came to America, where he received his high school and junior college training in Concordia College, Fort Wayne, Indiana. He graduated from Concordia Seminary, St. Louis, in 1887, and served as pastor in St. James Lutheran Church in Chicago (1887—89) and St. Andrew's Church in the same city (1889—1913). Besides serving on various boards and committees in the District and Synod, Kohn was Northern Illinois District President from 1909 to 1913 and chairman of Lutheran Army and Navy Church Board from 1914 to 1919. He was one of the leaders in the Lutheran Education Society, which promoted the move of the college to River Forest in 1913. Dr. Kohn became the fourth president of the college and the first at River Forest in 1913, serving till his retirement in 1939, after which he continued to teach until his death on March 13, 1943.

His many services to the church were recognized in 1929, when Concordia Seminary of St. Louis awarded him the Doctor of Divinity degree. He was also active in the community, serving as a life member of the Chicago Planning Commission, having been appointed by Mayor Carter Harrison in 1908.

Dr. Kohn was married to Sophia nee Bartling in 1888, and their family consisted of four sons, William, Herbert, Gerard, and Luther, and three daughters, Elsa, Paula, and Gertrude. Their first two sons became pastors.

Chapter 6

Pastor William C. Kohn was well acquainted with the college and its needs, having been intimately connected with it for four years. In 1907 he had declined a call to the Addison seminary.[1] By his election as President of the Northern Illinois District in 1909 he became an ex-officio member of the board of control of the Addison seminary.

The first major objective of the new president was to have the plant at River Forest ready for the new school year, 1913—14. According to the architects, John Ahlschlager and Son, the plant would be completed by Sept. 15. Now plans for dedication were greatly accelerated, and the date was set for Oct. 12. All students were told to report on Oct. 8 except the freshmen, who were to arrive several days later.[2]

Preparations had been made for a large crowd on dedication day. Although the ceremonies were not to start until noon, all car lines were overtaxed as early as nine o'clock, and a huge crowd estimated at from 30,000 to 45,000 was gathered between the buildings and Augusta Street. The Chicago *Tribune* reported on Oct. 13, 1913, that two special trains had come from Milwaukee and that 600 persons had attended from Fort Wayne.[3] Music was supplied by the brass band of Aurora, directed by Teacher Emil C. Hoffmann; a male chorus of 700 directed by Teacher Max O. Frieser; a mixed choir of 800 directed by Teacher Oscar F. Rusch, and a children's choir of 2,000 directed by Teacher Paul T. Buszin.

President Brunn of the Northern Illinois District officially opened the program and welcomed the huge throng. Three simultaneous services were held, speaker's platforms having been set up at Lindemann Hall, the administration building, and Krauss Hall. Dr. Francis Pieper, president of Concordia Seminary, St. Louis, President Max

J. F. Albrecht of Concordia College, Milwaukee, and President Martin
Luecke of Concordia College, Fort Wayne, gave the German sermons.
Professor G. Friedrich Bente of Concordia Seminary, St. Louis, the
Rev. William Koepchen of New York City, a son of Zion Congregation,
Addison, and President George Weller of Concordia Teachers College,
Seward, Nebr., addressed the people in English.[4] Since there were
no public address systems in those days, the speakers were forced to
exert themselves considerably to be heard.

The dedication ceremonies took place at about two o'clock, when
the chairman of the building committee, Paul Schulze, turned over
the keys to the Rev. John Strassen of Milwaukee, who represented
the President of the Synod, the Rev. Frederick Pfotenhauer. Pastor
Strassen then unlocked the doors and presented the keys to President
Kohn. After the dedicatory prayer was offered by the Rev. Theodore
Kohn, secretary of the board of control, President Kohn closed the
service with a benediction.[5] After the ceremonies the crowds pushed
into the buildings to view the rooms and equipment.

The building committee had carried out its assignment to the
satisfaction of the church, completing the five buildings at a total
cost of $224,389.33.[6] Members of the committee included the General
Board of Control of the Synod: the Rev. Charles F. Obermeyer of
St. Louis, Benjamin Bosse of Evansville, Ind., and F. G. Walker of
Cleveland, Ohio; and the local board of control: District President
Brunn, Rev. Theodore Kohn, Paul Schulze, L. Blecke, L. Leeseberg,
G. A. Fleischer, and C. H. Zuttermeister, augmented by William
Schulze, T. C. Diener, the Rev. Paul Sauer, William Schlake, Teacher
Ottomar Kolb, Alderman Albert W. Beilfuss, Prof. Albert Miller, and
President Kohn.[7]

The plant included five new college buildings running parallel to
Augusta Street facing south. In describing them a month after the
dedication Professor Miller said:

> From a distance the buildings appear unnecessarily severe. Upon
> closer approach, however, the classical lines of the individual build-
> ings make themselves felt, and one is impressed by the whole. The
> lines of the buildings will undoubtedly become very much subdued
> after the plans of the landscape architect have been carried out, since
> it has been decided to lay out avenues of trees and shrubbery ap-
> proaches to the college. The cost of defraying this work will be
> borne by the Lutheran Education Society, a body of men who are
> intensely loyal to the entire project, and who intend to spend many
> thousands of dollars in beautifying the whole tract.[8]

The buildings were well planned to suit the needs of the school. The westernmost was the Commons, containing the dining hall accommodating 240 students, the kitchen, the bakery, hospital rooms, and living quarters for the steward and kitchen help.

The next building was the dormitory now known as Lindemann Hall. It had three stories, each containing eight study-rooms for four students each, four sleeping rooms for eight students each, a lavatory, a toilet, and a clubroom, or lounge. Showers and trunk storage rooms were in the basement. All buildings had steam heat and electric lights, a far cry from Addison, where the only lighting had been with kerosene lamps.

The two-story administration building was designed to be the most prominent in the complex. Of classic design, it had 10 massive stone columns in front supporting a portico. Wide stone steps led up to the entrance. Inside were a reception room, a student library and reading room, a chemistry laboratory, lecture rooms, and classrooms for the training school. A faculty room, a faculty library, and six classrooms were on the second floor.

The dormitory now called Krauss Hall was a duplicate of Lindemann Hall in size and accommodations.

The fifth building was called the Music College. It had not been included in the Synod's appropriation for the new college plant but was the gift of 35 individual donors and cost $35,000. It contained 18 piano rooms, eight organ rooms, and a practice room for band and orchestra on the first floor. The second floor was an assembly hall with a seating capacity of 400. In it were a stage and a large organ. Electric blowers in the basement supplied wind for the organs, replacing the *Windfuchs* of the Addison period.

All the new buildings were connected by a corridor 567 feet in length, well lighted and heated. Severe weather need not disturb the students. They did not need to go out in it to get from one building to another.

Besides the college buildings in the central portion of the south side of the campus, nine brick homes had been built for the faculty members.

The Missouri Synod had grown very rapidly since its beginning in 1847, as the following statistics revealed: [9]

Churches and mission stations	4,061
Pastors	2,204
Members	934,199
Schools	2,216
Enrollment	94,167
Teachers (male, 2,235; female, 252)	2,487

Chicago Lutheranism in 1913 included 70,000 Missouri Synod members served by 71 pastors and 135 teachers. The dedication of the new plant was a reaffirmation that the educational objectives of the Synod were still a strong motivating force in the church body. There had been questions about the advisability of continuing support of the parish schools. Some of these had been frankly pessimistic, expressing the feeling that they were on the wane and would finally become extinct. A few schools had closed.

In a speech before the Lutheran Education Society on Jan. 22, 1914, Professor Miller touched on these matters and stated his conviction and also that of a majority of Lutherans, that if Lutheran pastors, teachers, and parents believe in the real value of a Christian training, working devotedly, unselfishly, and intensively for the improvement of the schools, a new era would undoubtedly be the result. In his estimation the future for Lutheran schools looked bright. He felt that the dedication of the new plant was a great stimulus to Christian education, and the great outpouring of gifts was proof of high interest in Lutheran schools. Other Lutherans (many of whom had long since dropped their parish schools) were looking in surprise and wonder on the faith here shown in this institution, he said. River Forest is a monument, he believed, to proclaim the earnestness with which the Missouri Synod regards its purpose to maintain institutions of higher learning through which it could secure men thoroughly competent to teach, who are themselves imbued with an intense desire to spread the Gospel of Christ throughout the land.[10]

Classes began in the new plant on Oct. 13, 1913, with 188 (20 below the estimate) students and a faculty of nine, including President Kohn, and Professors Backhaus, Rechlin, Kaeppel, Miller, Schmitt, Koehler, Eifrig, and Lochner (a son of one of the founders of the Milwaukee private teachers seminary).

The establishment of the college helped to increase land development in the surrounding area, and values of property moved steadily upwards, increasing as much as 25% in two years. Chicago newspapers began to advertise land sales to the north of the college property in an area known as "Green Fields." Property east and south of the college was being subdivided, and the streets and avenues were being planted with trees to make them more attractive. The residents of River Forest were proud to have the school in their midst, and it was mentioned in village promotional literature.[11] City officials welcomed the school, faculty, and students in a special meeting of the village trustees with the college faculty. The city also vacated the streets which would have continued through the property. A city ordinance was passed which required that all houses built in this area had to be set back 57 feet to give a parklike effect along the streets. These developments bore testimony to the wisdom of the Lutheran Education Society and the Synod in relocating the school.

Administration Building Burns

Tragedy struck the new college four and a half months after it was dedicated when, on Saturday, Feb. 28, 1914, the administration building was destroyed by fire. It had been discovered about 5:30 p. m. by President Kohn, who smelled smoke in the building as he was on a tour of inspection. He called several students to help him search for the source of the smoke, which was located in the northeast corner of an upstairs classroom.

The River Forest Volunteer Fire Department responded at once to the alarm, and fire departments from Chicago, Oak Park, Forest Park, and Maywood also were called. At first it seemed that the blaze had been brought under control, but the wind, which had been coming from the west, suddenly changed to the north, and the entire structure seemed to explode into flame. All that the firemen could do was to save the dormitories and music building. Lack of sufficient hose was a handicap. Although there were 14 fireplugs in the general vicinity, none were closer than 500 feet. One lead of hose was 950 feet long. Fire engines from Chicago pumped water from Harlem Avenue. President Einfeldt of Oak Park, Superintendent Mitchell of River Forest, and the four suburban fire chiefs were present. Several firemen were overcome with smoke, and there were numerous narrow escapes from falling walls and falling brick and stone.[12]

The fire chiefs were amazed to discover that there was no fire hose or firefighting equipment in any of the college buildings.[13]

The fire was brought under control by 9:00 p. m. As soon as it became apparent that the other buildings were safe, President Kohn at 9:30 called the faculty and student body together in the dining hall, dimly lighted by oil lamps. Supper had been waiting since 5:30. One of the students, Albert H. Beck, who later became a professor at the school, wrote an account of the meeting:

> We filed into the dining room. President Kohn was there ahead of us. He wept uncontrollably, and so did we. We sat down at our table. He told us we would pray. Never have I heard such an impassioned prayer of penitence. He began in German, "Lord, most merciful Father, have compassion on us, Thy poor children." His prayer was spontaneous . . . and heart rending. . . . There was no way for the president to know where the students were. . . . As it turned out, everybody was safe. . . . About a week later one student did die of pneumonia which he developed after having stood in the snow and water watching the fire. After the prayer President Kohn told us to put our faith in the Lord and everything would turn out well, and now we should eat our supper. Not many of us ate. We were too disturbed to eat. There were long sessions in the rooms that night. There was no heat because the heating system had been ruined. We sat huddled in blankets for awhile and then went to bed, talking late into the night.[14]

The firemen remained on duty nearly all night. The Chicago fire department left at 3:00 a. m. Sunday. A blizzard had added to the tragedy. The sinking temperature made the work difficult, and the blizzard blew burning embers far and wide, endangering property as far away as Harlem Avenue, two blocks away, where homeowners were spraying water on their houses. On Sunday a guard was placed around the ruins to keep visitors from risking their lives.

The cause of the fire was believed to be faulty electrical wiring. The entire building was gutted, seemingly a hopeless ruin. The total loss came to $85,000 in measurable items. Many priceless things were gone forever, including the libraries, the museum, and historical records of all kinds.

Sunday morning, March 1, the board and faculty met at the home of President Kohn and decided to rebuild at once. It was decided to send the students home temporarily, but they planned to resume classes in two weeks. Students who could not afford the trip were to be given financial assistance.[15] It was further decided to have the same building committee which had supervised the original construction in 1913 and also to secure the same general contractors, Menke and Thielberg. A special appeal was to be sent out to all congregations of the Synod for financial assistance in rebuilding. They met all day that Sunday and again on the next day. Work began on the heating plant on March 2 so that the rest of the buildings could be used as soon as possible. The reopening was set for March 16.[16]

The rooms on the first floor of the west dormitory (Lindemann Hall) were cleared for classrooms, and although conditions were difficult, the normal class routine was restored.[17]

The 50th anniversary of the founding of the college in Addison was celebrated on May 10, 1914. By this time the graduates of the school totaled 1,553. Approximately 20,000 people came to participate in the golden anniversary celebration held on the campus. Three German speakers included synodical First Vice-President Peter Brand of Pittsburgh, Pa., Pastor Hermann Speckhard of Saginaw, Mich., and South Wisconsin District President Sam. Wm. Hermann Daib of Merrill, Wis. The three English preachers were Professor Louis Wessel of Concordia Seminary, Springfield, Ill., Pastor William Schoenfeld of New York City, and Pastor Henry P. Eckhardt of Pittsburgh. As at the dedication on Oct. 12, 1913, there were three simultaneous services.[18] Music was furnished by the Aurora Brass Band directed by Teacher E. C. Hoffmann; the college choir directed by Professor Kaeppel; a children's choir of 2,000 directed by Teacher P. T. Buszin; a male chorus directed by Teacher M. O. Frieser, and a mixed choir of 1,200 directed by Teacher O. F. Rusch.[19]

The Lutheran Education Society took charge of all arrangements. The committee included Chicago Alderman Beilfuss as transportation chairman, G. A. Fleischer as treasurer, and Jacob Kirsch, who organized 300 ushers.

Restoration of the administration building had been proceeding rapidly. The roof was scheduled to be in place by the end of the 50th-anniversary celebration week. Seven of the 10 large stone columns had to be replaced; but as the work proceeded, it was found that a considerable portion of the original walls and concrete corridors were sturdy and safe for reuse. All corridors, stairways, the lobby, terrazzo floors and pillars, iron supports, and steel girders remained intact and are in the present building. Restoration costs were thus reduced considerably.

The general floor plan of the original building was followed, but the previous "boxy" look of the original building was to be improved by changing the front elevation.

The Lutheran Education Society had taken over the project of landscaping. In February they had transplanted 104 large trees, some of them over 25 years old. In April 600 shrubs and 800 bushes were to be set out during the week following the celebration.[20]

Shortly after the fire President Kohn had received a telegram from Theodore Lamprecht, a strong supporter of the college who was on a business trip to Cuba: STRONGER FAITH, LARGER DEEDS WILL FOLLOW. IT IS GOD'S TRIAL BY FIRE. CONFIDE IN GOD AND REBUILD. Soon he followed this telegram up with a check for $1,000, plus one for $200 he had received from a relative.[21] Lutherans from all over America were generous in supporting the rebuilding program. In three weeks sufficient funds were pledged to pay for the restoration costs.

The restored building presented several aesthetic improvements. The exterior walls had been raised 8 to 10 feet higher than the original, and stone ornamentation and trim were used to break the severe lines of the original. Every precaution was taken to make the building as fireproof as possible, especially in constructing the boiler rooms. Lines of fire hose and fire gongs were installed in all buildings.[22]

A number of valuable gifts were received to replace equipment which had been destroyed. Furniture and equipment was almost entirely new and far superior to that which had been brought along from Addison, some of which had been purchased many years before. The college was actually better equipped than before the fire.

On Oct. 17, 1914, almost exactly a year from the first dedication, the rebuilt administration building was dedicated with an estimated attendance of 13,000. Dedicatory addresses were given by the President of the Synod, F. Pfotenhauer, and by Pastors Guido R. Schuessler, Ernst Werfelmann, and Theodore Kohn. Special music was provided by a mixed choir directed by Teacher Gustav J. Guettler, a male chorus led by John F. Zitzmann, and the Aurora Brass Band.[23]

The first college catalog to be published in English was for the college year 1914–15. It announced an increase in student costs to $127 per year. During that year the enrollment reached 200, necessitating the addition of another instructor. Albert H. Beck, a graduate of 1914, was appointed to fill the position. An outbreak of smallpox in 1914–15 had caused the college to be quarantined by the village board of health, and two uniformed guards were posted to enforce it strictly. Two hundred students and nine faculty members were inoculated, and an epidemic was averted. Only one student, Frederick Kowitz, had to be placed in an isolation ward.[24]

The seminary property in Addison was sold to the Lutheran Children's Welfare Society in 1914. The professors' residences were sold separately.[25] However, the necessary renovation and remodeling for use as an orphanage was delayed because of World War I conditions, so that the buildings could not be used till December 1916, when the old dining hall was put into service.[26]

The war years 1914–18 had little effect on the college although a number of students did enter the armed forces. The enrollment was 200 in 1914, 237 in 1916, and 213 in 1919. However, in the wake of strong (and often irrational) anti-German feeling generated by that world struggle, federal authorities "spoke to" President Kohn in 1919 because he made a German speech at the graduation.[27] This was about the time of the foreign-language acts in Nebraska and Ohio which were later declared unconstitutional. The war did serve to break the last social and emotional ties with the Old World culture.[28] The thinking of the Synod was becoming distinctly American, and this made an important impact on the pattern of the teacher training program.

After the move to River Forest, the faculty became increasingly interested in accreditation. Contacts were made with the State Department of Education in Illinois and with local and state colleges and universities in the state to have the college accredited as a normal school. By September 1919 the Illinois State Educational Examining Board accredited Concordia as a normal school, and similar recognition was given by the University of Chicago.

In the following December the college was visited by representatives of the University of Illinois and several other colleges in the state.[29]

The Synod had instituted studies to improve educational standards in its colleges and seminaries. A committee was established in 1917 by the convention in Milwaukee to make a study and bring recommendations for such improvement.[30] By 1926 the various boards of control and the Professors' Conference of the Synod all strongly urged accreditation for all Synod's schools.

The wave of certification laws for teachers which followed World War I placed Concordia Teachers College under pressure to keep adjusting its curriculum to meet the needs of teachers for certification in various states. Numerous negotiations were instituted to have the college accredited by various state departments of education.[31]

The college became aware that the preparation of a number of applicants for admission to the high school was considerably below standard during the World War I years, and there was danger of a general lowering of standards as a result. In 1920 the Synod authorized the establishment of a special preparatory class to give boys of good character and ability the equivalent of an eighth-grade education.[32] Special instruction was given in religion, English, memorizing, German, arithmetic, geography, and penmanship. A new faculty position was established for this purpose in 1921. Improved admission policies made it possible to discontinue the class after several years.[33]

Building Additions

The enrollment, which had grown to 230 during 1920–21, increased to 315 by the following school year and to 416 by 1924–25. The original facilities, built to accommodate 200 students, were increasingly inadequate. Therefore additions were built in 1922 and 1924 which doubled the original plant capacity.

In 1922 an addition was built to the music building (now the Student Union) which added seven music rooms on the third floor, a chemistry laboratory on the first floor, and a physics laboratory on the second floor. Its cost was about $29,300. A large program of building expansion took place in 1924 which included the following additions: a dining hall and hospital extension at a cost of $16,569; Brohm and Kohn Halls, each costing $51,795 and providing six study rooms, three bedrooms, and toilet and lavatory facilities on each floor; two additions on the northeast and northwest corners of the administration building, identical in cost ($9,600) and space (two lecture rooms each).[34] The college now had facilities for 400 students.

From the time the college had been relocated in River Forest, attempts were made to raise funds for a gymnasium. In the summer of 1925 students made a special effort to interest relatives and friends in making donations for this purpose. Efforts were increased greatly when President Kohn announced that Theodore Fathauer of Chicago had given $25,000 for the gymnasium on condition that the college match this sum.[35] Since the Synod did not assume responsibility for providing such facilities, the needed sum of $95,000 had to be raised by soliciting gifts.

The gymnasium, with a seating capacity of 1,800, was completed in January 1927. Plans were made to have the formal dedication in spring to allow for greater participation. However, an informal dedication was held on Jan. 25, 1927, with the board, faculty, students, and many alumni and friends present. William Schlake, a member of the board, addressed the gathering and introduced Mr. Fathauer to a joyful and cheering student body as the man who had done more than any one person to get the building under way by his large gift.[36]

Formal dedication took place on Sunday, April 24. The pipe organ in the gymnasium was dedicated the same day by Professor Lochner. President Kohn made a strong appeal for donations to an endowment fund, the interest of which could defray the salary of an athletic director. The Synod did not provide for services in physical education or athletics.

New Training School Built

In River Forest the practice school for student teachers was in one of the college rooms. It included only the first four grades of Grace Lutheran Church, Oak Park. The four upper grades were taught by William Wegener in the church's one-room school at Bellaforte and Augusta Streets. Student teaching was done under the supervision of a college faculty member. The growing enrollment made it necessary to plan expanded facilities for practice teaching.

Grace Congregation and the Synod, together with the college, negotiated an agreement on March 19, 1929, by which the northeast corner of the college property, consisting of 3.7 acres, was sold to the congregation for $20,000 for the purpose of erecting a new church and school. According to the agreement, the Synod or the college could buy the plot back in case the congregation should want to dispose of it.

The new school was to house the training school of the college, including the four lower grades, which were then under the supervision of Professors Schmieding and Kuehnert, as well as the upper four grades. College students could now have the opportunity to practice teach in the upper grades also. The room which had been used for a training school could now be utilized for college curriculum needs.[37]

Work was begun on the new plant in October 1929, and the school was dedicated in September 1930 with a capacity of 80 pupils. The facilities were regarded as the most modern obtainable.[38]

A Final Farewell to Addison

From 1913 to 1924 the old seminary property at Addison had stood empty, with the exception of the dining hall. The Lutheran Children's Welfare Society of Illinois, which had purchased the property in 1914, decided to raze the old buildings and build a more suitable plant on the site. Wrecking activities began in October 1924, and by the end of the month all buildings except the dining hall had been leveled to the ground.[39]

Addison alumnus William A. Helmkamp, a teacher in Chicago, suggested that the alumni erect a memorial on the site of the old seminary. A number of older graduates, including Professor Albert H. Miller of River Forest, went to Addison and received permission from the wrecking company to use 75 stone window sills and the stone steps to the old north wing.[40] The stone name slab which had been above the door of the main building was also placed in the monument, and the original cornerstone was used as a capstone. The original contents of the seminary cornerstone had been removed and taken to the archives at River Forest. (They are no longer to be found.) A new box was placed into the cornerstone by the alumni. Its contents included a brief history of the memorial and the dedication program written by Professor Miller, a copy of the address given in German by alumnus William Wegener, numerous periodicals, a picture of the old seminary, and a list of donors including the River Forest Alumni Association and numerous individuals and teachers conferences. Hoefner Brothers, stonecutters of Elmhurst, donated the designing and cutting of the stone as well as supervision of the construction.

The monument was dedicated and unveiled on July 9, 1925, by John Richter, a teacher at Matteson, Ill., the oldest alumnus present, who had been teaching for 53 years. About 400 were present to see the memorial, which was at the center of the base of the "triangle park," just in front of the site of the original administration building.[41]

Curriculum Developments

Although the sixth year had been added to the curriculum while the college was still in Addison, the first class to complete the 6-year program graduated in 1914, at the end of the first year in River Forest.[42]

The curriculum had no electives. Piano and organ were required of all students. Other required courses were as follows:

Second Year Normal Class. Catechism, isagogics, church history, symbolics, pedagogy, German, English, arithmetic, geography, physiology, singing, and four weeks of practice teaching in the first four grades.

First Year Normal Class. Bible stories, Catechism, isagogics, pedagogy, German, English, arithmetic, history, chemistry, drawing, and singing.

Senior (High School) Class. Bible stories, Catechism, German, English, arithmetic, geography, church history, civics, physics, and handwriting.

Junior Class. Catechism, German, English, arithmetic, bookkeeping, geography, history, nature study, physiology, handwriting, drawing, and singing.

Sophomore Class. Bible stories, Catechism, German, English, arithmetic, geography, world history, nature study, handwriting, drawing, and singing.

Freshman Class. Bible stories, Catechism, German, English, arithmetic, geography, world history, nature study, handwriting, drawing, and singing.

President Kohn taught history of education to the first normal class in 1913–14 and Bible reading to the junior (high school) class. Civics was taught by Professor Miller, and methods in teaching by Professor Oscar F. Rusch. In 1916 United States history was added to the freshman curriculum. A course in psychology was added in 1919, and in 1922 general science, or nature study, was divided into chemistry and physics, and laboratory work was scheduled for both.

An additional year was added in 1920 for students whose preparation for high school was weak. About 18 students were enrolled in this course, taught by Professor Henry C. Gaertner, who had been called to become the tenth regular professor on the faculty.

Growing enrollment made it necessary to divide the classes into sections. By 1927 all six classes had been divided into at least two sections each, and professorships had risen to 18, besides two assistants. Faculty committees were working constantly to upgrade the instructional program because of a growing consciousness of standards needed in the American pattern of collegiate normal school preparation.[43]

The system of promotion was changed in 1927. Since the school was founded in 1864, promotion had been by classes. A student was advanced provided he had not failed more than two subjects. Under the new system promotion was given by courses and units alone. In the same year piano classes were inaugurated for beginning students, making it possible to eliminate two assistants. By 1932 new courses in school music and church organ were introduced in the second year normal class.

After the gymnasium was dedicated in May 1927, the demand for physical education became more urgent. In October the *Spectator* reported that gym classes would be instructed by the Rev. Luther Schuessler of Chicago and by Assistant Professor G. E. Rast. Each class would have two double periods of physical education weekly. The classes were required for high school students and elective for the normal classes.[44] By December it was announced that the gym program was in full effect, with Pastor Schuessler supervising freshman and junior classes and Professor Rast the sophomores and a senior class. Athletic Director Alfred F. Schmieding supervised the normal department and one of the senior classes.[45] The director of physical education and the coaches were referred to in the catalog for the first time in 1927–28.[46]

A new class in school library was organized in December 1930. Up to six lessons were given each division to help teacher graduates to learn about the library, its arrangement and management. Professor Paul Bretscher, the librarian, taught the course.[47]

During 1930 college facilities were used by a special committee which was to work out a complete curriculum in every subject taught in Lutheran elementary schools. Professors Schmieding and Arthur E. Diesing represented the college on this committee. Commercial arithmetic was added to the high school curriculum.[48]

In the catalog of 1930–31, as in other catalogs of the college from time to time, the purpose of the college was again pointed out. It recalls the fact that from its very beginning the Lutheran churches in the Missouri Synod maintained a system of schools to inculcate Biblical principles of Christianity in the education of children and that the college exists primarily for the purpose of training teachers for the elementary schools of the Synod.[49]

The country was on the threshold of the Great Depression, which would deeply affect the college and even challenge its single purpose to some extent.

The president was of course responsible for all supervision of the student body. Since he became president in 1913, W. C. Kohn made increasing use of student government to assist him in student supervision. He appointed a group of the second normal class for this purpose, even allowing them to pass judgment on offenders, although he held the guiding reins tightly within his grasp. Such privileges were unheard of in the Addison days, when the rule of the president was absolute. Although this was not student government in the 1964 sense of the term, it was a beginning.[50]

By 1930 the student body was allowed to elect 14 members who met with the president to discuss the general welfare of the school and to receive instructions from him. "Elders" (or "bucks," as they were popularly known) were appointed over each room and over each dormitory floor to oversee the order and cleanliness of each. Each table in the dining room also had a "table buck" to keep order. All students took part in work details to keep order in the buildings and on the grounds. Daily inspections were held by the president and by members of the faculty appointed to assist him. They also supervised the compulsory study periods daily.[51]

Two libraries were maintained, a faculty library of 5,500 volumes and a student library of 6,000 volumes.

The teacher training program required 120 hours of each second year college student, most of the time being spent in classroom teaching. This training involved not only teaching lessons, but close and careful consultation with the critic teacher, whose aim included the highest skill and the best attitude. The program was supervised by two faculty members (Schmieding and Kuehnert), one serving in the morning, the other in the afternoon. In addition to practice teaching, each student also had from 50 to 60 hours of observation to demonstrate practical application of the theories discussed in methods classes.[52]

A joint faculty and student committee directed the program of activities, including cultural programs at least twice a month, club work, and athletic events. Two outstanding musical groups had been developed, the college chorus (formed in 1923 by Professor Albert H. Beck) and the concert band (begun in 1925 by Professor Richard T. Rohlfing).

In 1930 President Kohn published a special appeal to the congregations of the Northern Illinois District for more students, pointing out that in that District alone 315 teachers were needed.[53]

Economy of operation was always a goal of the Synod in relation to its colleges. The need for this became more acute after the stock market crash of 1929. The college business manager, Professor Schmitt, described the economies practiced in the early 1930s. In the area of teaching-staff utilization, he pointed out that in addition to the regular courses each student had to be served by several weeks of teacher training and six years of organ and piano. By grouping 18–20 students in piano classes and limiting organ lessons to 12–15 minutes per week, four instructors could handle the music program while teacher training required one more. The Synod provided only 13 men, including the president, for all other instruction in high school and college besides all other supervisory and extracurricular work. The president also had many administrative matters which required his constant attention. Certainly the college was not overstaffed.

Schmitt described the maintenance program, giving great credit to the student labor program, in which all students were required to donate labor each year. The college employed one janitor, one repairman, and one fireman for the heating plant, who also assisted with repairs. The three men combined received pay of less than $9 a day. Upkeep of the 36-acre campus was done entirely by student labor, planned and supervised by the faculty.[54]

In describing the teacher training program of 1930, Professor Schmieding called attention to the need for professional training besides a strong academic training for teachers. He pointed out that in early years the opinion was held that a teacher need know very little more than his pupils; but fortunately this opinion was disappearing. The goals of teacher training must include a strong general academic program plus professional training, covering the theoretical and practical aspects of teaching and learning.[55]

Schmieding stated, "In all the learning through the mind which God has given man to use, the student is trained not to overvalue human learning, and never to forget that he is preparing to be a servant of the Savior in a special sense. He is led to appreciate that the main objective in Lutheran education must always be faith in Jesus, and that nothing must stand in the way of securing this objective in all of his teaching activities." [56]

Schmieding pointed out further that the training program included many individual conferences between the student and Professor Kuehnert or Schmieding, the critic teachers, over lesson plans which were carefully drawn up. The plans were thoroughly discussed after they were taught. The aim was to build a thinking teacher, not merely one who knows a few professional tricks which may be used over and over without much understanding and judgment.

On May 29 and 30, 1932, a special service of thanksgiving commemorated the 75th anniversary of the establishment of formal teacher training by the Synod. Two services were held on Sunday, May 29. The speakers were Dr. Frederick Pfotenhauer, President of the Synod, Dr. Walter A. Maier of Concordia Seminary, St. Louis, the Rev. Alexander Ullrich, President of the Northern Illinois District, and the Rev. Otto C. A. Boecler of Des Plaines, Ill. Music was provided by the college chorus, directed by Professor Beck, a mass chorus directed by Teacher John F. Zitzmann, a children's chorus led by Teacher Henry J. Lange, the Concordia College Band directed by Professor Rohlfing, and by Professor Lochner at the organ. The evening program included addresses by August C. Stellhorn, Synod's Secretary of Schools, and Dr. Ludwig E. Fuerbringer, president of Concordia Seminary, St. Louis. Besides the college band and chorus, students and alumni furnished special music for the program.

On Monday, May 30, the celebration featured special athletic events including baseball games with Valparaiso University and Luther Institute (High School), and a track meet with Chicago Normal College and Morton College, closing with a band concert and a play in the evening. [57]

Summer School Program Develops

Since the early 1920s there had been numerous suggestions by conferences and individuals that a postgraduate program in summer school or by correspondence be established. Many teachers wanted a study program which would give special attention to problems peculiar to the Lutheran school. In June 1931 the Western District of the Synod had conducted a special institute in St. Louis to help meet this need. The response was so encouraging that the suggestion was made to have another institute of this type at Concordia Teachers College, River Forest. A committee was set up to study the possibility, and its work resulted in the first summer session, held for one week, June 27 to July 2, 1932. The cost for two courses, library fee, and board and room was $10, a reflection of the depression economy.[58] The committee had petitioned the Synod in 1932 to approve the institute and to provide for its gradual expansion to a six-week summer school. The Synod approved the request.[59]

The first announcement stated:

> Just at this time, when the hand of the Lord is heavy upon the world, when He is teaching mankind to place the proper value on perishable and uncertain material things and to appreciate the ·incorruptible blessings offered in His Word, at such a time the Lutheran teacher ought to be aware of the great privilege he has in dispensing these incorruptible gifts to children. The more he realizes the greatness of his task, the more he studies the problems confronting him on every side, and the greater his love for serving his Master, the more ready and eager will he become to learn more about this important work and about possible ways of improving himself.[60]

Two hundred three teachers (of whom 48 were women) attended the first session. The courses met twice each day, one hour in the morning and another in the afternoon. Students could select only two of the 35 courses offered, with a minimum enrollment of 15 in a course. There were 23 instructors. For 1933 it was planned to have 57 courses and 33 instructors, extending the time to three weeks in response to an overwhelming demand.[61]

In September 1932 the *Lutheran School Journal* stated:

> The summer-school fills a definite need in our Church — it is to Lutheran education what a laboratory is to a manufacturing plant. The product of a factory improves as the findings of the laboratory point the way to new economies and refined methods of manufacture. The summer-school is the teacher's opportunity for new economies in learning, new refinements of method, a clearer understanding of the aims and objectives of Lutheran education, renewed inspiration and drive for the great work of leading souls to their Savior. The summer-school is not therefore a mere adornment to Synod's educational agencies, nor is it a luxury for the teacher or an extravagance for the congregation which assists the teacher in availing himself of the opportunity of attending. Properly conducted, the summer-

school as well as the regular teacher-training institutions may be looked upon as an agency which determines the character of our Lutheran schools.[62]

The summer session announcement of 1933 listed the objectives of the program as follows:

1. To improve teaching ability.
2. To help build understanding of the recent trends in education.
3. To provide systematic growth in religious and cultural subjects.
4. To offer special assistance to women teachers.
5. To help improve the ability of the teacher as organist, choir director, youth leader, and Sunday school worker.
6. To afford a more thorough study of Lutheran education.[63]

The second session was held three weeks, from July 31 to Aug. 18. The cost was $25. Even this was a considerable sum for many teachers during the depression, and the enrollment dropped to 113.

On the basis of experience in the first two years, the college faculty and board organized the summer school as a permanent feature in 1934, establishing a special summer school board to work out the plans for consideration by the college faculty and board. The summer school board should consist of five faculty members, a representative of the Lutheran District Superintendents Conference and two pastors and a teacher from the Northern Illinois District. The president of the college was assisted by a faculty member as chairman of the summer session and by a dean, a registrar, and a treasurer and business manager.[64] In 1934 a Sunday school teachers institute and a special institute for Lutheran teachers were held, each a week long. In 1936 the summer session was extended to five weeks.

The first summer-school board was organized in 1933 with Professor Kraeft as dean, Professor Schmitt as business manager, and Professor Diesing as registrar, besides President Kohn and the librarian, Professor Bretscher. Other faculty members were Professors Schmieding and Miller. The Rev. Martin Nickel of Lyons, Ill., Northern Illinois District School Superintendent Paul T. Buszin, and Teachers Karl Roemer and Arthur L. Miller completed the board.[65]

Third Year Added

The increasing tendency for American normal schools to grow up into teachers colleges was duly noted by the faculty and board of

Concordia Teachers College. As early as 1926 the Synod discussed the establishment of a 4-year college program.

A special Synodical Survey Committee recommended the addition of the seventh year because of the increasing needs of teachers and the pressures of accreditation requirements. The faculty at River Forest, while concurring in the recommendation, felt that it was essential to add the fourth college year as soon as possible. They believed also that it would be essential to separate the high school departments completely from all synodical colleges, from the standpoint of accreditation and administration and to offset the practical disadvantage of spending eight years on one campus.

In a report of the faculty to the 1932 Synod, it was pointed out that the general education of teachers before their professional training needed to be revised in consideration of the broadening needs of the day; also that the professional church worker could not be on a low level in important fields of human knowledge when congregation members have college training in such fields.[66]

Because of the depression it was often impossible to place graduates; some congregations were forced to close classrooms and even whole schools because of their inability to support them financially. The college faculty and board decided to provide for a third college year to be added in 1933–34 so that all members of the 1933 2-year graduating class who did not receive placement could be encouraged to return for another year of professional training. The third year would be optional, and the whole arrangement would be temporary until Synod could approve it in 1935. The faculty committee which was to make all plans included President Kohn and Professors Rusch, Schmitt, Koehler, Schmieding, and Diesing.[67]

Within a month they reported a tentative plan which required all 2-year college graduates who did not receive calls to return for the third year, unless excused by the president and the faculty. The high school freshman and sophomore classes were scheduled for only one section each, thus releasing instructors for the third college year. Courses offered included church history, German, public health, educational psychology, modern American and English literature, the novel, sociology, geography, history of the Renaissance and Reformation, and economics. Music was elective.[68]

In May President Kohn announced that the third-year normal class would operate on the honor system, being relieved of most of the rules that applied to all underclassmen. Separate housing would be provided in a third-floor dormitory under their own regulations and with many extra privileges.[69]

The apparent success of the venture was reported to the faculty on March 5, 1934. The students were pleased with the program and their privileges.[70] It was recommended that they be given preference in placement and that President Kohn encourage second-year normal students to remain for the third year in 1934–35. The faculty concurred in the committee report which recommended keeping the third year on the experimental basis until Synod could take definite action. Teaching positions were still very scarce.[71]

The faculty considered various ways of recruiting students to bring the plant utilization as high as possible. Pressure was exerted to gear the program for more general education and fill the school with students who did not intend to become teachers. This brought up a discussion of the purpose of the college and the possibility that an atmosphere might be developed which would be detrimental to the main purpose of the school. It was felt also that it would be too costly to develop a curriculum that would appeal to outsiders sufficiently. General students had always been accepted on an individual basis, and this could continue.

A special invitation was sent to graduates of Concordia Seminary, St. Louis, to study education at River Forest since most of them were not able to obtain placement and there was no other employment for them.

The faculty took note of the fact that adverse economic pressures caused many congregations to employ women as teachers, often without due regard to background or training, because they could be obtained for much lower salaries.[72]

In 1934 a special letter was sent to the Rev. Henry Grueber of Milwaukee, chairman of the Synod's Committee on Higher Education. The faculty pointed out the dangers in thinking that teaching in the lower grades did not require special training and that it was highly important to prepare women teachers carefully. Attention was also called to the practice which had developed by which congregations would engage men graduates on a "temporary call," thereby weakening the doctrine of the call in the church. A request was made to begin coeducation at River Forest.

It was pointed out that adequate training for teaching in Synod's schools could be given only in Synod's colleges and that the Synod should be vigilant in keeping control over the preparation of those who teach its children. Women who were not properly prepared should at least be required to attend summer school.[73]

The seriousness of the placement problem can be seen in the report made to the faculty that for 30 calls for pastors, there were 234 available candidates, and for 187 teachers there were 10 calls. All the rest but 46 were placed in temporary calls.[74]

A representative of the University of Illinois visited Concordia's high school department for accreditation in May 1934. He commended the students for their spirit and the school for fine facilities. Among his suggested improvements were further schooling for several professors, and a more rigid adherence to time schedule and the calendar of days taught. Nature study should now be called biology and be taught a whole year. These suggestions were to be implemented as soon as possible.[75]

Educational Policies Committee Formed

A committee on accreditation, which became known as the "Educational Policies Committee," was appointed in June 1934 with Professor Schmieding as chairman and Professor Walter O. Kraeft as secretary. Other members were President Kohn and Professors Diesing, Miller, and Rusch. Four goals were recommended and adopted by the faculty:

1. That high school accreditation be obtained in 1934–35 with the University of Illinois.
2. That high school accreditation be obtained from the North Central Association of Colleges and Secondary Schools as soon as possible thereafter.
3. That college accreditation be obtained for the 3-year program as soon as possible from the University of Illinois.
4. That the college be accredited with the North Central Association of Colleges and Secondary Schools.[76]

Contact was made with the American Association of Teachers Colleges with a view to accreditation with them as well. It was recommended that money be made available to help professors who might be asked to take courses.

In relation to accreditation of the high school the Educational

Policies Committee recommended that nature study be changed to biology and that it be a full year's course; that a classroom be equipped as a laboratory; that the teaching periods be 40 minutes in length with a 5-minute interval between periods; and that there be 180 full days of instruction, with makeup periods when a professor had to be absent.[76]

The third college year had been adopted as an experiment in 1933. The Synod would decide in 1935 whether to make it permanent. In the meantime the Educational Policies Committee was very active in studying the work of all departments in the college, the curricula of other schools, the specific teacher training requirements of some state departments, and the requirements of regional and national accrediting agencies. It was reported that the Synod's Committee on Higher Education would recommend approval of the third year to the Synod.[77] This recommendation was subsequently adopted by the faculty in 1935.

Studies had shown that there was a general trend in the country to extend the college preparation of teachers. Twenty percent of the larger cities in 1935 required a minimum of three years of college training for elementary teaching, and 15 percent required four years. Certification requirements in Illinois were being changed to require more training. The addition of the fourth year as soon as possible was strongly advocated.[78]

Curriculum Reorganized

In view of the changing needs and educational developments in the country, the Educational Policies Committee felt strongly that recent trends and changes in American life made a thorough reorganization of the college curriculum necessary.

The basic purposes of the college were carefully studied. Since 1864, when the school was founded in Addison, it had been engaged exclusively in the cause of Christian education, serving almost entirely the purpose of training of teachers for Lutheran day schools, although a small, unsolicited number of students had attended from time to time for the purpose of securing a general education. It was also noted that a new area of service in the church was arising in the position of director of religious education, who would direct part-time Christian education programs in congregations which did not have parish schools.[79]

The work of the Educational Policies Committee resulted in revolutionary changes in the college in curriculum and organization. At their recommendation a fivefold purpose was adopted by the faculty:

1. A broad general education as basic and preparatory to specialized training.
2. A specialized training for the regular teacher which will prepare him to meet the exacting and varied demands of the Lutheran school system.
3. A modified special training for the directors of religious education.
4. A liberal training for a small group of students who attend the institution for general educational purposes.
5. Development of a personality based on Christian principles, broad culture, and sound learning.[80]

In order to carry out the objectives seven curricular departments were organized: religion, languages, social studies, science and mathematics, music and fine arts, education, and physical education and recreation.

All departments met with the Educational Policies Committee to formulate objectives for each department and discipline, besides planning for elective courses in each department. A fundamental change was made in adopting the quarter system to replace the semester plan of course organization. The quarter system was used in about half of the teachers colleges in the United States.[81]

The first two years would now be largely devoted to general education, with professional training and practice teaching given in the third normal year. Classes were to be 50 minutes in length with 10-minute intermissions, and the number of courses to be carried by students was to be dropped to four or five plus instrumental music. The third college class would be divided into three sections so that one third of the class would register for practice teaching each quarter.

Further reorganization of the faculty and student personnel service was also planned after a thorough study of such organization in typical American liberal arts colleges could be made. Teaching loads were to be adjusted to a minimum of 16 hours per week and a maximum of 20. The subjects were to be limited to four courses in one or two related fields to conform to the standards of accrediting agencies.[82]

To prepare for accreditation, the high school was now completely separated from the college department. Its class periods were lengthened to 45 minutes with a 15-minute intermission. Professor Kraeft was appointed dean of the high school, and Professor Schmieding was named dean of the college. Student government of the high school was also separated from the college. By 1937 further curriculum changes had placed chemistry, church history, and trigonometry, which had formerly been first-year college courses, into the high school curriculum.[83] By June 1935 the high school was accredited by the University of Illinois as a preliminary step for accreditation with the North Central Association of Colleges and Secondary Schools in 1936.[84]

Continued study of trends and projected needs led to the approval of the fourth college year by the Synod in 1938, to become effective in September 1939. The fourth year was not to be compulsory at first. Half of the third college class of 1938 (about 25) registered for the fourth year, thus becoming the first class to receive degrees from Concordia Teachers College in 1940. The Educational Policies Committee had been in consultation with accrediting authorities in planning the program, and the final plans for the necessary curricular changes were complete by April 1939.[85]

Coeducation Comes to Concordia

The use of women teachers in the church schools was slow to develop since there was opposition to them in many quarters. There were but 13 women teachers in elementary schools of the Synod in 1884, but by 1923 there were 380, representing 18 percent of all teachers.[86]

The Survey Committee established by the Synod in 1917 had recommended the establishment of a ladies seminary to train teachers and other female church workers, but the plan was dropped by the Synod because of heavy opposition.[87]

The policy of the Synod had been to train its own pastors and teachers, and many felt that women should be included since the number in the teaching ministry was increasing. In 1926 a petition to train girls who wished to teach in Lutheran schools had resulted in the following action: Girls would be allowed to enroll for teacher training at Seward, Nebr., and Edmonton, Alta., Canada, and institutes for women teachers were to be encouraged elsewhere.[88]

During the depression of the 1930s many churches engaged women with very little training, if any, to teach for very low salaries. The faculty at River Forest repeatedly called attention to the great necessity for training women teachers if the parish schools were to prosper and remain true to their purpose. They requested permission to have coeducation at Concordia.

In September 1936 two professors' daughters, Ruth Bretscher and Ruth Kraeft, were allowed to enroll in the high school freshman class.[89] The board of control allowed them to remain that year only since the Synod had not given permission to enroll girls.[90]

Permission to have coeducation was finally granted to Concordia Teachers College by the Synod in 1938.[91] No more than 30 percent of the total enrollment could be girls. The enrollment of 335 included 38 coeds in September, 23 of whom were in the first college year. A special reception was held for them by Grace Lutheran Church. For the first time the college could have a mixed choir. Its first concert was held on March 12, 1939.[92] The first physical education classes for girls were taught by the women's supervisor, Miss Irma Beck.[93]

Correspondence and Extension

The convention of the Synod in 1935 requested Concordia Teachers College to offer correspondence courses for credit [94] and also encouraged the college to establish extension centers.[95] This convention also elected Rev. John W. Behnken President of the Synod to succeed President Pfotenhauer. In 1937 the faculty resolved to offer extension courses on campus and to investigate the possibility of establishing courses in Milwaukee. Over the succeeding years, courses were also offered in St. Louis, Fort Wayne, Sheboygan, Wis., Edwardsville, Ill., Cleveland, and Cedar Rapids, Iowa, besides Saturday courses at the college. By 1937 the faculty had one correspondence course ready.[96]

Depression Economies

President Kohn pleaded with·the students to exercise all possible economies, requesting that use of water be cut to a minimum; a regular bathing schedule was established to reduce costs. Students were asked to use no larger than 25-watt bulbs in their study lamps and to be very careful to shut off organ motors after use. To conserve electricity, organ students were to avoid playing full organ as much as possible, and to use organs only for practicing lessons.[97]

Decreasing enrollment caused the college to close down the third floors of Krauss and Lindemann Halls in September 1933. The Synod itself had run a deficit of more than a million dollars in 1932, but repaid $100,000 of it in 1933.[98] Salary cuts had been drastic for all personnel. All students at Concordia were required to donate 10 hours of work to the college instead of the usual five.

The college business manager, Professor Schmitt, was hard pressed to keep expenses low and the bills paid when due. During the summers of 1933 and 1934 he received permission from Synod's Board of Directors to provide lodging and breakfast for the Chicago Century of Progress visitors at a cost of 75 cents per day. This brought so many visitors that the college cleared over $10,000, which was used for badly needed repairs and improvements.[99] The college accepted Federal Emergency Relief Administration funds to aid 55 needy college students in 1934. The work done by the students helped maintain and improve the premises of the college. This assistance program was replaced by the National Youth Authority in 1935.[100]

Faculty and Administration Changes

The faculty growth kept pace with the growth of the college. Having begun operations in 1913 with nine professors and one assistant, the faculty more than doubled by 1939, numbering 18 professors and three assistants.

In 1915 Professor Backhaus retired. He was succeeded as professor by Teacher Ernst Henry Engelbrecht of New York City, who also became head of the training school. In December of 1915 Professor Rechlin died, and Teacher Oscar F. Rusch of Chicago succeeded him. Professor Kaeppel died in 1934. New professorships established over the years brought the following to the faculty: Henry C. Gaertner (1921), Alfred F. Schmieding (1922), Albert H. Beck, Paul M. Bretscher, and Arthur E. Diesing (1923), Richard T. Rohlfing (1925), Theodore C. Appelt and Walter O. Kraeft (1926), Theodore J. C. Kuehnert (1927), Otto J. Beyers (1936–37), and Wilfred F. Kruse (1938). Assistants during this period varied from one to five (1924), including some of the above, who were assistants before becoming professors.

When Concordia faculty members were confronted with the need to increase their own academic preparation to help in the accreditation of the college, they willingly accepted the task, enrolling in colleges and universities to work for advanced degrees. During the summers of 1925 and 1926 10 Concordia professors attended the University of Chicago. Several also attended during the regular term while teaching their own full loads.[101] Gradually the college gave financial assistance for such schooling. President Kohn was awarded the honorary degree of Doctor of Divinity by Concordia Seminary, St. Louis, in 1929.

The faculty of Concordia contributed numerous writings on various aspects of Christian education and of education in general, to keep Lutheran teachers posted on current developments. Many of these writings appeared as articles in the *Lutheran School Journal* (called *Evangelisch-Lutherisches Schulblatt* until 1921), and also through books, curriculum guides, and pamphlets. Professor Eifrig became known as one of the foremost naturalists in the state and was elected president of the Audubon Society of Illinois in 1929. He published a two-volume natural history called *Our Great Outdoors*. Other faculty members who wrote during this period included Miller (grammar, spelling, and science), Koehler *(Annotated Catechism)*, Kaeppel, Engelbrecht, Kuehnert, Kraeft, Schmieding, Schmitt, and Diesing.[102]

Traditionally the administrative structure had been based on a very strong faculty voice. The president was regarded as *primus inter pares* (the first among equals), although his influence was certainly great. Most of the decisions were made by the faculty. Business Manager Schmitt met directly with the board of control, as did other faculty members who had special appointments.[103] Members of the board of control also carried some executive functions.[104]

The first listing of an administrative staff appeared in 1928–29. The officers mentioned are W. C. Kohn, president; M. Lochner, secretary; F. H. Schmitt, purchasing agent; Albert H. Miller, registrar; Paul Bretscher, librarian; T. C. Appelt, assistant librarian; and Alfred F. Schmieding, director of physical education. In 1935 Professor Diesing was appointed assistant registrar, and in 1937 an assistant business manager was added. The 1929–30 catalog listed coaches for the first time. The faculty was divided into a number of standing operating committees, of which the Educational Policies Committee became the most powerful.

President Kohn's duties as head of the school included spiritual counseling and supervision of the student body, representing the school, being chief editor of the *Lutheran School Journal*, supervising at mealtimes and in study periods, counseling with faculty members, and acting as school doctor and nurse, besides handling correspondence and attending innumerable meetings. He was urged by the board of control not to overexert himself as they provided secretarial help in 1929.[105]

Two deans were appointed in 1935: Professor Schmieding as dean of the college and supervisor of athletics and Professor Kraeft as dean of the high school and extension department. These appointments were made by the faculty at the recommendation of the Educational Policies Committee.[106] Further recommendations of this committee for faculty reorganization were adopted as follows:

1. The president and business administrator were each to be regarded as one full-time position.
2. The librarian, registrar, and deans were to be allowed one period off their teaching load for their extra duties.
3. A central office was to be established with additional secretarial and clerical help to assist in coordination of administration.
4. The registration committee was to be abolished and its duties distributed.
5. Standing committees to be organized included the following: faculty, departments, administrative, policies, summer school board, extracurricular, placement, practice school faculty, and an editorial committee for the *Lutheran School Journal*.[107]

Assistant instructors were invited to be present for the faculty meetings for the first time in September 1935. There were but two ranks, professor and assistant, and the latter was not regarded as a full-fledged faculty member.[108]

Officers of the North Central Association of Colleges and Secondary Schools visited the college late in 1936 and made several recommendations to the faculty which were considered in January 1937. Areas to be improved were standards of admission, library books, especially in the sciences, and grading.[109]

In 1938 the college became an associate member of the Federation of Illinois Colleges, an association of non-tax-supported colleges. Full membership could be obtained after the school became a 4-year school.[110]

Because of advanced age Professor Miller asked to be relieved of the position of registrar in 1937, having served since 1916. Professor Schmieding was asked to assume the position in addition to his duties as dean, athletic director, and chairman of the Educational Policies Committee.[111] In May 1938 he requested relief from some of his duties, but no action was taken.[112]

The business manager, Professor Schmitt, was relieved of a portion of his teaching load in March 1938. With the opening of the fourth college year in 1939 it was necessary to establish a new faculty position. However, the Synod was not able to pay the salary of an additional professor. In order to make it possible to call another professor, Schmitt resigned as professor and accepted the position of full-time business manager, thus leaving one faculty position vacant. He was to keep the title of professor and be listed as an administrative officer.[113]

Professor Schmieding resigned as director of physical education, registrar, and dean in March 1939. The volume of work in these positions had grown so that it was too much for one person. He pointed out that he had not received a reduction in teaching duties so he could have adequate time for administrative duties. He felt the deanship was most troublesome because it had never been defined. He expressed willingness to accept any one of the three according to the wishes of the faculty and administration.[114]

In April 1939, at the end of 26 years of service, President Kohn announced that he had resigned as president effective in June.[115] The board of control named him honorary president and accepted his offer to continue teaching on a part-time basis. Professor Schmitt was appointed acting president.[116] He had served the college since 1905 as teacher of English and as business manager. Professor Kuehnert was assigned the administration of affairs regarding calls and placement formerly handled by President Kohn, Professor Schmieding was reappointed registrar, and Professor Kruse was appointed director of physical education. Both appointments were subject to change with the coming of a new president.

"The Old Man," as Dr. Kohn was affectionately called by the students, was honored at a banquet on June 7, 1939.

Women's Auxiliary of Concordia Teachers College

Throughout his term of office Dr. Kohn had busied himself in many ways to promote the college and its cause by means of speeches, written articles, convention essays and reports, and personal contact with people.

In the summer of 1934, at a social evening of the General Teachers Conference, President Kohn proposed the formation of a ladies auxiliary. There was general interest in this venture, and after considerable planning during the summer and early autumn, a meeting was called for Oct. 11, 1934, to organize such a group.[117]

The name "Women's Auxiliary of Concordia Teachers College, River Forest, Illinois," was chosen. The purpose of this organization as stated in the constitution adopted in November 1934 was "to promote an interest among the congregations of Northern Illinois for the college, to assist in making the library standard, and to aid the institution in general." All funds were to be raised through free-will offerings.[118] In December the Auxiliary sponsored the first annual Christmas party for students, faculty, staff, and their families.

Membership gains were steady, reaching a peak of 1,000 in 1941. Annual rallies were held in October to which women from northern Illinois and southern Wisconsin were invited. In 1937 more than 1,800 participated in the rally.

.Gifts to the college included food, books and equipment for library, offices, dining hall, and music department, and furnishings for the president's office and the girls' dormitories. In addition, the Auxiliary performed as a service organization for receptions and conventions of many kinds.[119]

Concordia Teachers College Men's Club and the Athletic Program

President Kohn also suggested the formation of a men's club at a banquet on May 2, 1936. More than a hundred signed up to indicate interest. The Concordia Teachers College Men's Club was launched Nov. 7, 1936.[120] Its purpose was "to arouse a deeper interest for Concordia Teachers College, River Forest, Illinois, in our Lutheran congregations of the Synodical Conference; to give the Board of Control of Concordia Teachers College moral and financial support in maintaining the physical education program; and to foster the spirit of Christian fellowship." [121] The Men's Club immediately began to consider one of the pressing needs of the college: to obtain a full-time physical education teacher and coach. The Synod itself made no provision for this kind of instruction, leaving the establishment and the financing of it to the college.

When the college moved to River Forest in 1913, sports and athletics continued at about the pace set at Addison, with students themselves taking the initiative and leadership. Baseball and basketball were well established by 1913. One of the prime movers in starting football was Arthur W. Gross, who as a student in 1917 persuaded the president of the student athletic association to buy a football. Within a short time a football series was started between the various buildings.[122] Ten years later Mr. Gross, then teaching in St. Paul's School, Austin, Ill., was secured as the new football coach by Athletic Director Schmieding, who had been coaching football since 1925.[123]

Professor Schmieding became athletic director in 1926, and in the following year Concordia was accepted as a member of the Northern Illinois Junior College Conference, participating in football and baseball, with basketball to be added in 1928.[124] Pastor Luther A. Schuessler was selected as basketball coach.

In 1928 the athletic council consisted of President Kohn, Professor Schmieding, athletic director; Pastor Schuessler, basketball coach and part-time physical education instructor; A. W. Gross, football coach; G. E. Rast, a part-time gym instructor and coach of tennis and track; and seven students. They were to make recommendations and policy suggestions to the faculty.[125]

In 1929 Mr. A. C. Koy was secured to coach basketball for Concordia High School. Students donated 4,500 hours of work in building a new baseball diamond, a new track, and new tennis courts in the same year.[126]

Although much progress had been made, the lack of a full-time physical education instructor and coach was felt more and more. The newly organized Concordia Men's Club in April 1937 offered to underwrite the costs.[127] The offer was gratefully accepted by the college board of control, and William A. Hedtke, a graduate of the University of Illinois, was selected as the first incumbent. Physical education became a required subject for all students for the 1937–38 school year,[128] each student having three periods per week.

Professor Schmieding continued as director of physical education, and in 1938 he completed negotiations for Concordia High School's admission into the Private School League.[129]

Before Professor Schmieding came to Concordia, athletic promotion had been largely done by the students themselves by the formation of clubs for the various sports. The class of 1924 organized a schoolwide club known as the Concordia Athletic Promoters

(C. A. P.) as a memorial to the school. Its chief purpose was to promote all sports at Concordia. Students and alumni could belong.

The C. A. P. developed into the C Club under the leadership of Paul W. Lange, a student. To the original objectives of the C. A. P. was added the aim of raising the standard for the major "C" award and the promotion of harmony among athletes. Its first project was to build new tennis courts in 1926. Members also bought bleachers for the field and uniforms for the teams and helped maintain the football field, besides donating for the gymnasium. The "C" Club presented certificates to "C" lettermen and a special certificate to graduating lettermen, adding a special gold emblem for a graduate who earned a letter in three sports. Over the years the club experienced many successes and failures as the interest waxed and waned.[130]

Library Development

The library showed very little progress before the 1920s, probably because very little use of the library was expected in the instructional program before then.[131] Growing interest in accreditation helped to focus attention on the need for adequate library facilities. A considerable number of books were purchased in 1926, and new furniture with a $1,000 gift of the Book Concern, which was still operated by Professor Koehler.[132] Since 1920 the bookstore had contributed $4,600 to the student library. An elementary textbook library section was introduced in that year in which all current texts were available for student use.

Library supervision had been by student-elected librarians until 1926–27, when Professor Bretscher was appointed librarian. He immediately began to reorganize the entire library system for better service and supervision. Aided by a staff of student helpers, he established regular hours of 3:00 to 5:00 p. m. daily, when he would be present.[133]

Although there had been some proposals to consolidate all libraries, there were still two libraries in 1930–31 — a faculty library of 5,500 volumes and a student library of 6,000 volumes.[134] Regular evening library hours were established in 1933 from 8:00 to 10:30 for special reference work. In 1934 it was reported that the Book Concern had given $500 for the libraries and that the grand total given for library use since 1909 was $10,535.[135] It was a timely donation since the newly begun third college year had increased the demand for library books and references. The graduating class of 1926 also donated their treasury of more than $400 for the library. The money represented profit they had made on their class book. The need for more books had been observed by a member of the class during the second summer session in 1933.

College and Community

When the college was first established, there were large areas of open fields surrounding it. The traditionally good relationship of the school to the Village of River Forest and surrounding municipalities was established from the beginning. During World War I the college band and student body participated in patriotic rallies and parades, and in 1929 the college board donated a large silk American flag to the Memorial Hall of Roosevelt High School in River Forest in memory of those who served in the war.[136] In 1936 Professor Rohlfing wrote an original musical composition in honor of the River Forest centennial celebration. Dr. Kohn was interested in the community and rendered service in various ways. He represented the college at civic affairs of Greater Chicago, as for example at the reception for the personnel of the *Graf Zeppelin* in October 1928.[137] He also served as a member of the Chicago Planning Commission.

Use of the college facilities for conventions, institutes, and summer sessions became more and more common and constant. In October 1933 it was estimated that over 6,000 people had used the premises during the previous summer.[138]

In November 1935 the new synodical Committee on Higher Education held its first meeting at Concordia. Here it organized itself into three subcommittees: Committee A, on higher education in general; Committee B, on training pastors; and Committee C, on teacher training.[139]

Developments in Music

After the college moved to River Forest, a band was organized under the leadership of Professor Engelbrecht. It gained much popularity by participating in numerous civic parades, patriotic gatherings, and at railway stations when servicemen were leaving during the war years of 1916 and 1917. Later directors were Assistant Professors Herbert B. Fehner, F. C. Rathert, Paul Boester, and Harold H. Pollex.

In 1925 Professor Rohlfing became director, and under his leadership the band became a highly skilled organization which was greatly in demand. His aim was to develop a full symphonic band. Annual tours took the band into many sections of the country.

Chorus work was done mostly by small groups until 1922, when a large 100-member chorus was organized by Professor Beck. In 1925–26 this chorus made its first radio broadcast. A touring choir, also organized by Professor Beck in 1929, gained the acclaim of Lutherans in all parts of the country. Both the choir and the band assisted in the program of recruitment of students. The first mixed choir was organized by Professor Beck in 1938, and its first concert was presented in March 1939.

A music library was established in 1930 so that students might be able to check out organ and piano music instead of buying every piece.[140] In addition to the pipe organs, of which there were 10 by 1935, the college also installed several reed organs in order to help those students who might serve in congregations which had only reed organs.

The "Spectator" Is Born

On Monday mornings during the school year 1924–25 a set of typewritten news notes was posted on the bulletin boards near the entrance to the dining hall. They carried the title "Concordia Concoctions." The editors signed themselves as "Tipsy" and "Eebel" and remained anonymous until the spring of 1925, when they were revealed as students G. E. Rast and Herbert H. Gross (now a member of the faculty and editor of *Lutheran Education*).

The purpose of this clandestine venture was to keep the students informed about campus events and athletics and to help build school spirit. Editors worked late Sunday nights and posted their news about one o'clock Monday mornings.

The bulletin-board publication was continued in autumn 1925, and in September a ballot was circulated on which students expressed their overwhelming desire for a school paper. This was followed by a petition to the faculty, and permission was granted.[141]

The first issue of the *Spectator* appeared on Nov. 2, 1925. Its lead story gave the following information on its origin and purpose:

> This, the second day of November, 1925, is to be regarded as an important date in the history of River Forest, Concordia, for on this

day the initial issue of the paper which is to represent the ideals of our college is being given to the members of the student body and to the alumni. During the spring of 1925, students placed upon the bulletin board weekly a sketch of college activities. The sheets commanded attention and this paper is a realization of one of the needs of 400 youths.

The staff of *The Spectator* was selected by the English Department of the faculty, the selection being based upon general character, class standing, and a literary try-out. The editors are to keep in mind the purposes of this publication, namely, to foster a spirit of loyalty for Concordia, to form a closer bond between the alumni and their Alma Mater, and to furnish wholesome publicity for the college.

The Spectator was the name selected by the staff and Professor Albert H. Miller, O. W. List having handed it to the staff for consideration. . . . We trust you will see our reflections on these pages and wherever necessary, criticize them.[142]

Professor Miller's great admiration for the *Spectator* papers by the English author Joseph Addison was said to have been an important factor in the selection of the name for the new school paper.

The first staff included Palmer A. Czamanske as editor-in-chief; J. Salmon, business manager; R. Korf, staff artist; W. Manske and E. Nickel, sports editors; W. Zahnow, F. Groth, R. Judish, E. Pflieger, A. Will, news editors; H. Steinkamp, alumni editor; W. Schalkofski, A. Wittmer, E. Sieving, O. Beyers, W. Metzger, R. Waldschmidt, and W. Marquardt, reporters. Professors Miller, Schmitt, and Diesing were "faculty consulting editors." The subscription rate was set at 50 cents per annum for students and $1.00 for alumni. The *Spectator* has continued to be an important forum for student opinion and chronicles of current events, using as its motto "Positive Christian Journalism." [143]

Alumni Relations

In the autumn of 1927 a special committee was established to study the floundering alumni association and bring recommendations as to its future. Questions had been asked as to the advisability of working to keep it alive. The committee recommended a complete reorganization of the association under the following purposes:

1. To sponsor and assist in college activities not directly under control of the Synod, working through faculty representatives.

2. All graduates are to be automatically members of the alumni association.

3. An annual meeting should be held in summer during the General Teachers Conference. District alumni meetings could be held at the time of District teachers' conferences.
4. Reports of meetings were to be reported in the *Spectator*.
5. Annual pledges were to be solicited from each alumnus and the prevailing dues system abolished.
6. The *Spectator* should be sent gratis to all alumni. (Actually only one issue was sent.)[144]

Most of the objectives were incorporated in a constitution revision in July 1928. An alumni endowment fund was set up which grew to $1,600 by March 1929. In 1937 the association made a donation for the expanded library facilities made necessary by the summer school program.

Yearbooks

Regular yearbooks were primarily graduating class annuals until 1924, when a college annual called "Concorifor" came into being. It experienced financial difficulty, and an $800 deficit became a problem for the board of control which was met by an appeal to members of the class.[145] During the depression years the annual was dropped.

Campus Life and Activities

Initially the life of a student at River Forest was not much different during the Kohn period than what he had known at Addison, excepting for the drastically improved facilities. Gradually modifications were made with the changing times. The growth of the curriculum to include three and then four years of college beyond high school brought a more mature student to the campus. For 74 years the enrollment was all male. In the 75th year, 1938–39, the last year of the Kohn administration, coeducation was introduced; but during that year it was still essentially an all-male school with special regulations governing the girls.[146] The effects of coeducation were gradually felt in succeeding years as girls began to be active in student body affairs.

Admission to the college in 1938–39 still stressed the same qualities enunciated by past administrations since 1864: the character of the applicant, his diligence, purpose, and intelligence. The purpose of developing the highest quality training obtainable in its graduates for the ultimate benefit of the pupil in the Lutheran parish school was not diminished in any of the catalogs and other publications during this period.[147]

Student Government. The choice of student leaders remained largely a faculty matter through most of this period.[148] They approved all candidates even when students were allowed to vote. However, gradually the students were drawn into school government and more independence of choice regarding their leadership. Printed ballots were used for the first time in the spring of 1935.

A special advisory council was created in 1935. Its purpose was to coordinate all the various college activities. Its membership included the student body president, the student food administrator, the editor of the *Spectator,* the chairman of the extracurricular committee, the chairman of the athletic committee, the president of the chorus and of the band, and the chief student librarian. This council had no executive powers but could discuss and clarify the various activities and their needs and make suggestions for improvement and for sponsorship of such special activities as the field day and homecoming programs.[149] President Kohn served most of the functions commonly handled by a dean of students.

Since the high school and college departments were separated in 1935, the student government was also separate, the college retaining the name "student council." The high school group was appointed by the council and was called an "order committee." In 1937 the student council was preparing to publish the first student handbook explaining the extracurricular program. In 1938 a special order committee was organized for the girls.

Club Activity. Numerous literary societies flourished during the 1920s. Each class organized a club and named it after one of the great authors, such as the "Lowell Society" or the "Whittier Society." These societies were encouraged by the faculty, and clubrooms were provided in the basements of Brohm and Kohn Halls through the efforts of President Kohn and Professor Schmitt.

The societies helped to create an important social outlet for the students. The meetings were held on Friday nights, and most of the students participated at various times in the entertainment, including literary and dramatic presentations, instrumental and vocal numbers, and organ recitals. One of the high school clubs, known as the "Mark Twain Society," developed an orchestra which was on demand for banquets and other functions.[150] Debating clubs were also popular among the students.

Dormitories Named and Mascot Selected. When the plant was built in 1913, the architect simply labeled the dormitories "A" and "B" as a matter of convenience, and when the annexes were built in 1924, the letters "C" and "D" were added. These designations were used till March 1933, when the student body voted to name them in order after the first four presidents.[151]

"Cougars," the name of Concordia's athletic teams, was selected by the student body in 1933 out of a number of names submitted by students.[152]

A Typical Day. The day started at six o'clock for everyone. By 6:20 all had to be at breakfast neatly dressed in coats and ties. President Kohn always took roll in the dining hall and led in the devotions after breakfast. By 7:15 the rooms had to be in order. At 8:00 classes began, closing at 3:30 p. m. A midmorning recess of 15 minutes was allowed at 9:30, and a lunch hour from 12:00 till 1:30. After 3:30 till suppertime at 5:30 the students were free. Attendance at supper again was checked by President Kohn. Band and chorus meetings were held after supper, and at 7:00 study periods began, as well as piano and organ practice hours strictly scheduled in half-hour periods. At 9:00 devotions were held in the chapel (called the *aula*). High school classes had to go to bed after chapel, but college men could stay up till 10:30, when all lights were put out. The president and frequently also another professor supervised the evening study hours.[153] They also "made the rounds" after lights were out to see that all were in bed.

Student Aid. At the River Forest dedication in 1913 President Kohn had pleaded for the establishment of an "Indigent Student's Endowment Fund." One donor gave $5,000 for that purpose. Over the years other gifts were given to this fund so that by 1928 the income for student aid from this endowment was $1,200.[154] In 1934 the Lutheran Laymen's League also began a program of scholarships for Concordia students.

By 1938 Professor Schmitt, the business manager, reported that about 150 students were employed in off-campus jobs. He also made a survey in 1938 which showed that the students' distance from home averaged 512 miles and they paid $8.79 to go home. The student farthest from home traveled 1,100 miles and paid $36.[155]

Miscellaneous. The ban on going out with girls, which had pertained throughout the Addison years, was rigidly enforced at first and very few risked the penalty — expulsion.[156] However, during the 1930s weekend dates were gradually permitted.

Until the gymnasium was built in 1927, the graduation ceremony was held in the chapel, on the third floor of the music building.

The idea of "benefactors" came along to River Forest with the college, and the students who had "benefactors" eagerly looked forward to weekend meals in their homes.[157] This gave opportunity for students to see girls socially.[158]

The Addison Orphan Home Festival was still an important social affair each year, as was also the annual College Field Day filled with athletics and entertainment.[159]

Food was generally good and ample. It was served family style. Donations to the college larder were still coming from various congregations. One at Conklin, Mich., continued to send truckloads of apples and potatoes even throughout the depression.[160]

The student body was thrilled to have the first radio (four tubes) installed in the chapel with an inside aerial in 1928. The donor was Paul Schulze, a member of the board of control.[161] By 1935 the crystal sets and other radios were declared contraband by college authorities, together with toasters which were often used for midnight snacks even after lights were out.[162]

President Kohn was very solicitous when students were ill, visiting them every day, diagnosing their illnesses, and giving his pills. When his pills failed, there were two Lutheran doctors (Schroeder and Brown) available. They often did surgery gratis to the students, the hospital charging only 50%. The total bill for one tonsillectomy in 1935 came to $5.63.[163]

The "sweatbox" was a term familiar to all student teachers. It was a special room in the basement of one of the buildings with lights on all night for those who had to prepare lesson plans for training school.[164]

Dr. Kohn originated the annual Reformation Day tradition of assembling the student body on the front steps of the administration building to sing Luther's "A Mighty Fortress Is Our God" led by the college band.[165]

"The Old Man"

When Concordia students referred to President Kohn, it was to "The Old Man." This was a title of affection which was accepted as such by him. His days were always long and were spent in supervising at mealtimes, during chapel and study hours, and after lights were out at night. He also taught classes in religion and education and acted quite efficiently as school doctor and nurse, as well as counselor for all sorts of other problems, social, spiritual, or emotional. When coeducation arrived at Concordia during his last year as president, he commented in the words from Goethe's *Faust: "Ich fürchte, die Geister, die wir riefen, die werden wir nicht wieder los"* (I feel that we shall never again be rid of the spirits we have summoned). A former student wrote: "All during the day he served as a firm but friendly father to the boys who were placed by trusting parents into his care. 'The Old Man' was always sensitive to his responsibility and discharged it with wisdom he prayerfully solicited from his heavenly Father." [166]

Summary

In the 26-year administration of Dr. W. C. Kohn, Concordia Teachers College experienced great changes. The size of the faculty doubled from 9 to 18, and the student body nearly did so, becoming coeducational by Dr. Kohn's last year, 1938–39. The college had moved from Addison to a new campus and had barely settled down when a disastrous fire destroyed the administration building, causing the immediate problem of rebuilding. The plant was enlarged in 1922 and 1924 to accommodate the growing enrollment, and a gymnasium was built in 1927. The teacher training program was expanded when Grace Lutheran Church of Oak Park built its new school and church on the northeast corner of the campus.

The inauguration of a summer school program and of a correspondence and extension program took place in the 1930s. In 1935 the first major curriculum revision since 1864 was effected, accompanied by the adoption of the quarter system and the establishment of institutional objectives. Economic needs of the depression years caused serious consideration of the addition of a general liberal arts curriculum to increase enrollment. The idea was rejected and the one purpose of the school reaffirmed. The third college year was added in 1933, and the high school and college departments were separated. Plans for the fourth year were completed, and it was to begin in September 1939.

Gradual reorganization of the faculty to conform more closely to the American collegiate pattern was a notable achievement of this period. The establishment of deans and other administrative officers paved the way for further gradual development of the office of the president as the executive officer of the board of control and responsible head of the school.

Accreditation was studied, and the beginnings were made in 1919, when Concordia achieved recognition as a normal school by the State Department of Education. In 1935 the high school department was accepted as a member of the North Central Association of Colleges and Secondary Schools. By 1936 the first two college years received full accreditation by the University of Illinois. It is striking to note the faculty's willingness to work for advanced degrees to help assure accreditation, especially also on the part of the older men.

The student activity program was vastly expanded from 1913 to 1939, not only in club work, but in sports, in choir and band work, and in student participation in the government of the college. In this area of college life the Addison student of 1913 would not have recognized his Alma Mater.

Additional support for the college was obtained by the organization of the Women's Auxiliary in 1934 and the Men's Club in 1936.

President Kohn had guided the destinies of the school through World War I and its aftermath, the great depression, up to the threshold of World War II.

In 1913 Concordia was a 6-year school. Twenty years later it became a 7-year school, and at President Kohn's retirement the eighth year was ready to begin, giving a 4-year high school and a 4-year college.

Dr. Kohn was made honorary president and continued to serve as part-time instructor in freshman religion. He died March 13, 1943.

Notes

1. *Synodal-Bericht,* 1908, p. 55.
2. Albert H. Beck, news report in *Alma Mater,* IV (Nov. 1913), 52.
3. Chicago *Tribune,* Oct. 13, 1913.
4. Theodore C. Appelt in *Northern Illinois Messenger,* VIII (April 1932), 5.
5. Dedication program, *"Einweihungs-Feier des Evangelical Lutheran Concordia Teachers College,"* River Forest, Ill., Oct. 12, 1913.
6. Henry W. Horst, "Important Facts and Figures." Reports of two surveys evaluating the property at River Forest for the Synod in 1918 and 1932. (Unpublished, bound in one book, unpaginated.)
7. Chicago *Tribune,* Oct. 13, 1913.
8. Albert H. Miller, scrapbook, undated clipping.
9. Dedication program, Oct. 12, 1913.
10. Albert H. Miller, "Our New College," speech delivered to Lutheran Education Society, Jan. 22, 1914, published in *Concordia* (monthly paper of the Concordia Mutual Benefit League), Feb. 1914. Clipping found in Albert H. Miller scrapbook.
11. Albert H. Miller, "Concordia Teachers College." Undated clipping from *Southern Lutheran,* probably around 1916.
12. *Concordia* (April 1914), p. 2.
13. Ibid., p. 2.
14. Albert H. Beck, unpublished autobiography, Aug. 20, 1962, p. 23. By courtesy of Mrs. Paula Eggers nee Beck.
15. Minutes, Faculty of Concordia Teachers College, Mar. 1, 1914.
16. Ibid.
17. Albert H. Beck, autobiography, p. 24.
18. Program, May 10, 1914. "Jubilaeums-Feier des Evangelisch-Lutherischen Lehrer-Seminars zu River Forest, Illinois."
19. Albert H. Miller scrapbook. Clipping from *Oak Park Events,* May 16, 1914.
20. Ibid.
21. Theodore C. Appelt, "Concordia Teachers College, River Forest, Illinois — a Historical Sketch," *Northern Illinois Messenger,* VIII (April 1932), 5.
22. Albert H. Miller scrapbook. Clipping from *Oak Park Events,* Oct. 15, 1914.
23. Ibid.
24. Albert H. Miller scrapbook. Undated newspaper clipping, source not indicated.
25. *Synodal-Bericht,* 1914, p. 34.
26. Twenty-fifth-anniversary program of Lutheran Children's Welfare Society (in Concordia Historical Institute, St. Louis, Mo.), p. 2.
27. Minutes, Faculty, Dec. 10, 1919.
28. Walter H. Beck, *Lutheran Elementary Schools in the United States: A History of the Development of Parochial Schools and Synodical Educational Policies and Programs* (St. Louis: Concordia Publishing House, 1939), pp. 324, 343.
29. *Der Lutheraner,* LXXV (Oct. 7, 1919), 326.

30. *Synodal-Bericht,* 1917, p. 44.
31. Lawrence G. Bickel, "The Period of Integration, 1914—1917," *100 Years of Christian Education,* Lutheran Education Association 4th Yearbook (Chicago, 1947), p. 190.
32. *Proceedings,* 1920, p. 21; *Synodal-Bericht,* 1920, p. 50.
33. Henry C. Gaertner, "A Brief Historical Sketch of Concordia Teachers College, River Forest, Illinois," *Lutheran School Journal,* LXVII (May 1932), 407.
34. Henry W. Horst, "Important Facts and Figures." See note 6.
35. *The Spectator,* River Forest student paper, I (Nov. 2, 1925), 3.
36. Ibid., II (Feb. 28, 1927), 1.
37. Ibid., IV (Jan. 22, 1929), 1.
38. Ibid., VI (Sept. 23, 1930), 1.
39. Albert H. Miller, "Addison," *Lutheran School Journal,* LX (Feb. 1925), 41.
40. Albert H. Miller, "Dedication of the Addison Memorial," *Lutheran School Journal,* LX (Sept. 1925), 333—336.
41. Alwin R. Roschke letter to Martin L. Koehneke, Sept. 4, 1962.
42. *The Spectator,* VIII (May 9, 1933), 2.
43. Ibid.
44. Ibid., III (Oct. 11, 1927), 1.
45. Ibid., III (Dec. 12, 1927), 1.
46. *Catalog of the Educational Institutions of the Evangelical Lutheran Synod of Missouri, Ohio, and Other States,* 1927—28, p. 33.
47. *The Spectator,* VI (Jan. 27, 1931), 1.
48. River Forest Catalog, 1930—31, p. 28.
49. Ibid., pp. 4, 5.
50. A. H. Beck, autobiography, p. 19.
51. River Forest Catalog, 1930—31, p. 6.
52. Ibid.
53. William C. Kohn, "Dr. Kohn Has the Floor," *Northern Illinois Messenger,* VI (April 1930), 2.
54. Ferdinand H. Schmitt, "What Does It Cost?" *Northern Illinois Messenger,* VI (April 1930), 5, 6.
55. Alfred F. Schmieding, "The Teacher Training Department at Work," *Northern Illinois Messenger,* VI (April 1930), 5, 6.
56. Ibid.
57. *Northern Illinois Messenger,* VIII (May 1932), 1, 2.
58. Summer-school catalog, 1932, p. 6.
59. *Proceedings,* 1932, p. 101.
60. Summer-school catalog, 1932, p. 5.
61. Summer-school catalog, 1933, pp. 7—14.
62. *Lutheran School Journal,* LXVIII (Sept. 1932), 21.
63. Summer-school catalog, 1933, p. 5.
64. Summer-school catalog, 1934, p. 4.
65. *The Spectator,* IX (Nov. 2, 1933), 1.

66. Unpublished report of faculty of Concordia Teachers College, River Forest, Ill., to the Delegate Synod in Milwaukee, June 15—25, 1932. Report signed by A. F. Schmieding and Theo. Kuehnert.

67. Ibid.

68. *The Spectator,* VIII (March 21, 1933), 1.

69. Ibid., VIII (April 25, 1933), 1.

70. Minutes, Faculty, March 5, 1934.

71. Minutes, Faculty, March 19, 1934.

72. Minutes, Faculty, April 9, 1934.

73. Letter of River Forest faculty to Rev. Henry H. Grueber, chairman of the Committee on Higher Education, April 24, 1934.

74. Minutes, Faculty, April 23, 1934.

75. Minutes, Faculty, June 11, 1934.

76. Minutes, Faculty, June 12, 1934.

77. *The Spectator,* X (March 7, 1935), 1.

78. Ibid., X (May 23, 1935), 1.

79. Ibid., X (April 4, 1935), 1.

80. Ibid.

81. Minutes, Faculty, Feb. 18, 1935.

82. Minutes, Faculty, April 15, 1935.

83. *The Spectator,* XIII (Oct. 7, 1937), 1.

84. Minutes, Faculty, April 16, 1936.

85. *The Spectator,* XIV (April 27, 1939), 1.

86. August C. Stellhorn, *Schools of The Lutheran Church — Missouri Synod* (St. Louis: Concordia Publishing House, 1963), p. 424.

87. Ibid., pp. 344, 345.

88. *Proceedings,* 1926, p. 77.

89. *The Spectator,* XII (Oct. 8, 1936), 1.

90. Minutes, Board of Control, Jan. 18, 1937.

91. *Proceedings,* 1938, pp. 61, 62.

92. *The Spectator,* XIV (March 23, 1939), 1.

93. Ibid., XIV (Oct. 6, 1938), 4.

94. *Proceedings,* 1935, pp. 39, 40.

95. Ibid., pp. 44, 45.

96. Minutes, Faculty, Sept. 8, 1937.

97. *The Spectator,* VI (Dec. 2, 1930), 1.

98. Ibid., IX (Nov. 2, 1933), 3.

99. Ferdinand H. Schmitt, autobiography in "Fifty-Fifth Anniversary Reunion of Addison Seminary Class of 1901," a mimeographed publication.

100. *The Spectator,* XI (Oct. 4, 1935), 1.

101. Ibid., III (Oct. 11, 1927), 5.

102. Appelt, p. 7.

103. Minutes, Board of Control, June 6, 1927.

104. Ibid.

105. Minutes, Board of Control, March 25, 1929.

106. Minutes, Faculty, April 15, 1935.

107. Minutes, Faculty, May 6, 1935.

108. Minutes, Faculty, Sept. 23, 1935.

109. Minutes, Faculty, Jan. 18, 1937.

110. Minutes, Faculty, March 21, 1938.

111. Minutes, Board of Control, April 26, 1937.

112. Minutes, Faculty, May 17, 1938.

113. Minutes, Board of Control, March 20, 1939.

114. Minutes, Faculty, March 20, 1939.

115. Minutes, Faculty, April 17, 1939.

116. Minutes, Board of Control, May 22, 1939.

117. *The Spectator*, X (Oct. 18, 1934), 1.

118. Hildegard Weiss, "Excerpts for Concordia Teachers College Women's Auxiliary Rally" (25th-anniversary rally), unpublished, 1959.

119. Ibid.

120. *The Spectator*, XII (Oct. 22, 1936), 1.

121. Concordia Teachers College Men's Club Constitution, 1936.

122. *The Spectator*, III (Oct. 11, 1927), 1.

123. Ibid., I (Nov. 2, 1925), 5.

124. Ibid., III (Jan. 18, 1928), 1.

125. Ibid., IV (Oct. 9, 1928), 1.

126. Ibid., IV (April 23, 1929), 1.

127. Minutes, Board of Control, April 26, 1937.

128. *The Spectator*, XII (June 3, 1937), 5.

129. Ibid., XIV (May 25, 1939), 4.

130. Ibid.

131. Arthur W. Gross, Class of 1919, "Reminiscences of River Forest Student Days," 1964.

132. *The Spectator*, I (Feb. 8, 1926), 2.

133. Ibid., Oct. 4, 1926, 1.

134. Catalogue, 1930—1931, p. 1.

135. *The Spectator*, IX (Jan. 25, 1934), 1.

136. Minutes, Board of Control, Dec. 17, 1928.

137. *The Spectator*, IV (Nov. 6, 1928), 1.

138. Ibid., IX (Oct. 5, 1933), 1.

139. Ibid., XI (Dec. 19, 1935), 4.

140. Ibid., VI (Oct. 7, 1930), 1.

141. Ibid., XXV (Oct. 28, 1949), 8.

142. Ibid., I (Nov. 2, 1925), 1.

143. Ibid.

144. Ibid., III (Oct. 11, 1927), 4.

145. Minutes, Board of Control, Dec. 12, 1927.

146. Ibid., Aug. 29, 1938.

147. Catalog, 1938—39, pp. 4, 5.

148. *The Spectator*, X (April 4, 1935), 1.

149. Ibid.

150. Ibid., I (Nov. 2, 1925), 4.

151. Ibid., VIII (March 21, 1933), 3.

152. Ibid., IX (Oct. 19, 1933), 1.

153. E. H. Engelbrecht, "A Day at Concordia Teachers College," *Northern Illinois Messenger*, VI (April 1930), 3, 4.

154. *The Spectator*, III (Jan. 18, 1928), 4.

155. Ibid., XIV (Dec. 15, 1938), 3.

156. Arthur W. Gross, Class of 1919, letter to the author, April 30, 1964.

157. Herbert D. Bruening, Class of 1919, reminiscences to author. Dr. Bruening is a grandson of Friedrich Lochner, one of the founders of the Milwaukee private teachers seminary in 1855.

158. Edwin T. Pingel, Class of 1927, reminiscences to author.

159. Albert V. Maurer, Class of 1921, reminiscences to author.

160. *The Spectator*, IX (Oct. 9, 1933), 1.

161. Ibid., III (April 3, 1928), 1.

162. Henry W. Steinweg, Class of 1935, reminiscences to author.

163. Ibid.

164. Ibid.

165. Ibid.

166. Herbert H. Gross, Class of 1925, "The Old Man" — article sent to the author in 1964.

President Arthur W. Klinck, 1900—1959

Dr. Arthur William Klinck was born January 19, 1900,
at Elmira, Ontario, Canada. He received his elementary schooling
in the public school and St. Paul's Lutheran School in Elmira.
After graduating from high school he studied pre-engineering
at Kitchener Collegiate and Technical Institute, graduating in 1918.
Thereafter he attended Concordia College, Fort Wayne, and
Concordia Seminary, St. Louis, graduating from the latter school
in 1924 with the Bachelor of Divinity degree. In 1925 he received
the degree of Master of Sacred Theology from the seminary,
and in 1935 he was awarded the degree of Doctor of Philosophy
by the University of Nebraska in the field of history and classics.

He served as a missionary in North Platte, Nebraska, from
1925 to 1928, organizing Our Redeemer Lutheran Church and School.
In 1928 he was sent to Lincoln, Nebraska, where he organized
Calvary Lutheran Church and School. In 1939 he was called
to be the fifth president of Concordia Teachers College, serving

till December 31, 1953, when he left this post to become professor of historical theology at Concordia Seminary, St. Louis, the second president of Concordia Teachers College to do so.

Dr. Klinck was a scholar of Biblical archeology, and wrote Home Life in Bible Times *and* Old Testament History *in the Sunday School Teacher Training series for the Synod. He served on several educational boards of the Synod and Districts, and also as associate editor of* Lutheran Education *and the* Lutheran Witness.

He was married to Flora Buettner in 1925, and they had one son, Robert, who preceded his father in death in 1957.

Dr. Klinck died August 9, 1959.

Chapter 7

ARTHUR W. KLINCK'S ADMINISTRATION 1939—1953

As the fifth president of Concordia Teachers College was being installed on Oct. 6, 1939, the evil forces of World War II had been unleashed and were gaining momentum in Europe, while in the United States there was a growing feeling of apprehension about the possibility of American involvement.

The college was now in its first year as an 8-year institution, which included a fully accredited 4-year high school and a 4-year college granting the degree of Bachelor of Science in Education. The fourth college year was elective, the 3-year curriculum still being the official required course of the Synod for teacher graduates.

One of the major concerns confronting the new president was the accreditation of the college. A great deal of work had been accomplished by the Educational Policies Committee and the faculty to prepare for regional accreditation of the college with the North Central Association of Colleges and Secondary Schools. As in the case of the high school, which was accredited in 1936, the first step toward this goal was to become accredited by the University of Illinois. Various data were sent to the university in November 1939,[1] and by the following February negotiations had begun with the Illinois State Department of Public Instruction.[2]

The development of the college curriculum since the early 1930s, when the third college year was being planned, was under the guidance of the Educational Policies Committee. This committee was charged with the responsibility of planning for the full accreditation of the college. From 1939, when the fourth college year was added, and through the war years, there were three main developments — a broadened curriculum on the junior college level to include more general cultural training; strong specialization in elementary education and religion on the senior college level; and a much freer system of electives in the senior college years. By 1946 graduates of Concordia who earned their bachelor's degrees were able to earn a major in any of five fields other than religion and education, including music, English, history, German, and geography.[3]

Efforts on behalf of accreditation had also made some progress during World War II, although plans for an early examination by the North Central Association of Colleges and Secondary Schools had to be suspended because of the war. By the close of the war the Superintendent of Public Instruction and the Illinois State Examining Board for Teachers' Certificates recognized Concordia as a 4-year teachers college whose graduates could qualify for certificates based on the bachelor's degree for which specific requirements had been met.[4] Departments of education in a number of other states agreed to grant certificates to graduates upon application provided specific course requirements had been met.[5]

Graduates with superior standing who had satisfied requirements for undergraduate majors could be admitted to full graduate standing at the University of Illinois.[6]

The college catalog of 1942–43 listed three educational objectives of teacher preparation for positions in the church:

1. A basic education aimed at the development of a devout Christian character and a balanced personality, capable of an intelligent approach to the problems of modern life.
2. Educational training which will prepare the candidate to meet the exacting and varied demands of the Lutheran elementary parish school system.
3. Specialized training in religion and music for additional service in the local church's broader program of religious education.[7]

In October 1942 a special committee of the Synod conducted a survey of Concordia Teachers College which covered all phases of the college's operation, including the administrative offices of president, deans (of high school and college), registrar, business manager, librarian, placement committee, training school, and all instructional personnel.

The Board of Control voted $200 in December 1943 to have Dr. John D. Russell of the University of Chicago make an advisory survey as an important step to obtain guidelines to full accreditation.[8]

On the basis of these surveys the faculty and administration kept constantly at work during the war years, adapting and revising the curriculum, the accounting system, the library, and also the physical plant to the ever-expanding needs of the Synod and in accord with the standards of accreditation.

New courses were added from time to time to strengthen the curriculum and to serve the students more adequately. As the fourth college year began in 1939, some of the new courses included psychology and personality, the family, composition, and United States history.[9] Since many graduates went to serve small schools, Professor Albert V. Maurer, director of teacher training and placement, introduced a special course in 1941 entitled "The Problems of a Small School."[10] In 1942 an "honors" reading course in Greek and Roman civilization was added to the curriculum for students of high quality.

A completely revised and enriched curriculum was put into effect in the fall of 1948, beginning with college freshmen. Sophomores, too, were generally registered in the new curriculum, and juniors and seniors were permitted to take advantage of the new plan wherever feasible. It was the culmination of many studies which had been conducted by Academic Dean Schmieding and the Educational Policies Committee to ascertain the needs of the graduates in the field. These studies also included careful evaluation of the teacher-training programs in several universities and analyses of the certification requirements of those states in which most of Concordia's graduates were placed, as well as the changes anticipated in the various states as supply and demand would become more equalized.[11]

An important feature of the new curriculum was the introduction and expansion of survey courses in science, social studies, English, music, and art, to strengthen the general education requirements in the junior college program. Standard courses were cut down from five to four term hours, thus allowing the average student to broaden his program.[12] The normal student load was 16 term hours per quarter.[13]

Concordia students had to fulfill the requirements in religion and music, besides all other academic and professional requirements. A minimum of 198 term hours was required for graduation, at least 64 hours of which were on the senior college level. In the sophomore year a subject-matter sequence of at least 28 hours was to be selected, with 12 hours reserved for the senior college level. Sequences could be selected from English literature, German, history, music, and geography. No less than one year's residence (usually the last year) was required for graduation.

A special study of Concordia Teachers College was made in the spring of 1948 by Dr. Paul W. Lange, superintendent of the St. Louis Lutheran High School, and Dr. M. Gordon Neale, professor of education of the University of Minnesota, an experienced examiner for the North Central Association of Colleges and Secondary Schools. Both men made many suggestions for improvements to prepare the college further for accreditation.[14]

Dr. Neale wrote his report along the lines followed by the North Central Association in evaluating applicants for membership, submitting it to Dr. Klinck on May 24, 1948, at the end of 3½ weeks of study. Some of his commendations of the college included:

1. A definite purpose of training teachers for the elementary schools of the church. He stated that it was "unusual to find an institution whose teacher-training objectives are not complicated by liberal arts objectives or the necessities of pre-professional training in such fields as law, medicine, and engineering." [15]

2. Faculty enterprise in publication of scholarly books and articles despite heavy teaching loads and extra duties.

3. Faculty tenure system which allows stability far above the average college.

4. Excellent provision for faculty housing.

5. Expanding library.

6. Recruitment of a superior student body.

7. Superior student discipline, placement of graduates, and general counseling despite lack of full-time employees in student personnel services.

8. Many self-studies and analyses of the school by the faculty and the use of such studies to determine educational policies.

9. The college had no indebtedness, operating on a balanced budget.

10. Intercollegiate athletics were fully controlled in line with the highest standards.[16]

Recommendations were made urging that faculty members teach only in their fields of competence, also that the teaching load of faculty members who had administrative duties be made lighter.

A system of professional ranks and promotions with salary increases was advocated, as well as a group insurance plan.

Dr. Neale recommended further that summer school should be coordinated with the regular program and that a more adequate loan fund and student-aid program should be established, together with a more aggressive policy of student recruitment.[17]

Especially significant was the recommendation for changing the organization of the administration, including clarification of the status of the president as the responsible executive officer of the board of control in accord with the unit concept of administration. More responsibility for recruitment and selection of faculty members should be given to the president and the departments. Such selection should be based on scholarship, teaching ability, character, and fitness to serve on the faculty. No one should be appointed without the president's recommendation.[18]

Dr. Neale encouraged the administration and faculty to continue policies of admission that would draw outstanding students. To that end a good scholarship program should be established. He stated: "Few teachers colleges now have the backing of a permanent career motive and strong denominational recognition to support student recruitment found at Concordia." [19]

Another suggestion dealt with the implementation of a faculty recruitment policy previously recommended. It involved the exercise of synodical authority and that of its boards and committees through setting up general policies and through the power of final approval. It also included the suggestion of leaves for faculty members with pay to earn advanced degrees and to study in the best universities.[20]

A beginning was made in 1946 to establish the unit plan of administration, following the Russell report, as the board of control informed the faculty that all academic matters for the board must be cleared through the president. This new policy gave the president the duties of an academic dean.[21]

Stimulated by the reports of Neale and Lange in 1948, the faculty took immediate steps to make improvements prior to filing application for accreditation by the North Central Association of Colleges and Secondary Schools. In 1948–49 the teaching loads of administrators were reduced, with further reductions planned for 1949–50. Teaching loads and subject assignments were made more nearly in line with the preparation of faculty members. Four faculty members completed master's degrees, one was awarded his doctor's degree, and others met major and minor requirements for their teaching areas beyond the master's degree.[22]

Other marks of progress included a full revision of health services, numerous institutional self-studies, the appointment in 1948 of Professor Schmieding as academic dean with full responsibility for supervision of the curriculum, and the completion of an important study clarifying the functions of all administrative officers. Many improvements were made to the plant, including the addition of a new library and a women's dormitory. New studies initiated included faculty group insurance plans and a follow-up of alumni. Recommendations were sent to the Synod and to the Board for Higher Education regarding the delegation of more authority to the local board of control, as well as the needed corrections in the synodical *Handbook* to implement them.[23] A new system of accounting was installed in conformity with current collegiate standards.[24]

In October 1949 Concordia Teachers College made formal application for membership in the North Central Association of Colleges and Secondary Schools. The examining committee consisted of Dr. Irwin J. Lubbers, President of Hope College, and Dr. Robert White, dean of Kent State University. The examination took place Dec. 15 and 16, 1949. In examining the purposes of the college they quoted from the college catalog for 1949–50:

> Graduates of Concordia Teachers College are called to unique positions in the church, and the teacher-training program embodied in the curriculum recognizes the special needs of these positions. Lutheran parish schools definitely integrate religious education with the entire school, curricular and extra-curricular. In addition to his classroom work the Lutheran teacher frequently functions as the church organist, as the director of the church choir, as a leader of young people's groups in the church, and as a worker in part-time agencies of religious education, such as the Sunday School, the Saturday School and the Vacation Bible School.
>
> Approximately sixty percent of the Lutheran Church schools are located in rural sections, or in towns having a population of less than 2500. Most of these schools are served by one teacher. Hence he must be a man of broad culture and training rather than a specialist in a narrow field. A further condition which makes the position of the parish school teacher unique is the fact that his work is regarded as part of the ministry of the church. His induction into office approximates in importance the ordination of a minister. A call given to a parish school teacher is not a contract in the ordinary

sense, but a solemn agreement between him and the local church, to
be abrogated only by regular transfer to another charge, by removal
for a cause, or by death. Thus the office of a Lutheran teacher is
a life-work, and the average term of office about 35 years. At the
present time Concordia graduates serve in approximately two-thirds
of the states, in Canada, and in various foreign fields.

In describing the school the report states:

There is no mistaking the purpose of Concordia Teachers College.
The institution knows exactly what it wishes to achieve and states
its purpose in unequivocal terms. . . . There is no question of the
acceptance of the objectives by the faculty, since only members of
The Lutheran Church — Missouri Synod can have faculty status. It
is obvious in all the activities of the college that its purposes are the
determining factor. . . . The institution receives 70% of its operating
budget from the Synod. Concordia Teachers College owes its unity
and stability to the full commitment of its clientele to the clearly
defined purposes of the college.[25]

The committee recommended the elimination of the 3-year diploma
and the requirement of the bachelor's degree for teaching in the parish
schools.[26]

How well Concordia Teachers College had profited from previous
studies made by Neale, Lange, and earlier by Russell may be seen
in the commendations and recommendations for improvement.

Eight elements of strength were noted:

1. Since the board, faculty, and students possess a common background and objective, many problems are simplified, and general
   loyalty and devotion to improvement of the college is assured.
2. The college possesses a marked clarity and singleness of purpose, with no evidence of any dilution of that purpose. This
   guarantees that the resources of the school will be used to support that objective.
3. Faculty organization assures deliberate study of educational
   policy under sound conditions.
4. The student body is such that would facilitate a sound educational program, since the students are evidently considerably
   above the average college student, highly motivated and sincere.
5. The college has subjected itself to numerous self-studies and
   has made important changes on the evidence obtained from
   such studies.
6. Strong financial support from the church.

7. Effective student personnel service.

8. Administrative officers and faculty of the college are competent to staff an institution with the purposes of Concordia Teachers College.[27]

In commenting on the "elements of strength," President Klinck pointed out that in some of those areas further significant improvements could and should be made.[28]

Three general areas were recommended for improvement:

1. Greater local autonomy for the board of control. It was made clear that the committee had found no evidence that lack of complete freedom by the board of control had been significantly harmful or demoralizing to the college. It was felt, however, that all agencies of the Synod concerned with the college study possible arrangements to give the local board more freedom without dissipation of the strong support the college receives from the united church.

2. Clarification of administrative positions. Special attention should be given to development of the position of academic dean and of the administrative committees into more assured leadership and strength.

3. The time needs of general and professional education, plus the additional needs imposed by the required courses in music and religion, worked a severe stricture on advanced fields of study or on possible future enlargement of the professional program.[29]

In his *President's Report to the Board* for 1949–50 Dr. Klinck was able to report that progress had been made on the recommendation. Action had been taken by the Delegate Synod and the Board for Higher Education in 1950 to grant the local board of control more autonomy, and membership on the board was broadened to include another professional educator.[30] The terms of office of the board members were staggered to allow for continuity, and the board was allowed greater freedom to set up and administer its own budget. The president was designated as the responsible executive officer of the board of control. Finally, synodical control was simplified by the establishment of a single Board for Higher Education to supervise all the colleges of the Synod.[31]

The second recommendation of the examining committee was also in process of solution. The scope of the academic dean's position was enlarged to include assistance in recruitment, educational budgeting, and curriculum, besides the chairmanship of the Educational Policies Committee. His teaching load was greatly reduced so that his time could be used mostly for curriculum development. There was a more definite delegation of responsibility to other administrative officers and to the Educational Policies Committee, thus freeing the faculty from time-consuming detail so that their time could be given more to institutional studies and policy making.[32]

President Klinck felt that the third point of the committee report could be met only by making the bachelor's degree the requirement for anyone wishing to enter the permanent service of the church. The problem of state requirements plus church requirements filled the curriculum so that there was no room for the addition of more courses in the 3-year program.[33]

One of the problems facing the college at this time was the possibility of retaining the traditional solid core of liberal education while giving a good basic professional training, without the proliferation of professional courses which seemed to be the developing pattern of many normal schools. President Klinck felt that ultimately a fifth year (one year beyond the bachelor's degree) would be needed for concentration in such specialized areas as religious education and church music. This would require more facilities of all types. He advocated the continued study of this problem by all groups concerned with the needs of the Synod.[34]

The North Central Association of Colleges and Secondary Schools met March 20–24, 1950, and voted to accredit Concordia Teachers College.[35] On March 27 Dr. Klinck conducted a special service of thanksgiving in the college chapel for the student body and faculty. In reporting this service the *Spectator* commented: "President Klinck thanked the student body, faculty, and administrative personnel for their sturdy devotion to the Lord which has brought such a good report . . . and urged us all to grow in the knowledge of God's Word." [36] By 1952–53 the college received a "Class A" rating by the University of Illinois.[37]

High School Department Closes

Besides achieving accreditation in 1950, the institution also saw the termination of the 86-year-old high school department, which had admitted its last freshman class in 1946. Concordia Teachers College

High School had been a vital part of the institution ever since it was founded in 1864, making possible a longer training period in religion and music. The high school had maintained high standards of scholarship, having been accredited by the North Central Association of Colleges and Secondary Schools in 1936. The separation of the high school and the college student body had taken place in 1934, and Professor Walter O. Kraeft was appointed dean and principal.[38]

The establishment of community Lutheran high schools in Chicago, Ill.; Milwaukee and Racine, Wis.; Detroit, Mich.; St. Louis, Mo.; and Cleveland, Ohio, was one factor that had influenced the Synod in its decision in 1947 to drop the high school at Concordia. It was felt that these schools would be "feeder schools" for the teachers college. Another factor was the greatly increasing need for more teachers and the space demands of a heavier college enrollment to serve these needs.[39]

The last senior class, consisting of 30 students, was integrated into the college as "sub-freshmen" in all activities, and after the final graduation in 1950 all assets of the high school department were given over to the college.[40]

Library Development

As the college developed a 3-year and later a 4-year curriculum, one of the great concerns was to maintain a library which would be adequate for the program and also fulfill the standards of accrediting agencies. Changes in the curriculum presupposed full student use of the library, and money for more acquisitions was provided in the budget and through the donations of various groups and individuals.

Dr. Paul Bretscher was librarian from 1926 to the spring of 1940, when he succeeded Professor Schmieding as dean of the college. During his tenure as librarian, over 12,000 books were added to the library, and many improvements were added, including a card catalog and the open-shelf service system. Bretscher was succeeded by Professor Edwin J. Wibracht.[41]

In December 1941 a campaign was launched to raise $15,000 for library books. This effort had been planned by the faculty and board of control and approved by the Synod's Board of Directors. In the meantime the Ladies' Auxiliary voted $500 annually to support this need. A request for assistance was sent to all alumni with the notice that such expansion was vital in the accreditation and certification program, and by October 1942 more than $7,000 had come in.[42]

The need for a new library building was presented to the Synod's Board of Directors in 1943. They recommended a campaign for funds which was also approved by the Synod in 1944 as the delegates voted $100,000 for it.[43]

The cornerstone of the library was laid May 16, 1948, and the building was dedicated May 29, 1949, although student use of its facilities had begun in April. The new building, which had a book stack capacity of 60,000 volumes, was the first structure on the campus to be air-conditioned. Allowance was made for future expansion according to the growth of the college. The library had added 1,728 volumes during 1948–49, bringing total book holdings to nearly 27,000. By July 1, 1950, the total was increased to 30,000.[44]

The development of the library was commended by the examining committee of the North Central Association in 1949 as they said: "The library of Concordia Teachers College seems to be in commendable condition with prospects of steady betterment under the present leadership of a young, able, well-trained librarian, with the added advantages of an adequately large, carefully planned new building and good financial report."[45]

Other Curricular Developments

Acceleration. In view of the great shortage of teachers during World War II, the board of control and faculty resolved to initiate a program which would accelerate the production of graduates. In February 1943 they resolved to close the school year on May 21 and offer a full summer quarter from May 23 to Aug. 6, besides a regular summer session beginning June 28. The accelerated program would also be helpful in case the wartime oil shortage should create special problems during the winter quarter. The summer program was modified to two specific terminal sessions in 1944, both of which could be taken together for a quarter's credit.[46] The program of acceleration continued throughout the war and postwar period.

Extension and Correspondence. Although correspondence courses had been offered since 1935, the number of courses grew quite slowly, reaching a total of 12 in 1948–49, with an enrollment of 111 which grew to 201 in 1949–50 and 640 in 1952–53.[47]

In 1950–51 the first correspondence catalog was published, announcing the purpose of this division to meet the needs of Lutheran teachers in both general and professional education. Recognition was given to the need of a broader background in religion and many other fields of knowledge, not only for teaching of various subjects but also for the teacher's own cultural growth, bearing in mind that the members of the congregations were also constantly attaining higher standards of education and cultural advancement. Other aims of the correspondence division included professional guidance in extra-school activities such as guidance, Sunday school teaching, church music, or youth work. Eighteen courses were offered at a cost of $15 per course.[48]

The extension division fluctuated in number from two or three locations, including one in River Forest, depending on the number enrolled. An extension center was organized in Concordia College, St. Paul, Minn., to prepare emergency teachers in 1949–50. Also Saturday extension courses were taught at the Walther Memorial Hospital in Chicago to 25 student nurses.[49]

Both the extension and the correspondence offerings were designed to help teachers who had graduated under the 2-year or 3-year college curriculum, so that they might complete requirements for the bachelor's degree. A significant development was the arrangement for the completion of the student-teaching requirement for emergency teachers with only partial training in summer school through the correspondence division. They were permitted to do additional supervised work in connection with their year of supply teaching and so receive full credit for student teaching. This was begun in 1949–50 with the approval of the examiner of the North Central Association of Colleges and Secondary Schools.[50]

Workshops. Additional services were offered to teachers in the various two-week workshops given for credit in the summer. In 1952, for example, offerings included arts and crafts, physical education and recreation, audiovisual aids, and kindergarten curriculum materials.[51]

Student Teaching. Until 1939 the teacher training program had been conducted by two professors of education, one of whom usually supervised in the morning and the other in the afternoon, each assuming the responsibility for all elementary instruction in the room and doing some of the teaching. Professors Schmieding and Kuehnert were the last "team" to operate the program in this fashion. It was decided to place this program in charge of one man.

Professor Albert V. Maurer was called to take over the program of student teaching and be teacher of the middle grades in the campus

training school at Grace Church. By the autumn of 1940 he was relieved of all teaching responsibility, thus being permitted to devote
full time to the development and administration of the student-teaching program and to teach college courses in education, besides becoming director of placement. By 1946 other Lutheran schools of
various sizes were being used for off-campus observation in addition
to Grace School, and observation was permitted by three cooperating
public elementary schools in Oak Park and River Forest.[52]

The first major change in the training school program was made
in 1943. Three activities were included: observation, participation,
and teaching. A student spent an entire quarter of 11 weeks in the
program, devoting two full days and three mornings each week to
teaching activities and related activities. In addition, each student
took the course in child psychology the remaining three afternoons,
and also scheduled a number of group conferences with Professor
Maurer. From six to eight weeks of the quarter were spent in the
campus training school. The remaining weeks were spent in observation in off-campus schools, both Lutheran and public. Three one-
room schools were included, as were both rural and urban types.[53]

As the enrollment kept increasing, not only at Concordia but also
in Grace Lutheran School, an extension was added to the training
school in 1951, so that it could serve the teacher training needs more
effectively.[54]

During 1951–52 several changes were made in this program. The
first four weeks of the teacher training program were spent in observation in the 13 cooperating Lutheran and public schools in the
Chicago area within a 50-mile radius of the college. Another eight
weeks were spent in observation and practice teaching in the campus
training school. The program was now enriched by the addition of
four special workshops to deal with problems discovered through
follow-up studies of graduates. Topics of the workshops included
"Youth Work for the Teacher," "First Aid Problems," "School Administration Problems," and "Pre-school and Primary School Problems,
Procedures and Materials."[55]

By 1952–53 students were to practice teach in two different grades
in the training school. St. John's Lutheran School of Forest Park was
developed into a second training school, and the observation schools
were increased to 15, including one Roman Catholic school.[56]

Development of Administration

President A. W. Klinck described his position in 1946 thus:

The president is the head of the institution and chief spiritual adviser, according to Synodical practice. His chief field of activity is the college department, where he serves as academic dean and instructor in the departments of religion and history.[57]

Dr. Klinck had been his own academic dean since 1944. After Professor Schmieding resigned as dean of the college in 1940, Dr. Paul Bretscher was appointed to succeed him, serving but a few months when he accepted a position at Concordia Seminary, St. Louis. Dr. Walter R. Roehrs became dean of the college in October 1941, serving until 1944, when he also accepted a call to the St. Louis seminary.

Other administrative officers in 1946 were Professor Wilfred F. Kruse, registrar, Professor Albert G. Huegli, dean of college students, and Professor Walter O. Kraeft, high school principal, who served as registrar and dean of the high school under the superintendency of the president. All the foregoing also taught part time. Since 1938 Professor Schmitt's position as business manager was a full-time position for which he was provided with clerical assistance.

The Synod adopted the unit type of administrative control for all its schools and colleges in 1947. This placed all departments of the school under the president's jurisdiction, making him the responsible head of the school, whose duty it was to carry out policies as determined by the board of control. Changing over to fit this new concept of administration became the task of the board, administration, and faculty.

Under the old administrative structure the president had been the executive officer of the faculty. Administrative officers often dealt directly with the board of control. The business manager, for example, also attended board meetings. When the board organized itself in two committees in 1942, the one was called the "Committee for Spiritual Matters," composed of Dr. Klinck and Pastors Ernest T. Lams and Adolf W. Bartling of the board. The other committee was called the "Committee for Physical Matters" and included Professor Schmitt, the business manager, and two lay members of the board, Christ H. Garbers and Fred O. Linstead. Professors Eifrig and Schmitt were appointed to advise the board on the matter of supervision of women.[58]

Study of the administrative structure of the college was stimulated by the move toward accreditation in the 1940s. Dr. Klinck submitted a report on his duties as president to the board in September 1943. Gradually the thinking of the board and faculty moved in the direction of unit administrative organization. As noted previously, in 1946 the board adopted a policy which referred all academic matters to the president's office before they could be presented to the board.

In December 1946 the board adopted the unit plan of administration recommended by the North Central Association of Colleges and Secondary Schools, which assigned the responsibility for determining the general policies of the school to the board and designated the administrative head of the school as the chief executive officer of the board. Subject to the approval of the board, the head of the school was thus responsible for the selection and assignment of all school employees, for the business management of the school including plant and equipment, for the educational program, and for public relations. He was responsible for delegating duties and authority and for supervising all individuals to whom duties were assigned.[59] A factor which helped bring about the unit plan of control was that the Synod's Board for Higher Education gradually preferred to deal with the president of an institution instead of the whole faculty.

Having been applied to the high school department at first, the plan was now inaugurated in the college also, so that in February 1947 for the first time the president was authorized to draw up the annual budget (for 1947–48), assisted by the business department. Previously this had been done by the business manager reporting directly to the board.[60]

The adoption by the Synod of the unit plan of administration for all its schools in its delegate convention in Chicago in 1947 quickly brought about many changes in view of the pending accreditation surveys.[61] It was deemed very desirable to retain the better features of faculty participation in the operation of the school and at the same time establish the proper relationship between faculty and the president and between the president and the board under the new plan of administration.

A new administrative office for recruitment, public relations, and alumni relations was established in 1948. The first director of this office was Professor Kraeft, who was also dean and principal of the high school department.[62] Professor John W. Klotz then was appointed assistant high school principal.[63]

The earlier position of dean of the college, held successively by Professors Schmieding, Bretscher, and Roehrs, had included a few elements of an academic dean's duties plus (and mainly) those of a dean of students. In 1944 Professor Huegli was appointed dean of students. When Professor Roehrs went to St. Louis in 1944, President Klinck assumed the duties of an academic dean until this office was officially established in 1948. The first to fill the position was the veteran Professor Schmieding, who had served long and capably as chairman of the Educational Policies Committee and had taken active leadership in the accrediting program of the college.[64]

Professor Kruse had accepted the position of registrar in October 1940,[65] relinquishing the office of athletic director to Professor Richard A. Lange.[66]

Professor Schmitt had become full-time business manager in 1938, having served the college faithfully as a professor and part-time business manager since 1905. In 1943 he submitted his resignation, but the board urgently requested him to reconsider in view of his intimate knowledge of wartime regulations and rationing.[67] He agreed to stay if some of his work load could be curtailed. In 1945 Professor Schmitt resigned because of poor health, making his final report on Oct. 16, 1946.[68] Elmer F. Jagow, who had been his assistant since November 1940, was appointed in April 1947.[69] In 1948–49 a new system of accounting was developed by Mr. Jagow, assisted by A. F. Scribner, to conform to the minimum requirements for accreditation. The new program was to go into effect July 1, 1949.[70]

Faculty Developments

It was reported to the faculty in 1940 that the Synod's Board for Higher Education was considering the problem of tenure of office and the ranking of professors.[71] In 1947 the new system of appointing instructors and electing professors was completed. The hierarchy of ranks included instructor, assistant professor, associate professor, and full professor. The new ranking system with salary differentials was to take effect on Feb. 1, 1950.[72]

Under the new system Dr. Klinck experienced some initial difficulty in securing faculty members out of the field who were well trained, experienced, and mature, because of the low rank and salary under which they would have to begin. He felt this problem would become more acute, especially in securing outstanding men below the rank of associate professor.[73]

With the adoption of the ranking system in 1947, all regularly called (tenure) professors were automatically given the rank of associate professor. All others (nontenure) were classified as assistant professors or instructors. The first appointees to full professorships at Concordia during 1948–49 were Theodore C. Appelt, chairman of the German department; Herman O. A. Keinath, chairman of the social studies department; Wilfred F. Kruse, registrar and chairman of the science department; Theodore J. C. Kuehnert, professor of education, editor of *Lutheran Education,* and also faculty representative on Synod's Board for Parish Education; and Alfred F. Schmieding, academic dean and chairman of the department of education. During that year the faculty consisted of five professors, 15 associate professors, and six instructors.[74]

During President Klinck's administration the last remaining members of the Addison faculty were retired, including Professors Albert H. Miller (1906–43), F. H. Schmitt (1906–47), E. W. Koehler (1909 to 1947 – died in 1951), C. W. G. Eifrig (1909–42 – died in 1949), and Martin Lochner (1912–45 – died in office).

Other former faculty members who died during this time included the former president, Dr. W. C. Kohn (1943), and Professors E. H. Engelbrecht (1944), O. F. Rusch (1940), H. C. Gaertner(1952), and G. H. Reifschneider (1944).

New faculty members during President Klinck's tenure were Professors Albert V. Maurer (1939), Herbert H. Gross (1940), Richard A. Lange (1941), Walter R. Roehrs (1941), Edwin J. Wibracht (1941), Herman O. A. Keinath (1943), Gustav H. Reifschneider (1943), Carl H. Scaer (1943), Victor G. Hildner (1944), Albert G. Huegli (1944), Walter E. Buszin (1945), Emil H. Deffner (1945), John W. Klotz (1945), Siegbert W. Becker (1947), Carl F. Halter (1948), Paul G. Bunjes (1951), John F. Choitz (1951), Walter A. Vahl (1951), Paul A. Mundinger (1952), and (in 1953) Martin C. Pieper, Daniel E. Poellot, and Neelak S. Tjernagel.

In 1951 Dr. Klinck announced that the faculty would begin a complete restudy of the department objectives during 1951–52. Each department was to make a one-hour presentation at a faculty meeting. The purpose of this program was to bring about greater interdepartmental understanding and harmony, as well as a generally deeper consciousness of the purpose of Concordia Teachers College to prepare consecrated and effective Christian workers for the church. The president commended the "consecration and industry of the faculty in their striving toward this end." [75]

Numerous institutional studies were conducted by the administration and faculty, and many curricular improvements were based on them. During 1948–49 there were 25 such studies alone,[76] 16 in 1949–50,[77] and 10 in 1950–51.[78]

The faculty also served the church at large in many ways, by membership on the various District and synodical committees, by delivering essays or being discussion leaders in conferences of pastors, teachers, and laymen, and by conducting workshops and seminars in and out of the church.

They continued to publish the *Lutheran School Journal,* which had been founded by Concordia's first president, J. C. W. Lindemann, in 1865. The name was changed to *Lutheran Education* in 1947. The editor was Professor Kuehnert, who was aided by Professors Gross and Klinck as assistant editors and by other faculty members as well as representatives from the field.[79]

Concordia faculty members also gained recognition in other areas of education. For example, early in 1952 Dr. Gross accepted the position offered by the National Council of Geography Teachers as chairman of the Committee of Research on Geographic Education, which was to embark on a project that would last four years.[80]

Dr. Gross in 1953 received an offer of a position at the University of Pittsburgh. This prompted Dr. Klinck to remark:

> The recognition that Professor Gross has received during recent years culminating in this offer is additional evidence of the growing esteem in which a number of our faculty members are held in academic circles. It is bound to be so as more of our men advance in training and participate in the work of the national organizations. Lutheran education cannot afford on any level to fall behind the training given in state and private institutions of the same rank. I am happy that quite a number of our faculty members are being recognized, and I am confident that this recognition will serve as a constant stimulus to them in the teaching of subject matter involved and their Christian interpretation of it. We confidently hope that Dr. Gross will remain with us and carry on his thinking, planning and teaching for the benefit of our school and its program of Christian education.[81]

Coeducation — The First 15 Years

The progress of coeducation as a normal and vital part of Concordia Teachers College was slow but steady. The quota of girls was originally limited by the Synod to 30 percent of the male enrollment.[82] Since it proved difficult to determine needs for woman teachers and the space available for them three years in advance, the Synod delegated responsibility for setting the annual quota to the College of (District) Presidents, who were to receive data for their decision from the college and from a committee on assignments.[83]

Provision was made for dormitory space for college girls only. High school girls were accepted in the first years if they could live at home or with relatives or friends.[84] From the beginning of coeducation in 1938 through the Klinck administration, women paid a higher fee than the men. In 1939—40, for example, men paid $135 for the year while women paid $185. General education students, though not solicited at all, were admitted on a space-available basis.[85]

College women gradually became active in student body affairs. During 1939—40 they organized a club to lead the cheering at athletic games, and in the same year girls found positions on various staffs and committees.[86] A new tradition was established in 1949 when Miss Elfrieda Friedrich was elected the first homecoming queen of the college.

Miss Irma Beck was appointed supervisor of women in 1938. She was succeeded by Miss Adele Stauske in 1940, Miss Lulu Noess in 1941, and Mrs. Laura Mackensen in 1945. Miss Noess became the first full-time supervisor of women in 1942.[87] This title was changed to dean of women in 1955.

Ground was broken in October 1947 for a new dormitory to house 80 women. It was to be ready for use by September 1948, but the construction was delayed and the college gymnasium had to be used as a women's dormitory during part of the school year 1948—49.[88] In July 1949 the women's quarters were finally moved to the new dormitory east of the music building.[89] Increasing enrollment made it necessary to build an addition to this dormitory to house up to 120 more women in 1952.[90]

In 1949 President Klinck evaluated the benefits of coeducation as follows:

> Coeducation had done much in the eleven years of its existence at Concordia to prepare not only our women for whom it was in-

tended, but our men as well for their place in Christian congregations as teachers of the boys and girls, counselors of the youth of
both sexes and co-workers with their colleagues of both sexes and
with men and women of their constituencies.

The sharp contrast between our regular men and the men of like
age and academic advancement who come to our summer sessions
from non-coeducational schools is too obvious to escape mention
here. We are very thankful that the Delegate Synod saw fit in 1938
to establish a coeducational environment for our teachers-in-training,
because of the wholesome attitudes which it creates and the high
moral tone of the coeds we have been able to recruit. The fine work
of our full-time supervisor of women, whose activities are carried
on directly under the guidance of the Dean of Students, as well as
that of the other part-time supervisors working with her, is to be
highly commended. Intelligent and Christian understanding in this
phase of our work is all the more necessary since our faculty members, with the exception of some instrumental music teachers, the
physical education instructor for women, and some of the practice
school teachers, are all men.[91]

As the need for more women teachers continued to increase, studies
were made to determine how the Synod could best solve the problem.
A synodical "Trends Committee" had been appointed to bring recommendations to the 1950 convention in Milwaukee. They reiterated .
the historic aims of the Synod, that every reasonable effort should be
made to reach the ideal of having every teacher in the Lutheran
schools trained according to the synodical requirements, that the male
teacher is one of the most important factors in the growth of the
schools, and that production of male teachers should be kept up to
the needs.

In order to realize the above aims, the committee suggested that
River Forest become an all-male school again with a capacity for 500
students, graduating 100 teachers annually, and that four of the
Synod's ministerial junior colleges — at Bronxville, N. Y.; Fort Wayne,
Ind.; Oakland, Calif.; and St. Paul, Minn. — introduce a 2-year terminal course in teacher training for women. One such program that
could be used as a pattern was already in existence at the junior college at Winfield, Kans. Another proposal had been advanced to establish synodical teacher training at Valparaiso (Ind.) University.[92]

At the request of Martin J. Neeb, Executive Secretary of the Board
for Higher Education, the faculty of Concordia Teachers College reported their views on the steps to be taken in order to provide a sufficient number of teachers for the church and gave their reactions to

the recommendations of the Trends Committee. The faculty unanimously opposed the propositions of the committee to drop coeducation and establish a 2-year terminal program for women teachers.[93]

They pointed out that the national trend for teacher education was for a minimum of four years for all teachers, that no less than four years could be considered in professional interstate reciprocity of certification, and that a 2-year program would be a backward step. The Synod had also expressed itself in 1950: "It is only natural to conclude that the longer our Church works in the American scene, the more necessary it becomes for us to approach the national educational patterns which influence the American public." [94] The faculty reminded the Board for Higher Education that certification requirements were constantly rising.

In commenting on these proposals, Dean Schmieding later wrote:

The widespread demand for woman teachers presented very specific problems. There were those who held that the answer to the problem was to convert most of the preparatory schools into two-year normal schools, granting terminal diplomas and considering the two-year candidates "graduates." This was a dangerous proposal which might have resulted in making our preparatory schools sub-legal institutions. Our board and faculty readily saw that such a policy might in time have been detrimental to our entire educational system.[95]

Led by the Educational Policies Committee, the faculty addressed itself to the problem of the best utilization of all college facilities of the Synod to train women teachers without reducing certification requirements or making outmoded normal schools out of the preparatory schools.[96] They recommended an emergency teacher training program of two years, plus at least one summer session before anyone was allowed to teach. A general diploma was to be given by the junior colleges but not a teacher's certificate. Three- and four-year diplomas were to be granted by the teachers colleges only, upon completion of the necessary credits.[97]

World War II Problems

Shortly after the Japanese attack on Pearl Harbor Dec. 7, 1941, the Concordia Defense Organization was formed at the college under the leadership of Professor Huegli. Its purpose was to plan the civil defense program for the college and coordinate it with the community. Professor Huegli presented preliminary plans to the board of control in February 1942, announcing that faculty members and students were required by the Selective Service Law to register at the college.[98]

Booths were set up in the administration building lobby to sell war bonds and stamps, and numerous bond drives were conducted throughout the war years. In 1943 the homecoming featured the general theme of love to country, and it was dedicated to alumni and former students in the armed forces. A war bond queen was featured at this homecoming,[99] and a goal of $1,000 was set to purchase a jeep for the army.[100] The students also resolved to install a special plaque for Concordians in the armed services.

In the autumn of 1943 Professor Gross served as part-time instructor of geography at the University of Chicago to help train army engineers to function in the postwar-period reconstruction program.[101]

Concordians who were drafted or who enlisted in the armed forces were to have the opportunity to complete their work later. A former Concordia student, Hugo Manges of Louisville, Ky., was one of the first American casualties at Pearl Harber.[102]

Wartime shortages were also felt at Concordia. In April 1942 the board of control appointed a special committee consisting of Professors Engelbrecht, Lange, Huegli, Coach Emory Bauer, and Schmitt to plan economy measures for the maintenance of grounds, buildings, and equipment, using voluntary student labor as much as possible, since adequate outside help could not be obtained.[103] It was becoming more and more difficult to secure meat and other commissary needs, and in the fall of 1942 Business Manager Schmitt announced that only two thirds of the previous year's fuel oil would be available for heating. He also suggested that a bicycle be purchased for the college if permitted by the local rationing board.[104] In December 1942 many of the buildings were insulated with rock wool, and storm windows were installed to conserve fuel.

A student labor system was inaugurated in September 1943 to assist in the manpower shortage. Professor Huegli and Elmer F. Eggold (instructor in the high school) were in charge of this program in which high school students were expected to give 15 hours and college students 20 hours of voluntary service each year. These services, fully supported by the student council, were to be used in maintenance and janitorial duties and in the library and various offices.[105]

Concordia Teachers College was included in the list of schools eligible to receive veterans of the armed forces under the "G. I. Bill of Rights," an educational benefits program. By September 1946 26 veterans were enrolled under the program.[106]

Scholarship Assistance and Student Work Programs

Since Concordia Teachers College was founded by The Lutheran Church — Missouri Synod for the sole purpose of training workers for its congregations, the church has always subsidized the college very heavily. Such a subsidy benefits the individual student in the form of reduced tuition. Despite this some students have needed financial assistance all through the years, and many of them have received direct support from their home congregations or Districts. Some have also found it necessary to earn part or all of their financial needs.

The first mention of a student work program at Concordia was in the 1942–43 catalog. The business office assisted students in securing employment both on and off the campus under special regulations. The work program was not to interfere with studies, while a reduced class load was prescribed for those whose work load was considered too heavy. Employers had to agree to release students for special tests and other activities outside the regular program as required by the college.[107] The work opportunities for students increased from year to year as rising costs made it imperative for more to work. In 1950–51, 366 students out of 559 were employed in the fall quarter; 383 out of 558 in the winter quarter, and 421 out of 568 in the spring quarter.

The scholarship and financial assistance program was largely a postwar development. The 1949–50 catalog announced two scholarships for $100 each, one for superior scholarship and one for superior work in religion. There was also a student loan fund which had been initiated by Dean Huegli and a student employment fund for students who worked at the college.[108] The number of scholarships began to multiply growing to 8 in 1950–51, 14 in 1951–52, and 23 in 1953–54.[109]

Building Activities

Extensive remodeling and renovating of the plant was carried on during Dr. Klinck's administration. Five departmental offices were constructed early in 1942 between the Administration Building and Lindemann Hall, to give the professors in each department an opportunity to meet students privately and thus to work for closer harmony between them.[110] Four more such offices were added by October 1942.

It was announced in December 1942 that a long-awaited student center was nearing completion as a result of the labors of volunteer students working under the supervision of student council president Edward Krafft. The students had agitated for years for a place to gather for refreshments during free periods.[111] The new lunch center was named Campus Corner.[112] Everyone was greatly pleased with it, including the board of control, which sent a special message of thanks to the students after a visit made during a recess in their meeting on March 27, 1943.[113] The profits from the operation of the Campus Corner were designated by the students to assist in the activities program. Accordingly a check for $200 was given to the *Spectator* to aid in its expansion program in 1943–44.[114]

In 1944 the Synod approved the erection of a new women's dormitory and a library, costing $150,000 and $100,000 respectively. However, construction could not begin until after September 1946. The faculty building committee included Professors Keinath, Rohlfing, Kraeft, Wibracht, and President Klinck. Considerable time was spent by this committee in studying the recommendations of the North Central Association of Colleges and Secondary Schools and of the American Association of Teachers Colleges in order to embody as many of their ideas as possible in the new buildings as well as in the remodeling program for the old buildings. Remodeling plans included partitioning of the large sleeping rooms, new lighting in all classrooms, lowering of most of the classroom ceilings, and complete redecoration of the plant.

The new library and the women's dormitory with a capacity of 80 were dedicated on May 29, 1949. The air-conditioned library had a total of 26,972 books at the time of dedication, with book space for 60,000 volumes.

The addition of the two new buildings made possible other changes. All administrative offices were now moved to the central part of the administration building, including those of the president, the academic dean, the dean of students, the registrar, the dean of the summer school, the director of extension, and the placement director. Secretarial offices and a fireproof storage vault were also added, and there was a general renovation of classrooms and corridors.[115]

A new music building was urgently needed to give adequate instruction to the growing enrollment. The Synod had allowed $375,000 for this building and its equipment in 1947, releasing the funds in

1950.[116] The building committee consisted of C. H. Garbers, E. F. Jagow, F. O. Linstead, and Walter Peckat, besides Dr. Klinck and Professors Rohlfing and Halter. The new facilities included 16 organ practice rooms and five organ studios, besides 40 piano practice rooms and eight studios, a choral room, a band room, various offices, and a faculty meeting room. Dedicatory services were held Oct. 28, 1951, followed by special concerts by the choirs and the band in honor of the occasion.[117]

The growing number of women applicants again made it necessary to build more dormitory space. In 1950 the Synod approved the request for $325,000 for the addition of a north wing to the women's dormitory to provide facilities for 120 more women, and an additional $78,500 for a classroom wing addition and equipment for the new music building.[118] The dormitory was dedicated Oct. 4, 1953.

The Synod also approved the cost of remodeling the old music building into a student union with offices for the Student Association, the Student Affairs Council, the *Spectator,* and the *Pillars* (yearbook), as well as headquarters for various clubs and activities. A spacious lounge was included in the plans, and the college bookstore was moved into a central location. These plans had been drawn up by a Student Union Committee together with Dean Huegli. The Student Union was opened in September 1952, and student reaction to both the bookstore and the Student Union facilities was enthusiastic, according to Dr. Klinck.[119]

During the summer of 1953 the food service facilities of the college were completely changed over to a cafeteria from the traditional family style used since 1864.[120]

The Synod considered the growing needs of the college in its 1953 convention in Houston, Tex., and voted $530,000 for a new men's dormitory and a new classroom building, besides the renovation of the original men's dormitories.[121]

Following a suggestion of the Men's Council, the board of control approved the procurement of name plaques for the dormitories, which had been named in 1933 after the first four presidents, and also for the new women's dormitory, named "Mary-Martha." [122]

College and Community

Relations with the village of River Forest were friendly and cooperative. College personnel were active in many civic projects. The college student body participated generously in Red Cross, Community Chest Fund, Blood Bank, and other civic responsibilities. Civic officials also were invited to participate in numerous college activities. When the new music building was dedicated on Oct. 28, 1951, Walter Gabel, president of the village of River Forest, was present personally to congratulate the college on behalf of the village.[123]

The college was also willing to accept its obligations in the community. Accordingly, when in 1943 a special assessment was levied against all property owners for improvements along Division Street, the college board declined to go along with other property owners to contest this levy, feeling it would be better not to dispute taxes. The tax board was so favorably impressed that they volunteered to grant the college the same reduction obtained by Lloyd's Property Owners Association of Chicago for the clients who had initiated the contest. The reduction came to 30%, and Lloyd's offered to handle the matter for the college gratis.[124]

The board of control approved a request by the United States Air Force to use campus facilities for their reserve training program in 1951, thus extending the use of the college buildings for the people of the community.[125] Concordia was named one of 1,000 testing centers for the Selective Service System. The tests were conducted by Professor Schmieding, who was awarded an honorary Doctor of Laws degree by Valparaiso University in June 1952.[126]

From January to March 1951 Concordia Teachers College conducted a regular Monday evening radio broadcast over Radio Station WOPA, a new station in Oak Park. The broadcasts were under the direction of Dean Kraeft, director of recruitment, public relations, and alumni relations, and his assistant, Victor Krause, instructor in education.[127] The board of control consented to the program with the understanding that it was to be a nonreligious program, that students did not sacrifice too much time, that there be no commercial sponsorship, and that no faculty member be relieved of any teaching load to carry on the work connected with the broadcasts.[128]

Student Activities

Student Council. Student government of the college continued to develop and become better defined during the Klinck administration under the leadership of Professor Huegli, the dean of students.

Participation in student life at Concordia was based on the premise that the college is a community in which students are guided in their conduct by Scriptural principles and the great heritage of American democratic tradition. Ultimate responsibility for the control of student activities was vested in the president. Students were encouraged to share in the direction of their own affairs as part of their training for effective American citizenship. This was the primary reason for establishing student government. The student body elected a senate consisting of a Men's Council and a Women's Council. Under the senate was a committee on student activities to integrate and correlate all activities of the different college clubs and organizations. Leadership in student activities was vested in a student body president and an executive board. The organization was under the supervision of the dean of students and was known as the College Student Body.[129] A special orientation program was inaugurated in 1944–45 and held at the beginning of each school year to acquaint new students with extracurricular opportunities. In autumn 1952 a "big sister" program was introduced, so that new girls could be helped in their orientation by someone familiar with Concordia.

The student body constitution of 1942 was revised in 1945, 1949, and 1953. The organization was now known as the Student Association of Concordia Teachers College.

The 1953 preamble to the constitution declared that the guiding purpose would be "the development of Christian living through the promotion of an efficient administration of student activities and the development of initiative and self-discipline. This shall be done according to Christian principles, thereby fostering good citizenship in the community, in the student body of Concordia, and in the Kingdom of God." [130]

On the recommendation of Dean Huegli and the Student Senate, a Lutheran Student Government Conference was invited to the campus in February 1950. Most of the synodical colleges and Valparaiso University responded by sending student representatives and faculty advisers. This was a successful conference, and delegates voted to continue it at Concordia Seminary, St. Louis, the following year.[131]

Clubs and Activities. All students were encouraged to participate in a well-rounded activity program as much as possible. The administration and faculty recognized the significant contributions of the cocurriculum for the social development of the students. Dr. Klinck reported on a 1949 survey which indicated that grade-point average as well as social competence seemed to be highest among those students who are active in a number of extracurricular activities, even when such students carried an additional personal work program.[132] Cultural activities included lectures, concerts, movies, and social functions. A strong program of interscholastic and intramural athletics was maintained, and three choirs and a band gave opportunity for musical participation. The biweekly *Spectator* and the college annual *The Pillars* provided outlets for journalistic talents. Clubs provided for a variety of interests, including the Mission Activities Group, International Relations Club, Scientific Research Club, Concordia Players, the "C" Club, the Art Club, the Veterans' Club, the Debate Society, the Literary Society, and others.

In 1950–51 the teams of the Debate Society, guided by Prof. Kenneth Heinitz, won second place in the National Collegiate Debate Tournament at De Paul University.[133]

Productions of the college musical organizations were widely acclaimed in the Chicago area and beyond. The College Choir directed by Professor Hildner was featured by the National Broadcasting Company on Good Friday, April 15, 1949.[134]

Health Services. President Klinck did not attempt to follow the footsteps of his predecessors in the role of school doctor and nurse. By 1939 the health service included a part-time registered nurse. This position was served for a few months by Mrs. Edwin Wibracht. Mrs. Adele Stauske succeeded her, serving two years, until she enlisted in the Army. Mrs. Ida Pfotenhauer served the following two years, being succeeded by Miss Lulu Noess. General guidance for the health program was furnished by a health committee of which Professor Kraeft was chairman. By 1950–51 Miss Noess was provided with an assistant, Mrs. Martha Moeller. A college physician was also on call to serve as needed.[135]

Veterans and Married Students. According to the 1952–53 catalog, veterans were cordially welcomed at Concordia, but they had to find their own living quarters off compus if they were married.

The same catalog pointed out that the college regarded marriage highly inadvisable during the student's school life. Students who expected to marry were to reach an understanding with the college authorities beforehand. Like the married veterans, all other married students had to find living quarters off the campus.[136]

Cars. Students were not permitted to have cars on the campus until September 1952. The Men's Council worked with the faculty to draw up regulations regarding insurance, license requirements, parking rules, etc. A special automobile club was organized on the campus to enforce the rules.[137]

Declaration of Intention. In 1944 the Synod ruled that all students at its colleges had to sign a "Declaration of Intention" to serve in the ministry as pastors or as parish teachers. This was an attempt by the Synod to assure itself that money it invested in the training of these students would serve the purpose for which it was intended. Students who were present for general education only had to pay additional tuition. By the Declaration of Intention the Synod was reemphasizing the single purpose of the college.[138] By 1952–53 space was so limited that the college was able to enroll only those who had signed the declaration. This made for a very homogeneous group. Through personal and academic counseling, students whose purpose could not conform to the Declaration and those who were not sufficiently gifted were guided into other fields.[139]

Enrollments and Fees. During President Klinck's administration the enrollment increased from 390 (including 175 in high school and 215 in college) in 1939–40, to 638 in college alone in 1953–54, including 353 men and 285 women. The year 1953–54 was also the last year the men outnumbered women on the campus. The student body had changed considerably after the high school was closed, becoming much more cosmopolitan in educational background since freshman students now came from many different high schools, and others came from other colleges and universities with advanced standing. Various tests given to the students bore consistent witness to the good recruitment standards of the college, running well above national norms.

Several studies were made of the holding power of the college. In his final report for the 1952–53 school year Dr. Klinck included some of the statistics of a late study which showed that in one class 76.9 percent of those entering as freshmen graduated, whereas the American college average at that time was about 50 percent.

Fees also had gone up over the years. In 1939–40 men paid $135 for the year and women $185. Any general students paid $80 additional. By 1952–53 the fees were $505 for men and $565 for women, the differential remaining practically the same.

Counseling Services. The first official mention of a guidance program was found in the 1945–46 catalog. Spiritual counsel was available from the president and other administrators, with the registrar and the supervisor of women assisting in personal and academic problems, and the director of student teaching and placement providing professional guidance. Personnel records were maintained including test results and other data on each student.

By 1949–50 the guidance and counseling program was placed under the dean of students, Professor Huegli. Students with special personal or emotional problems were referred to Professor Schmieding. Professor Maurer gave special counsel to those with vocational and professional problems.

During 1950–51 Dean Huegli organized a dormitory counseling system. He was assisted by Mrs. Laura Mackensen and Mrs. Edith Morrison in counseling women, while 10 professors and instructors counseled on the nine men's dormitory floors plus one special group of day students. Kenneth Heinitz, an English instructor, lived in one of the dormitories, serving as house counselor for all men students and adviser to the Student Senate and Men's Council.

Although the beginning had been made, it was still necessary for Dr. Klinck to say in 1953:

> The whole area of student guidance and counselling should receive a great deal more attention than the Dean of Students and his assistants can give it within the limitations of time and physical energy at their disposal. The results of such counselling do not show immediately, but they have a noticeable elevating effect on the morale of the student body, and will certainly bear fruit to eternity. Ways must be found to enable us to devote more trained and experienced manpower to this vital purpose.[140]

Other Services to the Church

The college often provided facilities for church conventions, as well as for smaller meetings of boards and committees. Leadership was also provided in other ways to benefit the church. In 1944 Professor Kraeft was commended by the board of control for his efforts to raise standards in Concordia High School and also to bring a greater degree of unity and cooperation among all Lutheran high schools, both those maintained by the Synod and those maintained by Lutheran congregations in various communities.[141] His efforts were very helpful in the formation of the Association of Lutheran Secondary Schools, which offered membership to all Lutheran high schools in America.

Lutheran Education Association. Concordia faculty members were very active in organizing the Lutheran Education Association. On

July 7–9, 1942, a group of laymen, laywomen, teachers, and pastors, interested in promoting Christian education at all levels by using existing agencies of the church, held its first convention in River Forest. The aim of this organization was to coordinate and fuse the educational thinking of individuals and groups. The Synod gave it full recognition and endorsement in its 1944 convention, at Saginaw, Mich. Headquarters of the LEA at the present time are at Concordia Teachers College.[142]

National Lutheran Parent-Teacher League. In 1953 this league was formed as a department of the Lutheran Education Association. Its purposes are similar to those of other parent-teacher groups in the country excepting that this organization is founded primarily on Christian principles.[143]

1953 Trends as Seen by Dr. Klinck

President Klinck's last report indicated that plans had been proposed to the Synod in 1953 for the inauguration of graduate study leading to a master's degree. They were to be presented to the next synodical convention in 1956 for final approval.

The adoption of regulations by the Synod making the third-year diploma provisional had cleared the way for making the bachelor's degree the only terminal certificate for teaching in the church.

Finally President Klinck observed that there had developed, almost imperceptibly, a definite beginning in the integration of the training program of pastors and teachers in the Synod, a policy which Concordia had favored since the early 1940s. It is interesting to note that the school was founded in Addison on an exactly opposite point of view. However, since the first two years of teacher training had been established at the various junior colleges, the Synod had placed both types of training together already, and it might be only a matter of time before the terminal teachers colleges would be permitted to add pastoral training.[144]

Klinck Accepts Call

President Klinck informed the board of control on Sept. 1, 1953, that he had received a call to Concordia Seminary, St. Louis, as professor of historical theology.[145] On Nov. 11, 1953, by his request he was granted a peaceful release to accept it, thus becoming the second president of the college to go to that seminary, following Dr. E. A. W.

Krauss, Concordia's second president. Dr. Klinck terminated his duties on Dec. 31, 1953. Dr. Schmieding was appointed acting president as of Jan. 1, 1954.

Summary

Dr. Arthur W. Klinck was the fifth president of Concordia Teachers College. Assuming the position at the time of the outbreak of World War II, his was the task of leading the school through many changes. He awarded the first bachelor's degrees in the history of the school in 1940, heading the 8-year institution until the 86-year-old high school was dropped in 1950. In the same year the college became accredited with the North Central Association of Colleges and Secondary Schools.

The development of the unit plan of administration and the establishment and definition of various administrative offices were major achievements. Curricular improvements following the various surveys and self-studies of the college were highlights of his administration.

New dormitories, a library, and a music building and modernization of the old plant aided in serving Concordia students better. President Klinck had seen the faculty grow to 50 and had directed the inauguration of the professional ranking system at Concordia. The student body changed from high school and college to college only, and coeducation, which had just begun at the outset of his administration, flourished so that the number of women rose to a point nearly equal with that of men. The Student Union, Campus Corner, and the development of student government had helped to build student morale.

Dr. Klinck could look back on 14 busy years of very fruitful promotion of Concordia Teachers College, for which he had worked diligently and given unsparingly of his time and efforts. He was noted throughout the church for his Biblical scholarship and for constructing a series of dioramas depicting life in Bible times which were used in his classes.

Notes

1. Minutes, Faculty of Concordia Teachers College, Nov. 6, 1939.
2. Minutes, Faculty, Feb. 26, 1940.
3. Arthur W. Klinck, "Concordia Teachers College During the Past Fifteen Years," unpublished article written in 1946, p. 4.
4. Concordia Teachers College Catalog, 1945—46, p. 6.
5. Ibid.
6. Ibid.
7. Ibid.
8. Minutes, Board of Control of Concordia Teachers College, Dec. 7, 1943.
9. *The Spectator,* River Forest student paper, XV (Dec. 14, 1939), 1.
10. Ibid., XVII (Oct. 9, 1941), 1.
11. Arthur W. Klinck, *The President's Report to the Board of Control of Concordia Teachers College, River Forest, Illinois* (1948—49), p. 6.
12. Ibid.
13. C. T. C. Catalog, 1948—49, p. 18.
14. Klinck, *Report,* 1948—49, p. 9.
15. M. Gordon Neale, *Report of a Survey of Concordia Teachers College, River Forest, Illinois* (May 24, 1948), p. 53.
16. Ibid., pp. 53, 54.
17. Ibid., p. 56.
18. Ibid., p. 57.
19. Ibid., p. 59.
20. Ibid., p. 61.
21. Minutes, Board of Control, Jan. 17, 1946.
22. Klinck, *Report,* 1948—49, p. 9.
23. Ibid., p. 11.
24. Ibid., p. 10.
25. Irwin J. Lubbers and Robert White, *Concordia Teachers College, River Forest, Illinois,* A Report to the Board of Review of the Commission on Colleges and Universities, North Central Association of Colleges and Secondary Schools, Dec. 14 and 15, 1949, p. 2.
26. Ibid., p. 7.
27. Ibid., p. 21.
28. Klinck, *Report,* 1949—50, p. 12.
29. Lubbers and White, p. 22.
30. The River Forest board was the first synodical board of control to include a Lutheran teacher, Alwin R. Roschke, on its membership, according to a comment made to the author by a former secretary of the board, Walter Hartkopf. Verified by a letter from Alwin R. Roschke to President Martin L. Koehneke, Sept. 4, 1962.
31. Klinck, *Report,* 1949—50, p. 12.
32. Ibid., pp. 12, 13.
33. Ibid., p. 13.
34. Ibid.

35. Minutes, Board of Control, April 4, 1950.
36. *The Spectator*, XXV (April 5, 1950), 1.
37. C. T. C. Catalog, 1952—53, p. 8.
38. *The Spectator*, XXV (May 26, 1950), 3.
39. Ibid.
40. Klinck, *Report*, 1949—50, p. 6.
41. Minutes, Board of Control, June 29, 1940.
42. *The Spectator*, XVIII (Oct. 8, 1942), 1.
43. Ibid., XX (Sept. 21, 1944), 1.
44. Klinck, *Report*, 1949—50, p. 7.
45. Lubbers and White, p. 9.
46. Minutes, Board of Control, Feb. 16, 1943.
47. Klinck, *Report*, 1952—53, p. 8.
48. C. T. C. Correspondence Division Catalog, 1950—51, p. 6.
49. Klinck, *Report*, 1952—53, p. 8.
50. Klinck, *Report*, 1949—50, p. 9.
51. Klinck, *Report*, 1952—53, p. 7.
52. Klinck, *Fifteen Year Report*, 1946, p. 7.
53. *The Spectator*, XIX (Nov. 18, 1943), 4.
54. Ibid., XXVI (Jan. 26, 1951), 4.
55. Ibid., XXVII (Oct. 12, 1951), 4.
56. Klinck, *Report*, 1952—53, pp. 6, 7.
57. Klinck, *Fifteen Year Report*, 1946, p. 6.
58. Minutes, Board of Control, May 19, 1942.
59. Minutes, Board of Control, Dec. 10, 1946.
60. Minutes, Board of Control, Feb. 11, 1947.
61. *Proceedings*, 1947, pp. 745, 746.
62. Minutes, Board of Control, Jan. 13, 1948.
63. Minutes, Board of Control, March 30, 1948.
64. Minutes, Board of Control, Jan. 13, 1948.
65. Minutes, Faculty, Oct. 7, 1940.
66. Minutes, Board of Control, March 11, 1941.
67. Minutes, Board of Control, Sept. 21, 1943.
68. Minutes, Board of Control, Oct. 16, 1946.
69. Minutes, Board of Control, April 8, 1947.
70. Klinck, *Report*, 1948—49, p. 10.
71. Minutes, Faculty, May 27, 1940.
72. Klinck, *Report*, 1948—49, p. 10.
73. Klinck, *Report*, 1949—50, p. 3.
74. Ibid., pp. 2, 3.
75. Klinck, *Report*, 1950—51, p. 4.
76. Klinck, *Report*, 1948—49, pp. 7, 8.
77. Klinck, *Report*, 1949—50, pp. 7, 8.

78. Klinck, Report, 1950—51, p. 5.
79. Ibid., p. 4.
80. *The Spectator*, XXVII (Feb. 1, 1952), 1.
81. Ibid., XXVIII (Jan. 30, 1953), 1.
82. *Proceedings*, 1938, pp. 61, 62.
83. *Proceedings*, 1941, pp. 49, 50.
84. C. T. C. Catalog, 1939—40, p. 6.
85. Ibid.
86. *The Spectator*, XV (Nov. 23, 1939), 1.
87. Klinck, *Fifteen Year Report*, 1946, p. 3.
88. Minutes, Board of Control, Aug. 3, 1948.
89. Minutes, Board of Control, July 12, 1949.
90. Minutes, Board of Control, Nov. 13, 1952.
91. Klinck, *Report*, 1948—49, pp. 5, 6.
92. *Proceedings*, 1950, p. 210.
93. *Report of Concordia Teachers College, River Forest, Illinois, to the Board of Higher Education, Lutheran Church — Missouri Synod*. Dec. 19, 1950.
94. *Proceedings*, 1950, p. 216.
95. A. F. Schmieding, *Fifth Annual Report of the Academic Dean of the School Year, 1952—1953*, pp. 1, 2.
96. Ibid., p. 2.
97. Ibid., pp. 4, 5.
98. Minutes, Board of Control, Feb. 16, 1942.
99. *The Spectator*, XIX (Oct. 21, 1943), 1.
100. Ibid., XIX (Nov. 18, 1943), 1.
101. Ibid., XIX (Nov. 4, 1943), 1.
102. Ibid., XVII (March 26, 1942), 1.
103. Minutes, Board of Control, April 10, 1942.
104. Minutes, Board of Control, Oct. 19, 1942.
105. *The Spectator*, XIX (Sept. 30, 1943), 1.
106. Ibid., XXII (Sept. 26, 1946), 1.
107. C. T. C. Catalog, 1942—43, p. 10.
108. C. T. C. Catalog, 1949—50, p. 14.
109. C. T. C. Catalog, 1953—54, pp. 13—15.
110. *The Spectator*, XVII (Feb. 19, 1942), 1.
111. Ibid., XVIII (Dec. 17, 1942), 1.
112. Ibid., XVIII (Jan. 21, 1943), 1.
113. Minutes, Board of Control, March 27, 1943.
114. *The Spectator*, XIX (April 1, 1944), 1.
115. Ibid., XXV (Sept. 30, 1949), 1.
116. Klinck, *Report*, 1949—50, pp. 11—14.
117. Dedication Service Program, Oct. 28, 1951.
118. Klinck, *Report*, 1949—50, p. 14.

119. Klinck, *Report*, 1952—53, p. 9.
120. *The Spectator*, XXVIII (May 28, 1953), 1.
121. Ibid., XXIX (Oct. 9, 1953), 1.
122. Minutes, Board of Control, Nov. 3, 1953.
123. Dedication Service Program, Oct. 28, 1951.
124. Minutes, Board of Control, Nov. 12, 1943.
125. *The Spectator*, XXVII (Nov. 9, 1951), 1.
126. Ibid., XXVII (April 21, 1952), 4.
127. Klinck, *Report*, 1950—51, p. 9.
128. Minutes, Board of Control, Sept. 5, 1950.
129. C. T. C. Catalog, 1945—46, p. 14.
130. Constitution of the Student Association of C. T. C., 1953 revision.
131. Klinck, *Report*, 1949—50, p. 5.
132. Klinck, *Report*, 1948—49, p. 6.
133. Klinck, *Report*, 1950—51, p. 7.
134. *The Spectator*, XXIV (Feb. 11, 1949), 1.
135. Klinck, *Report*, 1950—51, p. 7.
136. C. T. C. Catalog, 1952—53, p. 10.
137. *The Spectator*, XXVIII (Oct. 24, 1952), 1.
138. Ibid., XX (Oct. 5, 1944), 1.
139. Klinck, *Report*, 1952—53, pp. 5, 6.
140. Ibid., p. 6.
141. Minutes, Board of Control, April 10, 1944.
142. *Lutheran Cyclopedia* (St. Louis: Concordia Publishing House, 1954), pages 635, 636.
143. Ibid., p. 787.
144. Klinck, *Report*, 1952—53, p. 4.
145. Minutes, Board of Control, Sept. 1, 1953.

President Martin L. Koehneke, 1916—

Dr. *Martin Luther Koehneke was born April 11, 1916, in Dodge
Center, Minnesota. He attended Lutheran elementary schools in
Town Hart, Minnesota, and Milwaukee, Wisconsin. In the latter
place he also attended the high school and junior college of
Concordia College where his father, Paul F. Koehneke was
a professor. He graduated from Concordia Seminary, St. Louis,
Missouri, in 1939, after which he served as pastor of Mt. Calvary
Lutheran Church in Raymondville, Texas (1939–1943), and in
Mount Olive Lutheran Church, San Antonio, Texas (1943–1950).
From 1950–54 he was Counselor for Parish Education for the
Texas District of The Lutheran Church — Missouri Synod, with
headquarters in Austin, Texas. During this time he received his
Masters Degree from the University of Texas. He has served
since 1954 as the sixth president of Concordia Teachers College.*
*President Koehneke has been in great demand as a speaker,
essayist, and lecturer, and has gained wide recognition as a leader,*

thinker, teacher, and writer in Christian education. He is an associate editor of Lutheran Education. *He has also served the Synod as a member of the General Literature Board and of the Advisory Committee for the Inner-City-Mission Commission.*

In 1962 the president was awarded the degree of Doctor of Laws by Valparaiso University. The citation commended him for "inspiring leadership at the largest college of the Synod for the training of its professional workers. Under his guidance the college has broadened the scope of its service, multiplied its faculty, augmented its facilities, and established the first accredited graduate program in Synod. . . . His influence has been felt beyond the confines of his own campus, wherever Christian education is important, especially at the elementary and secondary levels."

In July 1963 Dr. Koehneke was one of 12 American college heads to be a guest of the Federal Republic of Germany for a four-week study tour of German educational trends and institutions with special emphasis on teacher-training.

The 25th anniversary of President Koehneke's service to the church and his 10th anniversary of service at Concordia were honored by the faculty and board of control, and student body on May 4, 1964.

Dr. Koehneke was married to Irma Ann Knippa in 1940, and they have four children: Barbara, a 1963 graduate of Concordia, who teaches in the Ebenezer Lutheran School (an inner-city project in Chicago); Richard, a divinity student at Concordia College, Ann Arbor, Michigan; Janice, a junior at Walther Lutheran High School; and Kathleen, an eighth-grader in Grace Lutheran School.

Chapter 8

MARTIN L. KOEHNEKE'S ADMINISTRATION 1954—
The Last Decade — Springboard to the Future

Martin Luther Koehneke was installed as the sixth president of Concordia Teachers College during the opening service for the 91st academic year, Sept. 17, 1954, in Grace Lutheran Church, River Forest, Ill. Although he was but 38 years of age, his background, training, and experience had equipped him well for the task. Having grown up on the campus of Concordia Junior College, Milwaukee, Wis., where his father, Paul F. Koehneke, was a professor, he completed his studies there and went on to graduate from Concordia Seminary, St. Louis, in 1939.[1]

President Koehneke had become well acquainted with the function and operation of parish schools during his years as a parish pastor. This acquaintance was expanded and intensified after 1950, when he became Counselor of Parish Education of the Texas District of The Lutheran Church — Missouri Synod. Here he had the opportunity to deal directly with the personnel and curriculum needs of parish schools.[2] He completed requirements for his master's degree in educational administration at the University of Texas.[3]

As President Koehneke assumed the duties of leadership in 1954, the college was at the threshold of an unprecedented period of expansion which presented many challenges not only to the new administration but also to the faculty and the board of control and to the Synod itself. The need to reorganize the curriculum to satisfy the requirements of the church and the constantly rising standards of teacher education in the various states presented a formidable task. Other problems, such as securing a competent staff and providing adequate plant and site facilities to serve the growing enrollment, became more acute as the first century drew to a close.[4]

Dr. Schmieding, who had served as academic dean since 1948 and as acting president since Jan. 1, 1954, had requested to be relieved of the deanship in July 1953.[5] Since Dr. Klinck received his call to the seminary in August, no action was taken on Schmieding's request, and he functioned in both capacities till Sept. 17, 1954, continuing as academic dean till June 30, 1955. President Koehneke announced his administrative appointments on Jan. 4, 1955: Prof. Huegli, who had been dean of students, was appointed academic dean, and Prof. Halter, who had been head of the music department, was appointed dean of students.[6] Both appointments were to be effective July 1, 1955.[7] Mrs. Laura Mackensen, who had served for 10 years as supervisor of women, was given the title dean of women.[8]

Dr. Maurer, who had been placement director since 1944, had asked to be relieved of this position in October 1953.[9] He continued to serve until Dr. Arvin Hahn was appointed to the position in January 1955.[10] Other new appointments included Dr. John F. Choitz, director of publicity and publications, and Prof. Victor Krause, director of recruitment and alumni.[11]

Curricular Developments

Plans had been initiated by the faculty in February 1950 to offer graduate courses at Concordia.[12] After the college was accredited by the North Central Association of Colleges and Secondary Schools in that year, the Board for Higher Education in its report to the Synod indicated interest in offering graduate studies at Concordia:

> Since this institution is now fully accredited with the North Central Association, the Church will need carefully to husband and extend the values which can accrue from this preferred status.
>
> As soon as feasible a graduate school should be developed so that the M. A. degree will be available (with majors in such specialties as administration, youth and adult education, music, etc.).[13]

The Graduate Program

In 1952 Dean Schmieding submitted a preliminary report on the graduate program which was adopted by the faculty as a basic plan for future discussion.[14] A year later the board of control approved the recommendation of Dr. Klinck to petition the Synod in its 1953 convention for permission to institute a graduate program at River Forest as soon as feasible.[15] The Synod referred the matter to the Board for Higher Education and to representatives of its terminal schools, requesting them to study the development of a graduate program for the Synod's professional training system.[16]

President Koehneke, Dean Huegli, and Professor Kraeft met in November 1954 with two representatives of the North Central Association, Dr. Norman Burns and Dr. Manning Patillo, to discuss the proposed graduate studies in the form of a 5-year program at River Forest. Dr. Patillo subsequently became a consultant to the college for the development of the graduate program.[17]

A Committee on Graduate Studies was appointed by the Board for Higher Education, consisting of two representatives from each of the two teachers colleges and the two seminaries of the church. President Koehneke and Dean Huegli represented River Forest.[18] This committee, together with the faculty, explored the various propositions which led to the first tentative proposals made to the faculty in May 1955.[19]

In 1955–56 a "Questionnaire on Graduate Study" was sent out to 2,300 alumni of both teachers colleges (River Forest and Seward) regarding the proposed graduate program. Of the 911 who responded, 92 percent expressed the conviction that the synodical teachers colleges should offer graduate studies, and 76 percent indicated they were ready to attend, with 37 percent showing interest in the master's degree program.[20] The most frequently selected area for graduate study was educational administration, with great interest also expressed in religious education.[21]

The faculty and board of control requested authorization of the Synod in 1956 to establish a 5-year graduate program. The beginning of the program would be made in the summer sessions. The reasons given were as follows:

1. The rising standards of education in our country underline the importance of the Master's degree for trained educators.

2. Surveys undertaken within our own church demonstrate that an increasingly large number of teachers in our parish school system have found it desirable and necessary to continue their studies on the graduate level at private and state universities and colleges.

3. The overwhelming majority of our teachers responding to a questionnaire on graduate work expressed a conviction that the synodical teachers colleges should offer graduate work and indicated a readiness to attend.

4. A fifth-year program leading to the Master's degree at the teachers colleges would enable the church to offer advanced training to its teachers, which would be directed toward the specific goals of

Christian education and which would offer a unique opportunity to broaden the training of its educators at the graduate level.

5. Investigations carried on by the faculty at Concordia Teachers College, River Forest, since 1950, and by a Committee on Graduate Studies designated by the Board for Higher Education after the Houston Convention in 1953, have demonstrated the feasibility of establishing a fifth-year program at River Forest with a minimum of additional cost and within the framework of the expectations of the accrediting agencies.[22]

The Board for Higher Education concurred with the request in its report to the Synod, recommending that graduate courses be offered primarily in summer sessions beginning in 1957, but that several courses could be offered as late afternoon or Saturday classes during the school year. All such graduate work was to meet the highest educational standards and be acceptable to the regional, state, and voluntary (such as the National Council for the Accreditation of Teacher Education) educational agencies.[23] The Synod approved the recommendations and the graduate offerings, and, modifying the synodical *Handbook*, it made the Board for Higher Education responsible for the authorization of graduate programs in the terminal schools.[24]

Formal authorization to begin the graduate program at River Forest was granted in a letter from Dr. Walter F. Wolbrecht, Executive Secretary of the Board for Higher Education, to President Koehneke, March 29, 1957.[25]

A Graduate Council was elected by the faculty in September 1956 to take full charge of the program under the general supervision of the faculty. Its members were Dr. Huegli, academic dean; Prof. Kruse, registrar; Prof. Kraeft, director of the summer session; Dr. Gross, professor of geography; and Dr. Klotz, professor of biology.[26]

Policies governing course offerings and graduate faculty qualifications were adopted. The academic dean was designated as director of the graduate division. In announcing that graduate courses would be offered for the first time in the summer session of 1957, the following general description was given:

Basically, the proposed graduate program is in the pattern of the fifth year programs of teacher training developed recently by some of the outstanding colleges and universities in America. It is constructed to prepare master teachers for more effective classroom and parish activity. It will also help to meet the needs of the church for principals, administrators, high school teachers, and parish musicians.

The program will offer a wide variety of educational opportunities, rather than a narrowly specialized curriculum. It will focus on the individual student's personal and professional growth, his requirements in general education, and his area of special interest.

The Master's degree program at Concordia has been developed with the advice of the accreditation authorities. Dr. Manning Patillo, formerly with the North Central Association of Colleges and Secondary Schools, served as special consultant. The program is intended to meet the highest standards prescribed for graduate education. At the same time it will be directed toward the particular requirements of teachers and leaders in the system of Christian education maintained by our church.[27]

Admission requirements included holding a bachelor's degree from an approved school and a recommendation from that school. The undergraduate transcript had to show at least 18 term hours in religion and 18 hours in education. Admission to candidacy for the degree could be granted by the Graduate Council only after the completion of 11 term hours of graduate study at Concordia. A total of 48 term hours with a grade average of not less than "B" was required for the master's degree. With the approval of the Graduate Council a limited amount of transfer credit from other schools could be accepted. Advanced courses were offered in education and psychology and in religion, besides the subject-matter fields of English, history, geography, biology, and music.[28] The degree to be granted was Master of Arts in Education rather than the traditional Master of Arts or Master of Science degrees, since the program was to be essentially a 5-year program of teacher training.[29]

In March 1957 the North Central Association adopted the requirement of a preliminary self-study for member institutions beginning new programs. Dr. Neelak Tjernagel was appointed to be director of the self-survey for the graduate program at Concordia,[30] which was completed by January 1958.[31]

Recognition of the graduate courses was granted by the Illinois State Teacher Certification Board in a communication received from the secretary, Luther J. Black, April 23, 1957.[32]

The first experience with the graduate program was very successful. Preliminary estimates seemed to indicate an enrollment of not more than 30, so the Graduate Council had planned two seminars and four "graduate only" level courses and had designated 13 undergraduate courses which could be taken for graduate credit with additional requirements. By July 8, 1957, there were 90 applicants, of which 80 were accepted, and 74 of these were on campus that summer.[33] These graduate students came from 15 states, according to Dr. Huegli's report.[34]

The importance of setting higher academic standards for teachers was stressed at the President's Forum Oct. 24, 1957. The speaker was Dr. Timothy M. Stinnett, Executive Secretary of the National Commission on Teacher Education and Professional Standards of the National Education Association. Speaking on "Crucial Problems in Teacher Education," Dr. Stinnett declared that more and more states were requiring degrees of elementary and secondary teachers, with 37 states requiring at least a bachelor's degree for both levels, and six more in the process of requiring it. He stated further that a definite trend was developing to require a master's degree for high school teachers and that four states were already doing so. He emphasized the need for quality teachers, predicting the need for 3,000,000 to 5,000,000 teachers in five to eight years.[35] The topic was of particular significance in view of the newly developing graduate program.

The self-survey of the graduate program which had been prepared under the direction of Dr. Tjernagel was examined by the Board of Review of the North Central Association in March 1958. Actual accreditation had to wait until the first master's degrees had been granted and the North Central Association had sent an evaluation team to visit the college.[36] However, college representatives were authorized and encouraged to proceed with the program, and several suggestions were given them to improve it.

In 1958 the total number of graduate students had increased to 125, of which 93 registered for courses, while in the following year the admissions totaled 187 with 127 registrations.[37] The first Master of Arts in Education degrees were awarded on Aug. 20, 1959, to William A. Hoffmann of Hammond, Ind.; Carl H. Ivey and Lloyd D. Liese of Hinsdale, Ill.; and Melvin E. Rotermund of Chicago, Ill. Dr. Walter F. Wolbrecht of St. Louis, Executive Secretary of the Board for Higher Education, was the speaker.[38]

Graduate courses were offered for the first time on Saturday mornings beginning Sept. 19, 1959. During 1959–60 four courses (two each in religion and education) were offered to 35 students.[39]

Dr. Rees H. Hughes of Pittsburg, Kans., was engaged as consultant on July 1, 1958, to give special guidance for the accreditation of the graduate program.[40] He was a former president of Kansas State Teachers College in Pittsburg, also a former president of the American Association of Colleges. His function was to advise the college on the improvement of its graduate division in order to bring it in line with the best thinking on 5th-year teacher education programs. The major goal of his guidance was to achieve accreditation of the graduate program by the North Central Association and of both the undergraduate and the graduate programs by the National Council for the Accreditation of Teacher Education.[41]

On Dr. Hughes's recommendation the Graduate Council was reorganized and its duties more clearly defined. Steps in the program toward the degree were clarified; some courses were modified, and limits were set on the number of hours to be earned in education and psychology. Graduate classes were limited to a maximum of 20 students, seminars to a maximum of 15. Admission policies were made more stringent as the applications multiplied. In 1961 Dr. Huegli wrote: "Today, admission to the River Forest master's program is more difficult than admission to many comparable graduate programs." [42]

Examination of Concordia's graduate program was made for the North Central Association by Dr. John S. Diekhoff and Dr. James W. Maucker, July 17–18, 1961. In October President Koehneke was advised by Dr. Norman Burns, secretary of the executive committee of the North Central Association, that the committee was recommending full accreditation of the graduate program to its plenary meeting in the spring of 1962. This was an interesting and very happy development, especially since the college had requested that preliminary accreditation be granted. The action was taken in view of the favorable impression gained by the visiting committee, who were especially impressed by the fact that financial support was given to faculty members for advanced study and that all graduate students were required to have at least one year of experience before they could enter the program.[43]

Final action on accreditation was taken by the North Central Association on March 29, 1962.[44] Considerable progress was made in organizing the graduate curriculum so that by the summer of 1962 there were 36 graduate-only courses and 50 senior-level courses available for graduate credit, provided that additional work was included. The master's degree program was conceived as a terminal program, offering a wide variety of educational opportunities designed to help the Christian educator improve the quality of his services to the church.[45]

In his final report as academic dean Dr. Huegli recommended the gradual integration of the total graduate program into the regular academic year. He also recommended the separation of the office of director of the graduate division from the academic deanship but that the dean should have overall responsibility for it.[46]

Secondary Education Begun

The college catalog for 1957—58 announced that for the first time a limited number of students would be admitted to a program for the training of teachers for Lutheran secondary schools. This program had been authorized by the Synod in 1956 at the same time the graduate program was approved. Since the Synod required all graduates to have fulfilled the training program for elementary teaching, students who wanted to prepare for secondary teaching had to be approved by a special screening committee to take additional work in a summer session. Sixteen hours were necessary above the bachelor's degree requirement, which was equal to one extra quarter.[47]

Students would normally apply for admission to the program at the end of the sophomore year. A major of 48 quarter hours and a minor of at least 30 quarter hours were required, and at least a "B" average had to be maintained in the field of specialization.[48] Each applicant had to agree to be placed for either the elementary or the secondary level as the church might need him.[49] The scope of the program was set to prepare beginning teachers for grades 7 to 10.[50]

Arrangements were made with two local high schools, Luther North in Chicago and Walther Lutheran in Melrose Park, for practice teaching in the autumn of 1958, as 11 students began their work in this program, and 18 more had been accepted for the fall of 1959. Twelve graduates were placed in Lutheran high schools in the spring of 1958.[51]

It was anticipated that the secondary program would interest a large proportion of male students as time went on, as well as those who desired to prepare for college teaching in the future. Dean Huegli recommended consultation with Lutheran high school principals in the matter of secondary placement.[52] The college adopted the practice of inviting qualified Lutheran high school administrators to serve on the summer school faculty and teach secondary education courses, so that students might have the benefit of their experience in the field.

Internship Program

In 1957 an experimental program of voluntary internship for male students was inaugurated, directed by the placement director, Dr. Arvin W. Hahn. Under this plan male students were able to teach one year between their junior and senior years. The objectives of the program were (1) to provide the church with more mature professional workers; (2) to develop basic instructional skills gained only by experience; and (3) to raise the professional quality of the Lutheran teacher. It was designed to develop in the student a better understanding of the Lutheran teacher's office and a higher sense of consecration to it.[53]

Freshman students were given some orientation on internship in a special program arranged by the Men's Council in which pros and cons of the program were discussed by returning interns together with the dean of students and the director of internship. A similar meeting was conducted for sophomores and juniors. Junior students were required to declare their intention to participate by Dec. 1, after which they received more intensive orientation as a group and individually. Placement of interns was made by the director of internship,[54] and in April 1959 the board of control approved a request to the Synod requiring a year of internship of all male students.[55]

Initially congregational participation was solicited, but as more of them gradually became aware of the program, the request for interns began to exceed the supply. Placement of the interns was made only after full information on the congregation, the school, and the staff was carefully considered.[56]

Quarterly reports must be submitted to the college by the supervising principal and an annual report by the supervising pastor. The student is required to register for the course with the director of internship, who also attempts to visit the intern during the year. On his return the intern participates in a special conference to discuss and evaluate the year's experiences.[57] For the 1964–65 school year, 60 Concordia juniors were assigned to positions in 14 states, including 42 men and 18 women.[58]

The New Curriculum

Since the college curriculum had been revised in 1947—48, many changes had taken place which reflected the changing standards of teacher education, changes in the expectation of congregations, adjustments in state certification requirements, as well as the introduction of graduate studies, secondary teacher education, and the internship program which was being proposed as a requirement for all male students. Since all of these changes had curricular implications, the faculty established a Curriculum Commission of 16 members as a subcommittee of the Academic Policies Committee. After considerable study of the literature and many investigations by its subcommittees, which enlisted the counsel of alumni and students, the commission presented the framework of a new curriculum in June 1959. Two more years of study and modification were required before the new curriculum was finally approved in the spring of 1961, becoming effective for freshmen entering the following September.[59]

The Curriculum Commission submitted the following statement of objectives, which were adopted by the faculty Dec. 8, 1958: [60]

Concordia Teachers College is committed to the task of preparing teachers for the schools of The Lutheran Church — Missouri Synod. In this task the college takes into account the requirements of teaching as a profession and the distinctive character and function of this profession in the life and work of the Church. It also recognizes that education is a lifelong process in which the student himself must be continually active. The college therefore seeks to provide the environment and the direction for the student as he prepares for the teaching profession through his pursuit of the following general objectives:

1. A firm faith in Jesus Christ as the only Savior from sin, a ready consent to the will of God in every life situation and a sense of wonder and appreciation for all the work of God.

2. A sincere acceptance of the Holy Scriptures as the revealed truth of God, an assent to the Lutheran Confessions as the correct expression of that truth, a growing ability to evaluate human learning and conduct in the light of God's Word.

3. A grateful consecration to the ministry of the Word and to the extension of the Kingdom of God, an active cooperation in promoting the purposes of The Lutheran Church — Missouri Synod, and a high standard of the ethics in the professional life of a Christian teacher.

4. A respect for the dignity and worth of the individual as a redeemed child of God, an understanding and development of the

resources of the human personality, and an effective practice of personal and professional stewardship of God-given talents.

5. A progressive development in the skills of study, research, and evaluation; an objectivity in the appraisal of data and opinions; and an increasing facility in the integration of learning and in the communication of ideas and knowledge.

6. A stimulation of intellectual curiosity; an acquisition of knowledge and skills in human affairs, the sciences, and humanities; and a refined ability to discriminate in aesthetic and cultural areas.

7. A broad acquaintance with the concept, vocabulary and practices of education; an increasing skill in teaching and a growing competence in specialized areas of teaching and service.

8. An understanding of the nature and needs of contemporary society, an increasing social competence, and a readiness to assume responsibility in the community.[61]

Since the graduates of Concordia Teachers College are called into unique positions in the church, the teacher education curriculum must be organized to meet the needs of these positions.

The following assumptions apply to all graduates of the college:

1. They will teach in a Lutheran elementary school or a Lutheran High School.
2. They will ordinarily be expected to teach religion in addition to the common subjects of learning.
3. They will teach all subjects in the framework of Christianity and in accordance with the doctrines and beliefs of The Lutheran Church — Missouri Synod.
4. In nearly all instances they will teach in self-contained classrooms if assigned to elementary school positions.
5. They will begin their teaching careers in grades 7—10 if assigned to high school positions.
6. They will need at least minimal skills in music, particularly sacred music, for their classroom teaching.
7. They will in most cases be expected to assist in the work of the various religious education agencies in addition to their classroom teaching.
8. They will make teaching a life-time career and will regard their positions as part of the educational ministry of The Lutheran Church — Missouri Synod.[62]

To effectively educate teachers to fit the foregoing assumptions the college believes that the curriculum should include:

1. A *general education* which demands both broad learning in all the common divisions of knowledge and Christian theology;

2. a reasonable depth in a narrower field of concentration or specialization;
3. professional education in the needs, growth, and development of children and in the aims, methods, and materials of teaching;
4. and some additional specialized training in the field of church music and for service in a variety of religious education agencies such as Sunday Schools and youth groups.[63]

Each of the six instructional divisions developed a set of objectives in harmony with the foregoing objectives, assumptions, and beliefs, and courses were designed to conform to them.[64]

The new curriculum retained some of the better features of the previous ones, continuing to emphasize general education at the junior college level. Requirements of the church and the state placed restrictions on much experimentation, but some new features were introduced. All students would now receive the Bachelor of Arts degree instead of the Bachelor of Science in Education which had been awarded since 1940. A foreign language was now required of all students who would find it possible to take at least 8 hours of advanced foreign language in German, Latin, or French with the aid of a language laboratory which was to be installed. Science requirements were reorganized as education courses were modified and a professional quarter was introduced. All divisions studied their offerings in order to provide new majors and minors. The new provision for the secondary school program reflected more realistically the requirements of high schools and their teachers.[65]

The new curriculum was inaugurated with the freshman class of 1961, and the first Bachelor of Arts degrees are to be awarded in 1965. In commenting on the work of five years which produced this curriculum, Dean Huegli wrote:

> The faculty . . . has already obtained much value from its studies. The efforts to formulate the objectives of the college and the various academic divisions were an educational experience of great help to members of the faculty. They have become conversant with modern trends in teacher education and more competent in their own offerings.[66]

Summer School and Extension

Under the administrative reorganization plan introduced by President Koehneke, the academic dean in 1957 was assigned the supervision of the summer school offering and its staff. When Dr. Kraeft terminated his services as summer school director in 1958, the operation of summer sessions was completely integrated with the regular school year. In 1959 the session was extended to 10 weeks so that credit for a full quarter could be earned. The summer school faculty increased from 27 in 1955 (including 7 visiting) to 75 in 1961 (with 30 visiting).[67] The enrollment increased from 502 in 1954 to a high of 795 in 1959.[68] By 1963 there were 107 course offerings in the summer session.

The Division of Correspondence and Extension was placed under the academic dean in 1959. Enrollment in the 35 courses increased from 425 in 1955—56 to 716 in 1959—60. A student could earn a maximum of 48 hours toward a degree. One-day institutes, devoted to one subject area, were offered at various intervals during the school year to teachers within a radius of 100 miles of the college. These institutes gave opportunity for the Concordia faculty to give service as expert resource persons for the elementary schools.[69]

On July 10, 1956, the board of control gave special recognition to the 25th anniversary of the summer school, presenting a scroll and a gift of $250 to Dr. Kraeft, who had played such a vital part in the founding and operation of this program.[70]

Numerous noncredit workshops and institutes conducted during summer sessions became increasingly popular. By 1964 10 one-week institutes were offered in a variety of subjects including organ, administration of District parish education, inner-city Christian education, a seminar in preaching, music composition, a lay institute of theology, and secondary school administration.[71]

As previously mentioned, the summer school assumed a new importance in 1957 as it became the chief means for graduate work leading to the Master of Arts degree. Beginning with four degrees awarded in 1959, a total of 56 degrees had been awarded by September 1963.

Accreditation

On recommendation of President Koehneke the board of control accepted an invitation to have the college join the American Association of Colleges for Teacher Education in January 1956.[72] This organization consisted of approximately 300 colleges in the United States engaged in teacher education, its members sharing in cooperative research, publication, and consultative services.[73]

We have noted previously the various steps by which accreditation was obtained for the graduate program with the North Central Association between 1957 and 1962.

On September 9, 1958, the board first resolved to apply for membership in the National Council for the Accreditation of Teacher Education.[74] This Council, known as NCATE, is an independent accrediting body organized exclusively for the evaluation and accreditation of programs for the preparation of professional school personnel at both undergraduate and graduate levels.[75] It supplements the services of regional accrediting agencies.

Accreditation by NCATE was highly desirable since graduates of member schools found it much easier to become certificated by the various states. Graduates of NCATE-accredited colleges and universities were granted certificates without most of the special requirements peculiar to each state.[76]

Preparation for NCATE accreditation took place over several years. The introduction of a new undergraduate curriculum in September 1961 was a part of this preparation.[77] Another phase was a 123-page self-study of the college compiled by Dr. James O. Roberts, admissions officer and assistant registrar, and other members of the faculty and administration. This report outlined the objectives and the program of the college.[78] Dr. Daryl Pendergraft, assistant to the president at the State College of Iowa, Cedar Falls, served as consultant to the college in planning for the examination by NCATE representatives.

A seven-member examination team visited Concordia Oct. 29–31, 1961. Subsequently accreditation of the elementary program was granted in May 1962, including the 4-year program and an optional one-year internship culminating in the degree of Bachelor of Arts.[79] Action on the secondary education and the master's degree programs was deferred since the Council wished to have more detailed information concerning them.

A communication to President Koehneke, dated Aug. 24, 1964, stated that NCATE had accredited the secondary teacher training program at the bachelor's degree level and the elementary program at the master's degree level.[80]

In January 1963 President Koehneke reported the receipt of a letter from the State Teacher Certification Board of the Illinois Department of Public Instruction which stated that the teacher education program of Concordia Teachers College was approved for elementary, high school, and special certificates, effective July 1, 1963.[81]

Student Teaching

Expansion of the student teaching program kept pace with the growth of enrollment. At the beginning of President Koehneke's administration in 1954–55 the enrollment of 651, which included 134 student teachers, required three practice schools, 17 supervising teachers, and one college supervisor. By 1960–61 the enrollment had mounted to 941, which required 15 schools, 54 supervising teachers, and 5 college supervisors.[82]

When the revised curriculum of 1961 was established, a new pattern of student teaching was adopted, which had two main features: (1) a coordinated program of methods courses with directed student teaching; and (2) a professional quarter selected by the student in the junior or senior year in which the 16 units earned consisted of elementary curriculum (6 quarter hours) for the first three weeks and student teaching (10 quarter hours) for the following eight weeks in one of the off-campus schools. During the professional quarter the student would take no other course work. In 1962–63 the program required 21 schools, 335 teaching stations, 85 supervising teachers, and 7 college supervisors to serve the 335 student teachers out of an undergraduate enrollment of 1,109.[83]

During 1963–64 the program included 28 schools which served 360 students. By this time the program had developed so that, besides classroom experience, students gained other professional experience by participating in various areas of life in a congregation, including local faculty and board meetings, athletic activities, musical events (such as operettas, etc.), organ and choir activities, administrative offices, Sunday school, parent-teacher activities, youth work, and conversations with the local pastor.[84]

Transportation was provided to the cooperating schools by the college, not only for the school day but as much as possible also for the evening and weekend parish activities of the congregation in which the student taught.[85]

Special activities were conducted for the in-service education and training of supervising personnel, including quarterly dinner meetings at the college and three seminars, including one each for experienced and inexperienced teachers and one for veteran supervisors.[86] In addition to these activities a midquarter informational newsletter, "Student Teaching Notes," was edited by the former (and first) director of student teaching, Dr. Maurer; and since 1959 a "Handbook of Student Teaching" was prepared by the director as a source book for the college coordinators and the supervising teachers.[87] A summer teaching program was conducted by some of the cooperating schools for the benefit of summer school students.[88]

The secondary practice teaching program was conducted with the cooperation of the two Lutheran high schools in Chicago, Luther North and Luther South, and Walther Lutheran High School in Melrose Park. The enrollment in the secondary program was limited to 25 students per year, because of the more limited needs of Lutheran high schools.[89]

Secondary student teachers earned four additional quarter hours of credit, requiring them to spend three hours each day at a high school for a quarter, for which students had to provide their own transportation. Besides observation and teaching, the student became acquainted with the administrative offices and officers. The final week was spent in visits to Roman Catholic and public high schools.[90]

Prof. Ralph L. Reinke, director of student teaching, reported in 1963 that there were 56 Lutheran schools within a 12-mile radius of the college with a potential of 322 classrooms which could be used as student teaching stations. He felt that if they could be staffed by teachers qualified to supervise, adequate provision for future growth of the student teaching program would be assumed.[91]

Other Curricular Developments

Three-Year Diplomas Dropped. The college catalog of 1955–56 announced the termination of the 3-year diploma program effective in 1958. The last students who would be able to exercise the option of a 3- or 4-year program were the freshman class of 1955–56.[92] Thus, after 25 years, this program closed on July 31, 1958, as three students received the last 3-year diplomas at the summer commencement.[93]

Evening Classes. In 1958–59 evening classes were begun on Tuesdays and Thursdays from 6:00 to 7:40 o'clock. The objective was to make better use of campus facilities to serve more students without conflicting with music, athletics, or other regularly scheduled afternoon programs. Twelve courses were offered in the evening program. Teachers of the area were invited to participate on a space-available basis after the undergraduate students had registered.[94] Evening classes became a regular feature of the curriculum, and by the school year 1961–62 classes were running almost continuously from 7:30 a. m. to 8:00 p. m. and from 9:00 to 11:00 a. m. on Saturdays.[95]

European Study Tours. A travel-study program was inaugurated by the board of control in the summer of 1961. The first tour, led by Prof. Daniel E. Poellot, was restricted to 10 students, six of whom were awarded special scholarships by the scholarship committee of the faculty. Scholarships were awarded on the basis of (a) the student's purpose in relating the tour to his vocation as a teacher and (b) his leadership ability as indicated by Christian service on campus. The tour was 40 days in length, exclusive of travel time.[96]

"CULT." The Committee for the Upgrading of Learning and Teaching, long a dream of President Koehneke, was a student-faculty committee established in September 1963 for the precise purpose implied in its name. CULT members were appointed by the president and included five faculty members and eight students, two representatives of each class. Their studies conducted by subcommittees, included the curriculum, instruction, student-faculty communications, and the relationship of student life to the total academic program. Two questionnaires were distributed: the one attempted to obtain student evaluations of teaching which might be helpful to the academic dean, the division chairmen, and the individual instructors; the other was aimed to gather data which might be improved to aid learning. It was planned to continue the work of the committee in 1964–65.[97]

Music Development. After considerable and elaborate touring activity had become almost a tradition with regard to the a-cappela choir and the band, the board of control determined to suspend such activity for the school year 1957–58 and to permit limited touring by such groups only when specific prior approval of the projected tour had been obtained from the faculty and board.[98]

The objectives and structure of the cocurricular music program were subsequently reviewed in 1957, and a new program was provisionally established. The music division and the faculty reviewed the program again in 1958–59 and established five choral organizations and a band to offer students opportunities to gain various musical experiences. Choral groups included a college chorus, a junior college choir, a senior college choir, a treble choir, and a chorale choir, but off-campus appearances were limited to the junior and senior college choirs and the band.[99]

Off-campus appearances continued to increase again, averaging about once a month according to Robert L. Busse, who organized and managed such appearances on behalf of the Office of Field Services.[100] The senior choir, directed by Prof. Thomas Gieschen, appeared on television programs over WGN-TV in 1960 and in 1961, and the 1961 Christmas television program was produced by Prof. Martin Neeb, Jr., director of field services, assisted by Prof. Walter W. Martin of the art department.[101] The senior college choir was heard nationally on radio several times, including the National Broadcasting Company's program "Voices of Christmas" in December 1962.[102] In 1963 the senior choir and the band (directed by Prof. Harold T. Rohlfing) toured in the midwestern states.[103]

Library Development. During the last decade the library at Concordia also experienced the growth and expansion in its holdings which reflected a nearly doubled student body plus the greater demands of a constantly higher quality demanded of Concordia graduates by the church, the state, and the accreditation agencies. It also reflected the addition of a graduate program and secondary teacher training. From 1958 to 1961 the library holdings increased from 55,142 volumes to 64,921.[104]

Faculty Development

Problems of Recruitment. The faculty had more than doubled in size from 1954 to 1964, numbering 116 full-time and 4 part-time instructors at the beginning of the centennial year.[105] In the final decade the pattern of faculty recruitment changed considerably. Throughout the first 90 years recruitment had been almost exclusively from among the pastors and teachers of the church. From 1955 on it became increasingly apparent that there were not nearly enough of these synodically trained men and women to supply the staff needs at Concordia, especially since its recruitment was in competition with the parishes of the Synod as well as with other schools and colleges outside the church. Rising academic standards set by the college for its professors further compounded the problem.[106]

In 1960–61 nearly a third of the new faculty members were not trained in the synodical colleges or seminaries. The college administration had been forced to explore many sources for prospects besides the files maintained by the Board for Higher Education, such as the Commission on College and University Service, and contacts with church leaders throughout the country. To obtain 74 new faculty members between 1955 and 1961, about 225 names had to be screened and nearly 150 interviews held.[107]

In his final report as academic dean, Dr. Huegli noted that 28 percent of new faculty members from 1955 to 1961 had come from elementary parish schools, a great benefit to a college whose primary aim is the training of elementary teachers. He pointed out the great need for adding more experienced college teachers since but 16 percent of the new faculty had had such experience and almost 25 percent of the new personnel had come directly from graduate schools with very little, if any, practice teaching.[108]

Dean Huegli called attention to the necessity for establishing new recruitment contacts and methods, pointing to needed changes in synodical procedures which would give the colleges a larger share of autonomy in the area of staffing.[109]

Orientation of Faculty Members. The growing heterogeneity of the faculty recruitment brought a greater necessity for effective orientation procedures. In recognition of the fact that many new instructors were relatively unacquainted not only with the college but also with the synodical college system itself, several steps were taken to orient them more fully to both.

The idea of a retreat to prepare for the duties of a new school year had been in use for the Student Council and Senate since 1950. This idea was applied in the first faculty retreat, held for faculty men at Lake Geneva, Wis., Sept. 5–7, 1956.[110] Topics discussed included Religion in the Public Schools, the Impact of Increased Enrollment on Higher Education, Federal Aid to Education, Desegregation, College Teaching, and the implications for the college of synodical actions at the St. Paul convention in 1956.[111] In succeeding years the program emphasized the work of a different academic division of the faculty each year, becoming an in-service training program as well as a means of orientation, and in 1957 woman instructors were invited for the first time.[112]

Another orientation feature was introduced in 1959, when a seminar in college teaching was conducted for new staff members at Concordia. As a special service of the college, it was broadened in the following years to include new faculty members from nine other synodical schools, including the two seminaries. In these seminars the philosophy of the college and the techniques of college teaching were emphasized.[113]

Advanced Study Programs. During the last decade college teaching began to be recognized as a separate profession, and the requirements for college faculty members were constantly increasing. Conditions under which pastors and teachers work in the church often conflicted with requirements for advanced study. Despite this, a number of them who had good potential as college professors had to be recruited for service, and gradually the college began to share in the responsibility of assisting faculty members in advanced degree programs. A small amount of aid had been given in the past to Concordia faculty members particularly after the movement for accreditation began. This increased sharply between 1955 and 1961, as 50 faculty members received assistance amounting to $17,375.80.[114]

Ford Foundation Grants. In July 1956 the college received $115,000 from the Ford Foundation. The money was to be placed in trust, the earnings to be used for salary increases.[115] A second installment of $115,500 was received in July 1957.[116]

Board of Control Scholarships. President Koehneke announced in April 1961 that the board of control had established a new fund called the Endowment for the Enrichment of Instruction. This fund was established to provide opportunities to enrich the instructional services of the college by aiding college faculty members in their personal and professional growth, by educational research, and by the improvement of instructional techniques and materials.[117]

A. A. L. Fellowships. The Aid Association for Lutherans, a fraternal insurance company, began a program in 1961—62 of awarding faculty fellowships valued from $1,000 to $2,000 to assist Lutheran college professors in advanced studies.[118]

Senior Class Faculty Fellowships. The graduating class of 1962 initiated a program of faculty fellowships as a farewell gift to the college. The awards were to be made by the board of control to assist professors in further study and research. The class of 1963 also adopted this program by presenting nearly $1,000 as their parting gift.[119]

Field Visits. One of the dangers prevalent in a professional school such as Concordia Teachers College is that the faculty may get too far out of touch with the work and world of the parish school or high school in which their graduates must function. As noted previously, many new members of Concordia's faculty (about 80 percent in one year) had had no previous experience in the elementary or high schools of the church.[120]

In order to become aware of the changing needs of the teachers in the classrooms, a program of one-week field visits was begun in 1955, under which two faculty members were sent out to the Districts of the church to visit selected schools, parishes, and District meetings. Special funds granted to the college by the United States Steel Corporation were used for this purpose.[121]

With the cooperation of the District Superintendents or Counselors of Parish Education and the Lutheran high school administrators, the faculty members received reports and impressions of the effectiveness of the college program and then reported back to the faculty as a body, also to each academic division of the faculty. Many new insights thus gained were of influence in bringing about curricular changes. The visits served to draw alumni closer to the college, and thus they also served as a general public relations medium.[122]

Reverse Field Visits. During March 11–16, 1962, two District Superintendents, Dr. L. J. Dierker of the Western District and Dr. E. E. Yunghans of the Central District of The Lutheran Church — Missouri Synod were invited to the college in a "reverse field visit" program. They presented a joint written evaluation of the college to the faculty and board of control. The program was to continue with two District Superintendents participating each year. The "reverse field visit" program was extended to include two Lutheran high school administrators each year beginning in 1962–63.[123]

Faculty Handbook. In order to assist in the orientation of new instructors and as a source of information to all faculty members, the first *Faculty Handbook* was prepared in 1956 and presented to the faculty. Various decisions, policies, and procedures of board and faculty, as well as administrative rules and regulations, were set forth and classified.[124]

International Studies Program. In an effort to seek out new ways for the college to serve the church in its worldwide mission through the most effective application of Christian education, the board of control and President Koehneke established an International Studies Program in 1962. Dr. Koehneke had written in 1961:

There is increasing evidence that the new nations of Africa and other regions are desperately in need of teachers. There seems to be evidence for the assumption that new nations may not welcome Christian missionaries concerned primarily with the establishment of a Christian culture through a kerygmatic approach to the dissemination of the Gospel. The didactic approach may be tolerated, permitted, or even encouraged on the grounds of educational need in these new nations.[125]

Dr. Arvin W. Hahn, director of the graduate division, and Prof. Kenneth R. Schueler were sent to Africa for six weeks from July 25 to Sept. 19, 1962, as the pioneer "team" of the new program.[126] They were to seek data which might enable the college to clarify its role in the mission ministry of the church to nations new and old in foreign lands. According to the preface the report is —

intended to show the relevance of Christian mission education and other formal Christian activities to the pattern of education, religion, and politics in Africa. It presumes to evaluate the scope, function, and status of the Christian Church, its ministry and program of education. Finally it intends to make recommendations toward the greater fulfillment of the Lord's command to go and teach.[127]

The two men visited the newly independent and emerging African states to study the current educational system and the possibilities of the future, meeting with educational and governmental officials, and attempting especially to assess the educational mission of the Christian church in Africa. Their 50-page report points up the urgent need for immediate action on the part of the Synod and the college to be of help to the African nations by a new approach to missions and mission education. They recommended the establishment of a direct tie of assistance between the college and the church-sponsored teacher training center in Nigeria to assist in the training of more competent Nigerian teachers. Guidance and help was also urgently needed in staffing the center and in general improvement of facilities. Africa presented a good opportunity for quality Christian education, properly used in the building up of a strong church.[128] The second international study program was being planned for the Orient.[129]

Other Faculty Benefits. The policy of granting study leaves to faculty members, frequently with pay, has been a factor in building strength and stability in the faculty. This policy was extended to include research leaves as well.[130] Sabbatical leaves had been initiated in 1952–53, but only one was granted that year. In 1954–55 a second sabbatical was granted. However, the pace increased dramatically over the next six years with 15 faculty members having had one by 1960–61. Ten years of service was required to be eligible for the sabbatical, which was to be used for study, travel, or research.[131]

During the Koehneke administration other improvements to benefit the faculty which were either inaugurated or expanded included the construction of faculty offices, the provision of duplicating services for faculty members, and adequate arrangement for expanded housing needs, including a provision for an allowance for housing to be used for rental or purchase of a home.[132]

Special Services of the Faculty, 1954–64. The faculty of Concordia Teachers College has always been "on call" to serve the Synod in many ways: as members of committees, as authors of elementary school materials, as research specialists in various synodical problems, and as essayists and lecturers for numerous District conventions and educational conferences. Since it is impossible to list all such services, we may illustrate with several examples. In May 1962, Dr. Walter M. Wangerin, professor of religion and education, was selected to direct a revised exposition of Luther's Small Catechism and to prepare graded materials based on the Catechism.[133] Also in 1962 Prof. Paul G. Bunjes, head of the music department, designed a 41-rank Casavant pipe organ for Peace Lutheran Church of Saginaw, Mich., which was dedicated by Prof. Herbert M. Gotsch.[134]

Besides the services to the church and its numerous branches, faculty members participated in the various general fields of education according to their specialities. In 1960, for example, Dean Albert G. Huegli was one of 15 men selected to participate in a leadership training program designed to train them as educational consultants and examiners for the North Central Association of Colleges and Secondary Schools.[135]

A list of typical activities of the faculty was included in the "Report of Concordia Teachers College, River Forest, Illinois, to the National Council for the Accreditation of Teacher Education," Aug. 1, 1962, on pages 67, 68. This list was a review of professional activities of 1961–62 and included the following:

1. Presentation of a paper at a reading conference at the University of Chicago.

2. Director of a seven-year program at Dyslexia Memorial Institute of Chicago (a clinic for normal and above average children with reading difficulties).

3. Consultant for the development of a reading pacer.

4. Chairman of the editorial committee of the Lutheran Education Association.

5. Two members serve as psychological consultants and are certified as psychologists or qualified psychological examiners in the state of Illinois.

6. Eight presentations of professional education papers at district teachers conferences, two of which were out of state.

7. Eight individual consultations with local schools and faculties.

8. Thirty-five parent-teacher presentations.

9. Articles published in educational journals such as *Lutheran Education, Basketball Guide,* and *Religious Education.*

10. Psychological consultations on a weekly basis at Dyslexia Institute on the campus of Northwestern University.

11. Service on the editorial board of *Lutheran Education.*

Concordia Recognized in Geography. Dr. Herbert H. Gross, professor of geography, was appointed by the Governor to be a member of the Illinois Planning Committee for the White House Conference on Education in 1955.[136] In 1959 he was elected president of the 3,000-member Chicago Geographical Society,[137] and in 1960 he was reappointed director of coordinators of the National Council for Geographic Education,[138] becoming its president in 1964. Dr. Gross also was a contributor to the 1962 edition of the *Encyclopaedia Britannica.*[139] Further recognition of Concordia's service in the field of geography came when Dr. Hahn, associate professor of geography and director of the graduate division, was appointed to serve for a year as the first executive officer of the Association of American Geographers.[140]

During the centennial year Concordia Teachers College was selected to edit the internationally known *Journal of Geography,* official publication of the National Council for Geographic Education. The transfer from Indiana University is to take place in 1965, with the first issue edited at Concordia in September. President Koehneke named Dr. Gross, editor; Dr. Hahn, associate editor; Prof. Merle L. Radke, assistant to the editor; and Prof. Roy V. Schoenborn, layout and design editor.[141] Commenting on the transfer, Dr. Koehneke remarked:

> The college counts it an honor and a privilege to be selected as headquarters for the *Journal of Geography* and to perform this professional service to the geographers of the nation. It is especially delightful to be given this opportunity to serve during our Centennial

Year, when we are trying to express our gratitude as a college in tangible and substantial acts of service to the academic community.[142]

Faculty and Administrative Changes. In the past decade six professors died, including the following:

Richard T. Rohlfing, April 13, 1958 (served since 1925), former band director and professor of music.[143]

Albert H. Miller, emeritus, July 30, 1959, age 95 (served 1906–43), Concordia's first registrar (1913–36).[144]

Former President (1939–53) Arthur W. Klinck died in St. Louis on Aug. 6, 1959.[145]

Walter O. Kraeft, March 30, 1960 (served since 1926), the first dean of the summer school and the first director of recruitment and public relations.[146]

Theodore C. Appelt, Jan. 15, 1961 (served since 1926), professor of German, religion, and music.[147]

Albert H. Beck, May 30, 1962 (served since 1914, a record 48 years), who had served the college as professor of music.[148]

Ferdinand H. Schmitt, emeritus, Sept. 24, 1962 (served 1906–47), the last member of the Addison faculty, the first business manager (1939–47), acting president (1939), professor of English and German.[149]

Alfred F. Schmieding, emeritus, May 4, 1963 (served 1922–62), the first dean of the college (1935–40), registrar (1937–40), the first academic dean (1948–55), and acting president (Jan.–Sept. 1954).[150]

In 1959 Mrs. Laura Mackensen retired as dean of women after 15 years of service.[151]. Eunice Heyne was appointed acting dean of women, succeeding Mrs. Mackensen in July 1960. Dr. Albert V. Maurer, director of student teaching for 20 years, asked to be relieved of the position in July 1960. He was succeeded by Prof. Ralph L. Reinke, assistant director of student teaching. Prof. Walter A. Vahl was appointed director of correspondence and extension after the death of Dr. Walter O. Kraeft in 1960.[152] In 1959 the veteran Professor Theodore J. C. Kuehnert was appointed archivist of the college. A graduate of Addison in 1903, he had joined the faculty in 1927, serving also on the staff of the *Lutheran School Journal* (renamed *Lutheran Education* in 1947) from 1928 to 1953. He was managing editor, 1939–1945, then editor-in-chief, retiring in 1953. Dr. Herbert H. Gross became editor-in-chief in 1954.

The office of field services was established in 1957, and Prof. Frederick H. Pralle was appointed the first director.[153] This office was responsible for publications and news releases and for processing requests for conventions and other campus facility use. Prof. Martin J. Neeb, Jr., succeeded Professor Pralle in 1961. Also in 1961 Prof. Paul Grotelueschen was appointed to direct the department of recruitment and alumni relations, and Dr. Arvin Hahn was assigned the responsibility for the office of development.[154]

A new position, that of dean of administration, was established on Feb. 1, 1963, as an important part of a plan to reorganize the business services division of the college. Dr. Waldemar Affeldt was appointed by President Koehneke and was to be responsible for all business operations services of the school.[155]

In 1961 Dr. Albert G. Huegli, the academic dean, accepted a call to Valparaiso University to become its first vice-president for academic affairs.[156] He was succeeded by Prof. Carl L. Waldschmidt, who had been assistant academic dean since 1958.[157] During Dr. Huegli's incumbency the office had expanded greatly to serve the growing college. In 1956 he organized an advisory council of division chairmen and had them begin to share in recruitment, promotion, in-service training, and planning teaching loads and plant expansion. In 1957 he was made director of the graduate division and was given supervision of the summer school and staff, integrating it with the regular program. In 1959 supervision of the division of correspondence and extension was also added to his office.[158]

Faculty committees were reorganized in 1958 when two principal committees were established. The Academic Policies Committee dealt with the curriculum, instruction, and research and consisted of one representative from each division, the registrar, and the academic dean, who serves as chairman. The Student Life Policies Committee dealt with scholarships, awards, and discipline, the dean of students serving as chairman. Other standing committees were a faculty welfare committee, a library committee, a colloquy committee, an honors committee, and the graduate council.[159]

Faculty Publications

From the beginning of the college in 1864 the faculty members had written numerous books and articles to help the classroom teachers. According to an analysis of faculty publications made in 1958 which covered the school year 1956–57, the faculty serving that year had written a total of 76 books, an average of 1.36 books per member. Thirty-seven of these were on Lutheran education and the elementary school curriculum, 13 on religious subjects, 13 original or adapted musical compositions, six general scholarly works, four in general education, and three in secondary education. Faculty members had also written 35 unpublished dissertations and 18 other unpublished works.[160]

In the same report it was stated that 26 magazines had published articles written by faculty members of Concordia Teachers College, averaging four per member, and that 23 members had contributed to *Lutheran Education.*

Housing an Expanding College

As the enrollment of the college continued to increase each year, the problems of providing facilities to house the curriculum, the student body, and the faculty multiplied greatly, and planning became a crucial issue. The beautiful 40-acre campus became more and more inadequate to carry on the educational program as the century drew to a close.

Housing the Curriculum

Ground was broken in January 1955 for the new science building, containing a biology laboratory, a mathematics room, and a science-physics lecture laboratory. It was dedicated Oct. 25 of the same year.[161] The board of control resolved to name it Eifrig Hall, in honor of Dr. C. W. G. Eifrig, who had served Concordia as professor of natural science from 1909 to 1942 (died 1949).[162]

Until 1953–54 the students of the college were able to have chapel devotions in the auditorium of the present student union building. However, in March 1954 it was announced that, in order to ease the overcrowded conditions, the freshmen, sophomores, and juniors would continue to use the auditorium and that the seniors and graduate students would have chapel in the basement of the girls' dormitory, Mary-Martha Hall, featuring outside speakers from local churches and schools.[163]

Beginning on the first day of school, Sept. 17, 1956, the faculty and 723 students gathered in the gymasium for chapel each day.[164] Bleachers had been installed to allow seating to be moved easily and quickly. The religious activities committee of the student body recommended commissioning Dr. Adalbert R. Kretzmann, pastor of Lutheran Church of St. Luke, Chicago, to design a mobile type of chapel center which could be used in the gymnasium to give a better atmosphere for chapel.[165]

In February 1958 the design of the mobile chapel was revealed. A curtain on a movable track would be suspended from ceiling to floor, delineating a sanctuary including a lectern, an altar, a special speaker's chair, and a 10-foot cross. All items would be quickly movable to make allowance for gymnasium use.[166]

Dr. Kretzmann had also designed a college seal which was officially adopted by the board of control in June 1956.[167] Later the same year he designed a stained-glass "Christus" window for the newly remodeled office of President Koehneke.[168]

During the summer of 1954, Krauss Hall, one of the original men's dormitories, was completely remodeled, changing from the old pattern of eight students in a bedroom and four in a study to two-student rooms, each combining living room, bedroom, and study. The Campus Corner in the basement of the student union was also completely refurbished.[169] The growing enrollment made it necessary in 1956 to vacate five professor's homes on the campus, converting them into dormitories housing 14 students each,[170] necessitating the purchase of off-campus housing for faculty members.

Kohn and Brohm Halls were remodeled after the pattern of Krauss Hall in 1958, with the addition of counselor's quarters and new entrances. Remodeling was also carried out in the gymnasium balcony to accommodate a new pipe organ donated by a friend of the college. In the summer of 1958 the art department was moved to the north wing of the college union,[171] and new offices were built for faculty and staff members. Lindemann Hall was refurbished during the summer of 1959 to complete the project of remodeling all the original dormitories.[172] Both Lindemann and Kohn Halls were women's residence halls.

After the death of Dr. Arthur Klinck, Concordia's fifth president, in August 1959, the board of control accepted President Koehneke's recommendation to name the college library the Klinck Memorial Library in his honor.[173]

In 1959–60 a new men's residence hall, housing 168 students, a central heating and service building including office space for the superintendent of buildings and grounds, and an addition to Eifrig Hall consisting of six classrooms and laboratories and 13 faculty offices were constructed at a cost of $1,500,000. The new men's residence hall was named David and Jonathan Hall.[174] The new additions, representing the largest addition to the plant since 1913, when the original complex was dedicated, were dedicated on Oct. 9, 1960.[175] President Koehneke performed the rites of dedication, and the Rev. Paul Hansen of Denver, Colo., preached for the occasion. Special music was furnished by a massed choir of 800 children and 400 adults, besides a massed band composed of the college band and three Lutheran high school bands. Approximately 5,000 attended the service.[176]

In the spring of 1960 the post office of Oak Park, in cooperation with the college authorities, established Post Office Station No. 2 in the basement of Brohm Hall for the convenience of the students and faculty.[177] Relief in providing food services for the rapidly expanding student body came in 1960–61 as a second dining hall was built in the basement of Kohn Hall.[178]

Ground was broken Oct. 11, 1963, for a new gymnasium and swimming pool, to be joined to the original gymnasium to form one unit, and also for an addition to the music center, including remodeling of the south wing of the original building. The new construction was part of a long-range master plan of campus development which would eventually include central heating, air conditioning, and electrical systems for all buildings on the campus. The groundbreaking was a part of the 50th-anniversary observance of the college on the River Forest campus.[179] The target date for dedication was set for Oct. 11, 1964, which was designated Concordia Teachers College Centennial Sunday by synodical President Oliver R. Harms.[180]

Chapel Drive

Despite all arrangements to provide the appropriate atmosphere for worship in the gymnasium, such as the movable altar and the organ, the general inadequacies became more and more impressive as time went on. The need of a chapel-auditorium was noted by the Northern Illinois District, which met annually at the college. In its 34th convention on June 26, 1958, the District voted a thankoffering of $875,000 for this purpose in recognition of the college's centennial in 1964, approving a three-year fund-gathering period beginning with

1961. According to President Koehneke, this was the largest gift provided by a District for a synodical college in the history of the Synod.[181]

The location proposed was the southwest corner of the campus at Augusta and Monroe Streets, the site of the president's home. The chief function of the 1500-seat chapel-auditorium would be worship for the student body, faculty, and staff. Besides worship services, it would afford a center for many cultural events and convocations, besides furnishing some additional instructional facilities.[182]

A campaign for $1,000,000 was set up as a two-hour telephone "blitz" to take place March 12, 1961, 2:00—4:00 p. m. Every home in the Northern Illinois District was to be contacted for subscriptions in honor or in memory of someone whose guidance in Christian education was remembered with thanksgiving. The Rev. Victor C. Rickmann of St. Philip's Church, Chicago, was the campaign director. Assisting him as a steering committee were President Koehneke, Dr. Paul L. Kluender, member of the District Board of Directors, and Walter H. Hartkopf, representing the college board of control. Dr. Ernest T. Lams and Dr. Arthur H. Werfelmann, two former District Presidents, and Dr. Theodore F. Nickel, incumbent President of the District, gave support to the campaign.[183] By May 1964 the total raised was $670,500.[184] Plans were being made to continue the effort.

The board of control had started to plan for the purchase of a new president's home in 1958, so that the site of the original president's residence could be used for the proposed chapel.[185] In 1962 a new home was found for the president across Augusta Street at the corner of Clinton Street.[186] The former president's house was converted to offices for faculty until the new chapel construction could begin.

Other Campus Improvements

During the last decade the outdoor athletic facilities were generally improved, especially the running track and tennis courts. Other campus improvements consisted of fencing, a parking lot, landscaping, and improved campus lighting. New offices were built for business services, field services, and instructional division chairmen. Remodeling and refurbishing to keep abreast of the demands of a growing enrollment and staff included seven on-campus student residences, the library, rotunda offices and classroom, student association offices, the remaining faculty homes on campus, and 17 more faculty housing units which were acquired by 1961.[187]

The Search for More Facilities

A survey of the physical plant and space utilization was conducted in 1958 by the architectural firm of Perkins and Will of Chicago, and a separate study of space utilization by the staff of Registrar W. F. Kruse. The surveys showed an above-average degree of efficiency in building use and class assignment. The Perkins and Will study indicated that Concordia uses its space to a higher degree than the more than 80 institutions surveyed.[188] It was further stated that although Concordia's spaces were intensively used, every effort was being devoted to still more efficient space use before new construction was contemplated.[189]

The report went on to show that between 1957–58 and 1961–62 enrollment had grown from 795 to 1,027 full-time students and five additional classrooms and laboratories had been built. Other plans for greater space utilization provided for lengthening the school day, including evening classes, and scheduling Saturday classes.[190]

At the 1959 convention of the Synod, the board of control requested permission to open a junior college branch in the Chicago area to train both future pastors and teachers. The plans provided for the consolidation of administrative services, a core faculty for both schools, and the unification of public relations and business services. The River Forest campus was to be used for the senior college and graduate school, and a new campus would be found for the proposed junior college campus within a reasonable distance.[191]

A special study in 1962 of the Lutheran "hinterland" revealed that within a 100-mile radius there were 8.5 percent of the Synod's congregations, 15 percent of its baptized souls, 15.5 percent of its communicant members, 10.3 percent of its pastors, 20.3 percent of its male teachers, 16.8 percent of its female teachers, 13.7 percent of its elementary schools, 19.6 percent of its elementary enrollment, 12.4 percent of its Sunday school teachers, 11.8 percent of its Sunday school enrollment, 15.3 percent of its junior confirmands, 26.3 percent of its Lutheran high schools, 43.9 percent of its high school students, and 41.4 percent of its Lutheran high school teachers.[192] These statistics indicated that future expansion of a second college campus in that area was well warranted, and college authorities continued to propose the establishment of a second campus. Efforts were made to locate suitable sites within 10 minutes of the existing campus.

The college filed a special report with the Board for Higher Edu-

cation on Nov. 8, 1961, entitled "Outline of Major Building Request
for a Balanced Campus, to the Board for Higher Education, The Lutheran Church — Missouri Synod." The cost for complete maximum
development of the River Forest site for 1,500 students was shown
to be $8,886,430 and for a second campus $36,797,500, of which
$14,500,000 would be needed by Sept. 1, 1968.[193] It was now pro-
posed to use the River Forest campus as a junior college and the new
campus for the senior college and graduate school.

During the 100th academic year the Synod, acting through Concordia's board of control, purchased an 80-acre site at Harlem Avenue
and Cermak Road in North Riverside, Ill.[194] The specific use to which
it would be put was not announced, but this site was one of four
which were analyzed for the college by the Real Estate Research
Corporation in their "Preliminary Report, Locational Criteria for
a Second Campus, Concordia Teachers College, River Forest, Illinois,"
in March 1962.[195]

It was anticipated in 1962–63 that enrollment would increase from
1,082 to 2,725 in 1972–73, partly as a result of the increased enrollments in the junior colleges of the Synod, many of whose graduates
would attend Concordia for the third, fourth, and fifth years of college work.[196] The enrollment of the fifth year would also increase,
since the Synod had decided in 1962 to require that, beginning in
1966, all male teachers should have five years of preparation before
they could be placed permanently.[197] These factors, plus the growing need to increase the number and quality of teachers, presented
the great challenge to continue to provide the needed facilities for
service in the second century.

Student Body Affairs, 1954–64

Student Government. Two important changes were made in the
student government structure. During the 1958–59 school term a student activities board was established to supervise the cocurricular and
extracurricular program with the exception of athletics.[198]

On March 13, 1964, the student body voted to ratify a new constitution which replaced the student activities board with a college
union organization which would assume responsibility for all campus
activities. It would function through a senior board composed of
a chairman, treasurer, faculty director, and chairmen of the service
committees including house, public relations, social, cultural, religious,

personnel, and cocurricular. There was also a junior board composed of chairmen of various subcommittees. The executive board of the student association would now include the president, vice-president, secretary, and treasurer. The chairmen of the men's and women's councils would no longer be included. The senators, who had been elected from the various dormitories and living areas, would be elected by the classes.[199]

Special efforts have been made by the administration and faculty to keep student leaders informed about administrative affairs in special, informal meetings.[200] "Fireside chats" were begun in which professors invited students for an informal social evening to promote better student-faculty relations.[201]

The College Union. In his report of Jan. 8, 1963, Dean of Students Carl Halter stated his belief that the most pressing need for facilities lay in the development of the college union as an instrument to allow students and faculty to meet in curricular, cocurricular, and extracurricular situations. Curricular use would not include classroom instruction but rather facilities in which groups of students from various classes and their professors could meet to discuss and implement classwork.[202]

Concordia students had been concerned about building a new college union since 1957, when the student senate recommended that the students assess themselves $10 each for the third quarter of that year and also $10 for each quarter during the next year for that purpose.[203] The estimated cost of this project, which will include both remodeling and an addition to the present structure, was estimated to be $700,000 in 1962, and at that time $200,000 had been committed for the purpose.[204]

Scholarships

The number of scholarships and grants as well as the amount of money available through them increased greatly since 1954, when Dr. Klotz, chairman of the scholarship committee, announced that $4,250 was to be given out in scholarships at the annual honors convocation on Nov. 10.[205]

By January 1963 Dean Halter reported that $10,875 in scholarships had been awarded by the college in an honors convocation, besides $6,400 in grants, and that the total of scholarships and grants granted to Concordia students from all sources totaled $150,000.[206]

Sports

With the addition of cross-country, the number of interscholastic varsity sports offered at Concordia rose to seven, including football, basketball, baseball, track, tennis, and golf. The college did not belong to an athletic conference but joined the National Collegiate Athletic Association. Competition was carried on with schools having a similar enrollment and athletic program. The athletic program is controlled by the faculty through the student life policies committee. A diversified program of intramural sports is also offered through the physical education department.[207]

Of all sports, basketball brought the highest laurels with the winning of the Concordia Invitational Tournament (CIT) in 1960 and again in 1963. This tournament is conducted each year by the four terminal schools of the Synod, including the two Concordia Seminaries for pastors at Springfield, Ill., and St. Louis, Mo., and the two Concordia Teachers Colleges at River Forest, Ill., and Seward, Nebr.

At the close of the tournament in 1963, the Concordia Cougars accepted an invitation to play in the Great Lakes Regional College Division National Collegiate Athletic Association (NCAA) tournament in St. Louis, where they finished in third place. The Cougars, one of 21 teams chosen from among all colleges for the tournament, were the first of the synodical colleges to be invited.[208]

Student Activities

Concordia Teachers College has made a distinction between extracurricular and cocurricular activities. The former includes primarily student government activities which coordinate the various programs related to student life, such as Student Senate, Men's Council, Women's Council, Student Activities Board, Ambassadors for Christ, College Union, Cultural Activities Committee, Publicity, Social Activities, Religious Activities Committee (including subcommittees on education and information, worship, and fieldwork), *The Pillars* (annual), *The Spectator* (student newspaper), and Married Couples Club.[209]

The cocurricular program is actually an extension of classroom teaching, having its budget set through the curricular division to which it is related. Its purpose is to give students the opportunity of handling creatively the subject matter which interests them most. The following groups are included: Concordia Players, Human Relations Club, International Relations Club, Science Research Organization,

Student Teachers Activities Group, Women's Athletic Association, Youth Leadership Training Group, Art Activities Group, Speech Club, German Club, French Club, "C" Club, College Chorus, Senior College Choir, Junior College Choir, Chorale Choir, Treble Choir, Band, String Group, and other small musical groups.[210] All groups, cocurricular and extracurricular, have faculty advisors or leaders.

Students Serve. In his 1963 report Dean Halter stated: "Concordia students are deeply religious, as is evidenced by the tremendous growth of religious activity experienced in the last six or seven years." [211]

The activities mentioned gave Concordians opportunity to serve in various ways. In 1958 students began to give assistance in Sunday school instruction and music at Ebenezer Church, which is in a large, low-class Negro community on the west side of Chicago.[212] "Send Forth Laborers," a division of the religious activities committee, worked on a series of service projects which included supporting a seminary student who vicared three months at the Chicago Medical Center, and supporting inner-city mission work at First Immanuel by paying the salaries of two youth workers.[213]

Through a "mission emphasis week" the students were given information on various types of mission work. In order to assist the church in recruiting young people to enter full-time church professions, "Ambassadors for Christ," a new campus club, was chartered by the student senate in 1962. The members planned to speak to groups and individuals about church vocations. They hoped to cooperate with similar committees in other synodical schools.[214] Under the sponsorship of the religious activities committee, Concordia students assisted at the Hines Veterans Hospital twice a month by pushing wheelchair patients to midweek worship services and on alternate weeks to see movies. Concordia choirs gave special service in the worship services. The American National Red Cross awarded a citation of merit to Concordia students for their help.

Enrollment and Admissions

During the last decade the enrollment increased from 665 (1954 to 1955) to 1,109 (1963–64), while student costs in the same period increased from $545 for men and $595 for women to $995 for both men and women.[215] Charging higher fees for women stopped in 1958–59, when the fee schedule was changed from annual to quarterly charges.

Other costs included an initial enrollment fee of $50 and a synodical church work deposit of $120 charged at the initial enrollment which is refunded on graduation. The $120 was a sort of token guarantee that the student would complete the program of studies and enter a church profession. Since the Synod heavily subsidized the college's operating costs (nearly 46 percent in 1960–61), it virtually gave a subsidy of $739 in 1960–61 to each student.[216]

The caliber of students admitted to the college has been consistently high. A profile of the freshman class in 1961–62 showed that 84.3 percent of them ranked in the upper two quintiles of their high school class. However, 509 qualified applicants were denied admission between 1958 and 1962, because of the enrollment pressures and lack of facilities.[217]

Since 1960 students have been able to apply for admission at four different times a year, at the beginning of each regular quarter and in the summer quarter. A special four-year study on admissions counseling research was begun in 1962. Dr. James O. Roberts, admissions officer, and a team of faculty members interviewed new students admitted for the following school year in order to gather data on personality and general attitude toward the teaching ministry. Interviews were scheduled near the student's home. It was hoped that this study would give information that would aid the college in making more accurate predictions concerning the probable success of the students.[218]

Campus Living

Housing. By the centennial year the college was able to provide 815 spaces for housing students on the campus. Facilities included six dormitories and seven converted faculty homes. The sophomore class was housed off campus in various homes up to 4 miles from the college and brought to the campus by college vehicles each morning and evening. In 1962–63, 206 students were so housed.

In the summer of 1957 President Koehneke wrote to the pastors of congregations in the vicinity of the college asking assistance in the critical housing shortage created by the increasing demand for more teachers. Members of various congregations responded by renting rooms to the college.[219] Thus the program of housing students off campus began in September 1957 with 53 students in 25 homes, including seven homes for 14 men and 18 for 39 women. These were within 3 miles of the college, the maximum distance originally agreed on. Station wagons were secured for student transportation.[220]

At the college special facilities such as individual lockers, bookshelves, showers, study rooms, and recreation areas were provided for off-campus students.[221]

On the campus the dormitories were under the direction of residence counselors, who were responsible to the dean of men and the dean of women. In September 1960 housemothers were used as counselors in men's dormitories for the first time when Mrs. Leonora Schoepke and Mrs. Clara Pankow were secured for this position.[222] A floor council in each dormitory was responsible for the religious, social, and athletic program for students on each floor.

Personal Counseling. The fact that many Concordia faculty members have been experienced pastors and teachers has been to the benefit of the students, who very frequently choose their own counselors. Since the faculty members have been concerned for the total welfare of the individual student and since all are available for counseling, the personal counseling program has been regarded as superior in quality. The dean of students and the residence counselors have also been available for counseling.[223] Daily chapel devotions set up under a precisely planned program gave constant opportunity for all students to exercise their own faith.

Health Services. The college operated an infirmary of 16 beds, employing the services of a part-time doctor, two full-time nurses, a nurse's aide, and student assistants. Psychiatric examinations were available to students on referral by the dean of students. In his report of January 1963 Dean Halter called attention to the great need for renovation and for equipment for examination, consultation, and treatment of patients.[224]

Placement

The placement of Concordia graduates is carried out according to a method prescribed by The Lutheran Church — Missouri Synod for all its terminal schools. The College of (District) Presidents, acting as the Board of Assignments, meets at the synodical headquarters in St. Louis and determines where the graduates will be placed. These meetings are held three times a year, in April or May, July, and December. Information about each graduate is supplied to them by the college placement officer, who approves and authorizes all initial placements.[225] After all the calls have been assigned, they are taken back to the college and distributed to the graduates in a special "call night" service of consecration and dedication, in which graduates hear of their appointment for the first time. The whole student body and faculty join the graduating class in the devotional service.

In the spring placement of 1963, 600 men and women were placed as Lutheran teachers, of which River Forest supplied 345, or 57.5 percent of the total. Since the Synod needed 847 teachers, 247 calls could not be filled with graduates, so some were filled temporarily with supply students.[226]

Dr. Waldemar W. Affeldt, director of placement, observed in 1963 that although the number of graduates was increasing each year, the number of teachers needed was increasing even more, so that the percentage of supply as compared with demand was actually decreasing. In 1962, 73 percent of the requests were filled, but in 1963 only 63 percent could be supplied. He noted a continuing heavy demand for women teachers, attesting to a short initial tenure of many of them, largely because of marriage. He also noted that many of them in later life came back to help in the shortage.[227]

A study had been made of the service records of woman graduates between 1941 and 1956 by Dr. Maurer, Concordia's first placement director. He received a return of 83.3 percent from the 534 graduates to whom questionnaires were sent. He found that 28 percent had taught continuously since graduation. The first-class graduates had served an average of 6.82 years as teachers. Married teachers continued to be active as leaders in parishes and in their communities in many activities such as Sunday school, music, and youth work. Often married teachers returned to teaching after their families were of school age.[228]

A new orientation program for placement was introduced in 1962 to 1963 in which small groups of about 20 students met in the home of the placement director to discuss placement procedures. These meetings were followed up by personal interviews with each individual. Data from these interviews, plus the evaluations of counselors and faculty members, gave helpful data for the optimum in placement.[229] Dr. Affeldt's report revealed a growing demand for teachers in foreign fields (10 percent of the male graduates had been placed in them in a recent year) and also for school-teachers, graduates with a master's degree, church musicians, youth leaders, and directors of religion and education. The great benefit of the internship program for principalship candidates and for personnel needed to start schools was emphasized.[230]

College Services to Its Communities

Town and Gown. As noted earlier, Concordia Teachers College has been conscious of its geographical community as well as that of the church. Its facilities and personnel have been in service on numerous occasions to help both. In August 1954 the board of control granted permission for Walther Lutheran High School to use classrooms at the college because their new building in Melrose Park could not be finished in time for school opening in September.[231] They were able to use it without cost till Nov. 5.[232]

Active interest in community affairs has increased considerably in the last 10 years. In December 1954 the board of control voted to have the president and business manager become members of the Oak Park Rotary Club.[233] A civic dinner was held Dec. 1, 1960, for the service clubs of River Forest and Oak Park, including members of the Rotary, Lions, Optimists, Exchange, Sertoma, and Kiwanis clubs and their wives. They were entertained by the musical organizations, and information of the activities and plans of the college were presented.[234] This dinner became a traditional Christmas offering of the college to these civic organizations and their leaders.

In a special feature on Concordia Teachers College a local newspaper, the *Oak Leaves,* noted that Concordia students and faculty members participated in various civic projects, stating that it was not uncommon to see 40 or 50 men and a few professors giving a hand in such things as community chest drives. The entire student body was considered a valuable asset to the community.[235]

President Koehneke announced that on March 26, 1956, the village board of River Forest had authorized the college to make a land-use survey to assist the board in revising a 1931 zoning code, allocating $2,500 for this purpose. Dr. Gross, the appointed director, expressed the feeling that mutual relations between the college and the community would be strengthened by the project, which was to be completed by December.[236]

"MPATI." In January 1963 the college announced it had become a charter member of the Midwest Program on Airborne Television Instruction (MPATI). This was an experiment in which an aircraft flying 5 miles above the earth telecast 23 different courses for elementary, secondary, and college students on two channels. The program covered the six states of Illinois, Indiana, Kentucky, Michigan, Ohio, and Wisconsin, an area of 144,000 square miles including seven million students in 15,000 schools, among them 513 Lutheran elementary schools with 80,220 pupils taught by 2,852 teachers. Concordia's representative to MPATI was Prof. Martin J. Neeb, Jr., director of field services.[237]

Guidance Center

In February 1956 the faculty adopted a recommendation to establish a child and youth guidance center on the campus. Drs. Schmieding and Krause had been informally assisting children and youth with educational or social problems before this time. Concordia students would thus have the opportunity to observe and practice psychometric technique and counseling.[238]

Promotional Activities

In April 1956 the first issue of *The Forester*, a new college publication, appeared. Its purpose was to give information about college activities and plans to alumni, pastors, and teachers of the Synod.[239]

In 1955 the college began to grant honorary doctorates to distinguished leaders in Christian education. The first recipients were two alumni, John A. Klein, superintendent of the Lutheran School for the Deaf, Detroit, and William A. Kramer, Secretary of Schools of The Lutheran Church — Missouri Synod. In 1956 honorary degrees were also awarded to Albert H. Miller and Ferdinand H. Schmitt, professors emeriti of Concordia, and to Walter P. Wismar, veteran Lutheran teacher in Holy Cross Congregation, St. Louis. All were alumni of the college.[240]

Two anniversaries were observed besides the centennial activities. On Nov. 13, 1957, a special convocation in the gymnasium was designated as "100 Years of Teacher Training." This was the century mark for teacher education by the Synod, begun in 1857 in Fort Wayne. The program was developed by Dr. Theodore J. C. Kuehnert, professor emeritus of education and social studies.[241] The 50th anniversary of the establishment of the college in River Forest was observed in a special convocation on Oct. 11, 1963, when the author addressed the students, faculty, and alumni. Groundbreaking for the new gymnasium and swimming pool and an addition to the music building also marked this occasion.[242]

Closing a Century

As the centennial year, 1964, approached, a number of special activities were planned to carry out five major aims:

(1) To thank God for a century of blessings to and through the college and to stimulate this spirit of thanksgiving in the campus community and the entire Synod.

(2) To translate our thanksgiving into acts of service by the faculty and students, to the Synod and to the civic and academic communities.

(3) To provide a special measure of spiritual and intellectual environment through special convocations and cultural events, supplementing the on-going instructional program of the college.

(4) To give vigorous emphasis to the cause of Christian education in the Synod, with special emphasis on Lutheran elementary and secondary education.

(5) To contribute to the literature of the church and to the program of teacher education in the Synod and the nation.[243]

The faculty centennial committee included Carl L. Waldschmidt, chairman, Frank B. Miller, executive director, Ralph L. Reinke, Daniel E. Poellot, Arvin W. Hahn, William H. Lehmann, Jr., Martin J. Neeb, Jr., Paul G. Grotelueschen, Theodore J. C. Kuehnert, and President Martin L. Koehneke.

President Koehneke set the general theme of the entire year in his message to friends and supporters of the college:

When a college celebrates its centennial, it is tempted to glorify the past without capturing the true glory of the past, the exciting opportunities of the present, or the necessary dreams of the future.

Concordia has chosen to use its centennial observance as its way of saying "thank you" to its many friends and staunch supporters, and most particularly to The Lutheran Church — Missouri Synod, the sponsoring body of the college's program for 100 years.

It wants to express its thanks by a higher commitment to its single task of Christian education, and by acts of service performed in behalf of the academic, civic and ecclesiastical community.

The Centennial Year 1964 will find the college, therefore, sincere in its quest of the objectives it has set for itself as a college, and as a college celebrating a century of grace. The underlying motif is thanksgiving. The pervading spirit will be thanks-living.[244]

The various activities and special observances of the centennial programs are listed in the appendices of this book. During the year all publications were to display a special seal which was designed for the centennial by Prof. Roy V. Schoenborn. It consists of a triangular shield symbolizing the eternal truths of the Trinity, valid for all times, past, present, and future. It features the college monogram, "CTC," and a cross over water, the latter to symbolize both the diffusion of Christian knowledge to the world by Concordia's teachers and the efficacy of the Lutheran Church.[245]

The college student body, besides participating in the religious, academic, and cultural events of the centennial year, also decided to present a gift of appreciation for a century of blessings. They voted to provide a "Concordia Chapel" in a foreign mission field in the Philippines, Korea, India, or Formosa, the exact area to be chosen later.[246] Students also took part in the production of a movie entitled *College with a Cause*, planned as a special documentary recruitment film aimed at high school students and their parents. It depicts campus life in sound and color through the voices and actions of students and faculty. The centennial film committee which supervised this production included Prof. Martin Neeb, Jr., as chairman and Professors Thomas Gieschen, Paul Grotelueschen, Arvin Hahn, Henry Lettermann, and Henry Latzke.[247] It was planned to show this movie at all District conventions and also at recruitment conferences, rallies, and individual congregations in the Synod.

The awarding of diplomas to 253 seniors at the close of the 100th academic year in June 1964 brought the total number of graduates of Addison and River Forest to 5,485 since 1864. It is significant that 1,888, or slightly more than 32 percent, graduated in the last decade.

Although the supply had been growing, it was still far short of the demand for teachers. In 1962 the college reported that less than 50 percent of the demand for teachers for the churches of The Lutheran Church — Missouri Synod were being supplied by the Synod's system of higher education. Total expansion was greatly needed, and plans were drawn which provided for expansion of teacher education at the 10 existing junior colleges and at also four additional ones to be established in the future. This implied, however, that the terminal teachers colleges at Seward and River Forest would also have to expand to accommodate the graduates of these schools.[248]

In a special 20-year projection report to the Board for Higher Education in 1962, *The Role and Function of Concordia Teachers College, River Forest, Illinois, in the Synodical System of Colleges and Seminaries, 1962–1982*, Dr. Koehneke presented a plan which included the establishment of a second campus to serve a combined enrollment of

4,500. The plan called for an enrollment of 1,500 junior college students on the existing campus and for 3,000 in a senior college and graduate school which he called the "professional school."

The junior college, the president felt, should provide ministerial training to both future pastors and teachers. The idea of integrating the training of future pastors and teachers had been growing almost imperceptibly in the Synod as teacher training was gradually begun in some of the pastoral preparatory schools. In the Fort Wayne days (1857–64) the two programs had been integrated, but when Addison was founded, it was decided to separate them. The proposal to re-unite both at River Forest again on the junior college level was an interesting development, and, through its integration of the pastoral and teaching ministries, one which was designed to benefit the general ministry of the church.

At the close of the first century President Koehneke called attention to one of the most pressing problems facing the church's system of higher education — the great lack of long-range planning for the future in plant expansion, enrollment, and the enlistment of the faculty to assist in meeting the needs of the Synod.[249]

The Role of a College Facing a New Century

Addressing himself to the role of Christian higher education in the church, Dr. Koehneke stated that the college should not be merely a reflector of the *status quo* in the church, but that faculty and student body should be free, collectively and individually, to pursue the truth. In an interview with Carl N. Poole he said: "The college should be a friendly, loving critic on the contemporary church scene . . . on the cutting edge without cutting persons."[250]

Summary

During Dr. Martin Koehneke's administration Concordia Teachers College experienced a period of expansion unparalleled in its history and engaged in a dynamic search for self-improvement to better serve the church and nation. The curriculum was completely revised, and the instructional departments were reorganized into six divisions in order to develop a broader concept of curriculum. Summer school and correspondence offerings were increased as the curriculum was expanded to include both secondary teacher education and a 5th-year program leading to a master's degree (mandatory for all students beginning in 1966). An international study program was introduced by President Koehneke to discover new ways in which the college can serve the church in its program of missions.

The graduate program was accredited by the North Central Association of Colleges and Secondary Schools in 1962, and the elementary curriculum received accreditation by the National Council for the Accreditation of Teacher Education in 1963.

The college plant underwent an extensive building program which included a new science building, a new men's dormitory, a central service and heating plant, and offices. Ground was broken for a new gymnasium and a fine arts building during the 100th academic year. The Northern Illinois District resolved to give a new chapel to the college as a centennial gift. Extensive remodeling of the older college buildings and many other improvements to campus facilities were achieved during this last decade of the first century.

Improvements in the organization of administration were introduced for greater efficiency in service as the unit plan of administration was more clearly defined and completed. Faculty benefits during this period included expanded sabbatical-leave and study-grant programs, Ford Foundation grants for salary improvement, and the establishment of an endowment for the enrichment of instruction.

At the close of the century the college faced a serious space problem. The proposal was made to establish a second campus of the school, maintaining a junior college division on the present location and a senior college and graduate school on a new site.

The calendar year 1964 was designated as a year of thanksgiving and praise to God. The activities of the centennial on the campus were designed to stimulate faculty and student body to a deeper commitment to service in the church and community.

Under the dynamic leadership of President Koehneke, Concordia Teachers College completed its first century as an institution dedicated to exploring more avenues of service to its single purpose — providing for the teaching ministry of the church. Plans were being developed to meet the challenges of the second century in a spirit of an exciting adventure for Christ.

Notes

1. Program — The Installation of the Rev. Martin L. Koehneke at the Opening of the Ninety-First Academic Year, Sept. 17, 1954.
2. Ibid.
3. Carl N. Poole, "Men on a Mission: Dr. Martin L. Koehneke, President, Concordia Teachers College; Pursuer of the Truth," *Correspondent*, Bulletin of the Aid Association for Lutherans, Appleton, Wisconsin, Winter 1963, pp. 2 to 6.
4. *The Forester*, a quarterly bulletin of Concordia Teachers College, River Forest, Illinois, April 1956, p. 1. A quotation by Dr. Martin L. Koehneke.
5. Alfred F. Schmieding, *Fifth Annual Report of the Academic Dean, 1952— 1953.* July 1953, p. 19.
6. Minutes, Board of Control of Concordia Teachers College, Jan. 4, 1955.
7. *The Spectator*, River Forest student paper, XXX (Jan. 14, 1955), 1.
8. Minutes, Board of Control, Jan. 4, 1955.
9. Minutes, Board of Control, Oct. 6, 1953.
10. Ibid.
11. *The Spectator*, XXX (Feb. 18, 1955), 1.
12. Albert H. Huegli, *Six Year Report of the Academic Dean*, 1955—61, p. 12.
13. *Proceedings*, 1950, p. 195.
14. Minutes, Faculty, Feb. 11, 1952.
15. Minutes, Board of Control, Feb. 3, 1953.
16. *Proceedings*, 1953, p. 146.
17. *Self-Survey of Concordia Teachers College, River Forest, Illinois*, Jan. 25, 1958, p. 14. Prof. Neelak S. Tjernagel was the director of this survey, which was prepared for the North Central Association of Colleges and Secondary Schools.
18. Ibid., p. 14.
19. Minutes, Faculty, May 23, 1955.
20. *Self-Survey*, 1958, pp. 16, 17.
21. Ibid., p. 46.
22. *Proceedings*, 1956, p. 60.
23. Ibid., pp. 230—233.
24. Ibid., pp. 204, 205.
25. *Self-Survey*, 1958, p. 23.
26. Minutes, Faculty, Sept. 24, 1956.
27. *The Forester*, I (Oct. 1956), 2.
28. Ibid., p. 4.
29. *Self-Survey*, 1958, p. 26.
30. Huegli, *Report*, p. 13.
31. *Self-Survey*, 1958, Preface, p. ii.
32. Ibid, p. 24.
33. Ibid., p. 34.
34. *The Forester*, II (Sept. 1957), 1.

35. Ibid., II (Dec. 1957), 1.
36. Ibid., II (April 1958), 1.
37. Huegli, *Report*, p. 3.
38. *The Forester*, IV (Sept. 1959), 1.
39. Huegli, *Report*, p. 13.
40. Minutes, Board of Control, July 1, 1958.
41. *The Forester*, IV (Dec. 1959), 1.
42. Huegli, *Report*, p. 13.
43. *The Spectator*, XXXVII (Oct. 6, 1961), 1.
44. Ibid., XXXVII (April 1, 1962), 1.
45. *The Forester*, VI (May 1962), 4.
46. Huegli, *Report*, p. 14.
47. Concordia Teachers College Catalog, 1957—58, p. 51.
48. Minutes, Board of Control, April 2, 1957.
49. C. T. C. Catalog, 1957—58, p. 51.
50. Huegli, *Report*, p. 10.
51. *The Forester*, III (Nov. 1958), 1.
52. Huegli, *Report*, p. 10.
53. *The Forester*, V (Sept. 1960), 4.
54. *Report of Concordia Teachers College, River Forest, Illinois, to National Council for Accreditation of Teacher Education*, 1962 (NCATE), p. 85.
55. Minutes, Board of Control, April 7, 1959.
56. *Report of C. T. C. for NCATE*, p. 85.
57. Ibid.
58. *The Spectator*, XXXIX (Feb. 21, 1964), 3.
59. Huegli, *Report*, p. 11.
60. Minutes, Faculty, Dec. 8, 1958.
61. C. T. C. Catalog, 1963—64, p. 23.
62. *Report of C. T. C. to NCATE*, pp. 6, 7.
63. Ibid., p. 7.
64. Ibid.
65. Huegli, *Report*, p. 11.
66. Ibid., p. 12.
67. Ibid., p. 15.
68. M. L. Koehneke, "Blueprint for the Sixties," 1961, p. 7. (A mimeographed report.)
69. Huegli, *Report*, pp. 15, 16.
70. Minutes, Board of Control, July 16, 1956.
71. *The Spectator*, XXXIX (Feb. 7, 1964), 1.
72. Minutes, Board of Control, Jan. 17, 1956.
73. *The Spectator*, XXXI (March 2, 1956), 1.
74. Minutes, Board of Control, Sept. 9, 1958.
75. *The Forester*, VII (July 1963), 1.

76. *The Spectator,* XXXIX (Oct. 19, 1963), 2.

77. *The Forester,* VII (Oct. 1962), 5.

78. *The Spectator,* XXXIX (Sept. 20, 1963), 2.

79. *The Forester,* VII (July 1963), 1.

80. Letter of Rolf W. Larson, Acting Director, National Association for Accreditation of Teacher Education, to President Martin L. Koehneke, Aug. 24, 1964.

81. Minutes, Board of Control, Jan. 3, 1963.

82. Ralph L. Reinke, "Concordia Student Teaching Program — Its Past, Present, and Future" (a mimeographed report, Feb. 1963), p. 5.

83. Ibid.

84. *The Forester,* VIII (May 1964), 3.

85. Reinke, *Report,* p. 8.

86. Ibid., p. 14.

87. Ibid., p. 16.

88. Ibid., pp. 20, 21.

89. Ibid., p. 22.

90. Ibid., pp. 22, 23.

91. Ibid., p. 27.

92. C. T. C. Catalog, 1955—56, p. 39.

93. *The Forester,* VI (May 1962), 3.

94. Ibid., III (Nov. 1958), 3.

95. Ibid., VI (May 1962), 2.

96. Ibid., V (Dec. 1960), 3.

97. *The Spectator,* XXXIX (May 22, 1964), 2.

98. Minutes, Board of Control, May 21, 1957.

99. *The Forester,* III (April 1959), 5.

100. Ibid., IV (April 1960), 3.

101. Ibid., VI (Dec. 1961), 3.

102. Ibid., VII (Jan. 1963), 1.

103. Ibid., VII (July 1963), 6. Professor Rohlfing is the son of Prof. Richard T. Rohlfing, who organized and directed Concordia's first touring concert band in the 1930s.

104. *The Forester,* VIII (Aug. 1963), 4.

105. C. T. C. Catalog, 1964—65, pp. 105—115.

106. Huegli, *Report,* p. 3.

107. Ibid.

108. Ibid., p. 2.

109. Ibid., p. 4.

110. Minutes, Board of Control, Sept. 11, 1956.

111. *The Forester,* I (Oct. 1956), 2.

112. Minutes, Board of Control, April 2, 1957.

113. Huegli, *Report,* p. 5.

114. Ibid., p. 6.

115. Minutes, Board of Control, July 10, 1956.

116. M. L. Koehneke, "Blueprint for the Sixties," 1961, p. 5. (A mimeographed report.)
117. *The Forester,* V (April 1961), 3.
118. Ibid.
119. Ibid., VII (April 1963), 2.
120. Huegli, *Report,* p. 5.
121. Ibid., p. 7.
122. *The Forester,* VI (May 1962), 5.
123. Ibid.
124. Huegli, *Report,* p. 8.
125. M. L. Koehneke, "Blue Print for the Sixties," 1961, p. 12.
126. *The Forester,* VII (Jan. 1963), 3.
127. Arvin W. Hahn and Kenneth W. Schueler, "International Studies Program: Africa." Preface. (A mimeographed report.)
128. Ibid., pp. 47—51.
129. *The Forester,* VII (Jan. 1963), 3.
130. Huegli, *Report,* p. 8.
131. Ibid., p. 9.
132. Ibid.
133. *The Spectator,* XXXVIII (Oct. 12, 1962), 3.
134. Ibid., XXXIX (Nov. 22, 1963), 3.
135. *The Forester,* V (Dec. 1960), 2.
136. *The Spectator,* XXX (Feb. 18, 1955), 1.
137. *The Forester,* III (July 1959), 2.
138. Minutes, Board of Control, Jan. 18, 1960. ·
139. *The Spectator,* XXXVIII (Nov. 12, 1962), 3.
140. Ibid., XXXVIII (May 3, 1963), 1.
141. *The Forester,* VIII (May 1964), 4.
142. Ibid.
143. Ibid., III (July 1959), 3.
144. Ibid., IV (Sept. 1959), 3.
145. Ibid.
146. Ibid., IV (July 1960), 3.
147. Ibid., V (April 1961), 3.
148. Ibid., VI (July 1962), 4.
149. Ibid., VII (Jan. 1963), 6.
150. Ibid., VII (July 1963), 4.
151. Ibid., III (July 1959), 2.
152. Ibid., IV (July 1960), 2.
153. Ibid., II (Sept. 1957), 3.
154. Ibid., VI (Oct. 1961), 3.
155. *The Spectator,* XXXVIII (Feb. 8, 1963), 1.
156. Ibid., XXXVI (April 14, 1961), 1.

157. Minutes, Board of Control, July 1, 1958.

158. Huegli, *Report*, p. 16.

159. *The Spectator*, XXXIII (March 28, 1958), 1.

160. *Self-Survey*, 1958, pp. 57, 58.

161. Minutes, Board of Control, July 5, 1955.

162. Minutes, Board of Control, Sept. 6, 1955.

163. *The Spectator*, XXIX (March 19, 1954), 1.

164. *The Forester*, I (Oct. 1956), 1.

165. *The Spectator*, XXXII (Oct. 12, 1956), 1.

166. Ibid., XXXIII (Feb. 28, 1958), 1.

167. Minutes, Board of Control, Nov. 6, 1956.

168. Ibid.

169. *The Spectator*, XXX (Oct. 1, 1954), 1.

170. Minutes, Board of Control, March 22, 1956.

171. *The Forester*, III (Nov. 1958), 1.

172. Ibid., III (April 1959), 1.

173. Minutes, Board of Control, Sept. 15, 1959.

174. Minutes, Board of Control, June 7, 1960.

175. *The Forester*, V (Dec. 1960), 1.

176. Ibid.

177. Minutes, Board of Control, June 7, 1960.

178. *The Forester*, V (April 1961), 3.

179. *The Spectator*, XXXIX (Oct. 11, 1963), 1.

180. Ibid., XXXIX (Jan. 17, 1964), 1.

181. *The Forester*, II (July 8, 1958), 1.

182. Ibid.

183. Ibid., V (Dec. 1960), 2.

184. *The Spectator*, XXXIX (May 22, 1964), 1.

185. Minutes, Board of Control, Nov. 18, 1958.

186. *The Spectator*, XXXVIII (Sept. 22, 1962), 3.

187. M. L. Koehneke, "Blueprint for the Sixties," p. 10.

188. Application of Concordia Teachers College, River Forest, Illinois, for Hines Surplus Property, April 2, 1962, p. C-78.

189. *The Forester*, III (Nov. 1958), 3.

190. Hines Application, p. C-79.

191. *The Forester*, III (April 1959), 3.

192. Ibid., VI (May 1962), 2.

193. Hines Application, p. C-75.

194. *The Spectator*, XXXIX (May 22, 1964), 1.

195. Hines Application, p. C-63.

196. Ibid., p. C-51.

197. *NCATE Report*, p. 83.

198. Carl H. Halter, Dean of Students, "Student Personnel Services at Concordia

Teachers College, River Forest, Illinois," Jan. 8, 1963, p. 4. A mimeographed report.

199. *The Spectator,* XXXIX (March 20, 1964), 1.

200. Ibid., XXXIV (April 17, 1959), 1.

201. Ibid., XXXVI (Feb. 17, 1961), 1.

202. Halter, *Report,* p. 19.

203. *The Spectator,* XXXII (Feb. 22, 1957), 1.

204. "College with a Cause," undated brochure published in 1962. (Pages not numbered.)

205. *The Spectator,* XXX (Oct. 15, 1954), 4.

206. *The Forester,* VII (Jan. 1963), 1.

207. Ibid., VII (April 1963), 4.

208. Halter, *Report,* pp. 9, 10.

209. Ibid., p. 8.

210. Ibid.

211. Ibid., pp. 22, 23.

212. *The Spectator,* XXXIV (Nov. 21, 1958), 2.

213. Ibid., XXXIX (Dec. 19, 1963), 3.

214. Ibid., XXXVIII (Sept. 11, 1962), 1.

215. Ibid., XXXIX (March 20, 1964), 3.

216. *NCATE Report,* p. C-86.

217. Hines Application, p. C-73.

218. *The Forester,* VII (July 1963), 3.

219. *The Spectator,* XXXVIII (Oct. 6, 1962), 3.

220. Minutes, Board of Control, Sept. 17, 1957.

221. *The Spectator,* XXXVIII (Oct. 6, 1962), 3.

222. Ibid., XXVI (Sept. 30, 1960), 2.

223. Halter, *Report,* p. 6.

224. Ibid., p. 19.

225. C. T. C. Bulletin, 1964—65, pp. 13, 14.

226. Waldemar W. Affeldt, Director of Placement, Annual Report on Teacher Placement, 1962—1963." (Pages not numbered.)

227. Ibid.

228. Albert V. Maurer, "Women Teachers in the Church." An institutional study of the women graduates of Concordia Teachers College. Sept. 1957, pp. 39 to 46.

229. Ibid.

230. Ibid.

231. Minutes, Board of Control, Aug. 9, 1954.

232. Minutes, Board of Control, Dec. 7, 1954.

233. Ibid.

234. *The Spectator,* XXXVI (Nov. 18, 1960), 1.

235. *Oak Leaves,* Oak Park, Feb. 26, 1959, pp. 22, 23.

236. Minutes, Board of Control, March 22, 1956.

237. *The Forester*, VII (Jan. 1963), 3.

238. Ibid., I (April 1956), 3.

239. Ibid.

240. Ibid. (July 1956), 1.

241. Ibid., II (Dec. 1957), 1.

242. *The Spectator*, XXXIX (Oct. 11, 1963), 1.

243. *The Forester*, VIII (May 1964), 2.

244. M. L. Koehneke, "Message of the President," p. 2. Centennial brochure.

245. *The Spectator*, XXXIX (Jan. 17, 1964), 1.

246. Ibid., XXXIX (May 22, 1964), 1.

247. Ibid., XXXIX (Oct. 11, 1963), 1.

248. Hines Application, p. C-83.

249. Carl N. Poole, p. 5.

250. Ibid., p. 3.

Pictures

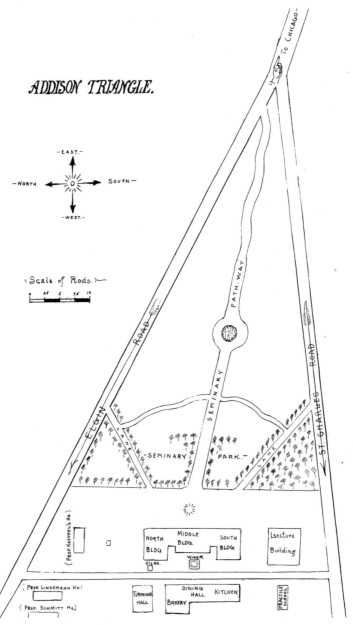

Map of "Triangle" campus at Addison, Ill. (about 1907). Concordia Teachers College was founded here in 1864, remaining until the move to River Forest, Ill., in 1913

Main building on the Addison campus, the center section
and north wing (right) erected in 1864, the south wing in 1873

The lecture hall at Addison, built in 1885, referred to as the
Neubau (new building); part of the main building shows at the left

Part of the Addison faculty in 1893: seated (from left): Eugen A. W. Krauss, Theodore Brohm, C. August T. Selle; standing: Ernst Homann, Friedrich Rechlin, Johann L. Backhaus

Rear view of main building at Addison (taken in late 1910s or early 1920s)

Dining hall at Addison about the turn of the century

Student campus cleanup crew at Addison, 1910 or later

Annual field day at Addison, 1911

Addison seminary band, 1890

Arthur E. Diesing, Martin J. Roschke, and Martin A. Krueger, with their 1912 diplomas in their luggage, bid farewell to Addison and to their close friends M. C. Thieme and Karl F. Roemer, who will not graduate till 1914

Dr. Theo. J. C. Kuehnert (1903 graduate) at the Addison Alumni Memorial, holding the cornerstone box given to the college for its centennial by the Village of Addison

*Part of the crowd of 45,000 who attended the dedication service of
Concordia Teachers College, River Forest, Ill., Oct. 12, 1913*

1921

Aerial views of River Forest campus

1964

Views of administration building after the fire of Feb. 28, 1914

Side and Rear View of Main Building of River Forest College after the fire

The present administration building at River Forest,
rebuilt after the fire, dedicated on Oct. 17, 1914

Concordia Library, dedicated May 29, 1949,
renamed Klinck Memorial Library in 1959

The music building at River Forest

Krauss Hall, a men's dormitory

The gymnasium

Mary-Martha Hall, a women's dormitory

Grace Lutheran Church and School, the campus church and training school

*Concordia's first graduate council (l. to r.): Dr. Walter O. Kraeft,
Dr. Albert G. Huegli, Dr. John W. Klotz, Dr. Martin L. Koehneke,
Dr. Herbert H. Gross, Dr. Wilfred F. Kruse*

*A "Call Night" tradition:
graduates pin location of their calls on a map*

Bibliography

PRIMARY SOURCES

Annuals

1962 Statistical Yearbook of The Lutheran Church — Missouri Synod. St. Louis: Concordia Publishing House, 1963.

The Blue and Gold. Class annual of the Addison Class of 1912.

Autobiographies, Letters, Reminiscences

Beck, Albert H. Unpublished autobiography and memoirs, August 1962.

Bewie, William H. Treatise of his life in Addison, Ill., in 1879. Undated.

Bruening, Herbert D. Reminiscences to author, April 25, 1964.

Fechtmann, Daniel. Letter to 50th-anniversary committee, Concordia Teachers College, May 1, 1914.

Gross, Arthur W. "Reminiscences of River Forest Student Days," 1964.

————. Letter to author, April 27, 1964.

Helmkamp, William A. "Reminiscences from the Middle of Concordia's (River Forest) Century," Oct. 27, 1962.

Kastner, J. Postal card to Paul Sauer, May 17, 1911.

Kohn, William C. Postal card to Paul Sauer, Feb. 11, 1911.

Kuehnert, Theodore J. C. Reminiscences to author, Dec. 3, 1963.

Luecke, Martin. Letter to Paul Sauer, May 6, 1911.

————. Postal card to Paul Sauer, April 22, 1911.

Markworth, Karl A. Autobiography in "Fifty-fifth Anniversary Reunion of the Addison Seminary Class of 1901," 1956.

Maurer, Albert V. Reminiscences to author, April 30, 1964.

Miller, Frank B. Letter to author, Feb. 19, 1964.

Pingel, Erwin T. Reminiscences to author, April 25, 1964.

River Forest Faculty. Letter to Rev. Henry H. Grueber, April 24, 1934.

Roschke, Alwin R. Letter to Martin L. Koehneke, Sept. 4, 1962.

Rosenwinkel, Adolph C. "Notes and Reminiscences on the Addison Teachers Seminary, 1908—1913," Oct. 31, 1962.

Schmidt, Jacob. Letter to author, March 9, 1962.

Schmitt, Ferdinand H. Autobiography in "Fifty-fifth Anniversary Reunion of Addison Seminary Class of 1901," 1956.

Sebald, John G. Letter to Albert Miller, March 14, 1932.

Steinweg, Henry H. Reminiscences to author, April 26, 1964.

Stellhorn, August C. "Recollections of Addison," to author, April 1963.

College Catalogs

Katalog der Lehranstalten der deutschen evang.-lutherischen Synode von Missouri, Ohio und anderen Staaten, 1875—1917.

Catalog of the Educational Institutions of the Evangelical Lutheran Synod of Missouri, Ohio, and Other States, 1917—32.
Concordia Teachers College Summer School, 1932—34.
C. T. C. Correspondence Division Catalog, 1950—51.
Concordia Teachers College Catalog, 1932—64.

Convention Reports, The Lutheran Church — Missouri Synod
Proceedings (Synodal-Berichte)
  A. *Verhandlungen der Allgemeinen Evangelisch-Lutherischen Synode von Missouri, Ohio und andern Staaten,* 1847—1938.
  B. *Proceedings . . . of The Lutheran Church — Missouri Synod,* 1917—62.
  C. *Zweiter Bericht des Oestlichen Distrikts,* 1856.

Minutes
Minutes of the Board of Control of the Addison Seminary, Addison, Ill.
Minutes of the Board of Control of Concordia Teachers College, River Forest, Ill.
Minutes of the Faculty of the Addison Seminary, Addison, Ill.
Minutes of the Faculty of Concordia Teachers College, River Forest, Ill.

Newspapers
Chicago *Tribune,* Oct. 13, 1913.
Oak Park Events, May 16, 1914.
Oak Leaves, Feb. 26, 1959.

Periodicals
Concordia Historical Institute Quarterly, I—XXXV (1928—61).
Der Lutheraner, I—CXVII (1844—1961).
Evangelisch-Lutherisches Schulblatt, I—LV (1865—1920).
Lutheran School Journal, LVI—LXXXII (1921—47).
Lutheran Education, LXXXIII—XCIX (1947—61).

Reports
Application of Concordia Teachers College, River Forest, Illinois, for Hines Surplus Property, April 2, 1962.

Affeldt, Waldemar W. *Annual Report on Teacher Placement,* 1962—63.

Faculty report of Concordia Teachers College, River Forest, Ill., to the Delegate Synod in Milwaukee, June 15—25, 1932. Unpublished.

Hahn, Arvin W., and Kenneth W. Schueler. *International Studies Program: Africa.*

Halter, Carl H. *Student Personnel Services at Concordia Teachers College, River Forest, Illinois.* Jan. 18, 1963.

Horst, Henry W. "Important Facts and Figures." Unpublished report to the Missouri Synod, 1918 and 1932.

Huegli, Albert G. *Six Year Report of the Academic Dean,* 1955—61.

Klinck, Arthur W. "Concordia Teachers College During the Past Fifteen Years." Unpublished report, Jan. 26, 1946.

Klinck, Arthur W. *The President's Report to the Board of Control of Concordia Teachers College, River Forest, Illinois, 1948—49.*

Koehneke, Martin L. *Blueprint for the Sixties,* 1961.

Lubbers, Irwin J., and Robert White. *Concordia Teachers College, River Forest, Illinois,* 1949.

Maurer, Albert V. *Women Teachers in the Church,* September 1947.

Neale, M. Gordon. *Report of a Survey of Concordia Teachers College, River Forest, Illinois,* May 24, 1948.

Reinke, Ralph L. *Concordia Student Teaching Program — Its Past, Present, and Future,* February 1963.

Report of Concordia Teachers College, River Forest, Illinois to National Council for Accreditation of Teacher Education, 1962.

Report of Concordia Teachers College, River Forest, Illinois to the Board of Higher Education, the Lutheran Church, Missouri Synod, Dec. 19, 1950.

Schmieding, Alfred F. *Fifth Annual Report of the Acadamic Dean of the School Year,* 1952—53.

Self-Survey of Concordia Teachers College, River Forest, Illinois, Jan. 25, 1958.

Others

Bartling, Henry. Account sheets from year 1864. Concordia Historical Institute in St. Louis.

College with a Cause, brochure published in 1962 by Concordia Teachers College.

Complete record of one year's expense at Addison, 1884. Unsigned.

Concordia Teachers College Men's Club Constitution, 1936.

Constitution of the Student Association of C. T. C., 1953 revision.

Dedication Program, "Einweihungs-Feier des Evangelical Lutheran Concordia Teachers College," River Forest, Ill., Oct. 12, 1913.

Dedication Service Program, River Forest, Ill., Oct. 28, 1951.

Die Verfassung der deutschen, evangelisch-lutherischen Synode von Missouri, Ohio und anderen Staaten — 1846.

Marquardt, E. W., F. Rittmueller, and Louis Leeseberg, *An die Brueder der Evangelisch-Lutherischen Synode von Missouri, Ohio, und anderen Staaten.* Undated.

Program, "Jubilaeums-Feier des Evangelisch-Lutherischen Lehrer-Seminars zu River Forest, Illinois," May 10, 1914.

Program, The Installation of the Rev. Martin L. Koehneke at the Opening of the Ninety-First Academic Year, Sept. 17, 1954.

Der Stadtmissionar, Dec. 15, 1912. Celebration of the cornerstone laying of the new Teachers Seminary in River Forest. Clipping in the Theodore Kohn Scrapbook in the archives at Concordia Teachers College, River Forest, Ill.

Twenty-fifth-anniversary program of the Lutheran Children's Welfare Society, 1941. Copy in Concordia Historical Institute, St. Louis.

SECONDARY SOURCES

Articles

Alma Mater, II—IV (1912—13).

Concordia, February 1914.

Northern Illinois Messenger, VI—VIII (1930—32).

Southern Lutheran, 1916.

The Correspondent, Bulletin of the Aid Association for Lutherans, Winter 1963.

The Forester, quarterly bulletin of Concordia Teachers College, River Forest, Ill., I—VII (1956—64).

The Spectator, college paper of Concordia Teachers College, River Forest, Ill., I—XXXIX (1925—64).

Books and Pamphlets

Beck, Walter H. *Lutheran Elementary Schools in the United States.* St. Louis: Concordia Publishing House, 1939.

Coates, Thomas. *The Making of a Minister.* Conference essay, published in 1954.

Dau, William T., ed. *Ebenezer.* St. Louis: Concordia Publishing House, 1922.

Fuelling, Daniel W., ed. *Zion Lutheran Parish.* (A Review of the History of Zion Church, Bensenville, Illinois, 1838—1963, on its 125th anniversary). Published by the congregation.

Grosse, T. Johannes. *Geschichte der deutschen Evangelisch-Lutherischen Gemeinde zu Addison, Du Page County, Illinois.* Chicago: Franz Gindele Printing Co., 1888.

Krauss, E. A. W. *Auskunft ueber das deutsche ev.-luth. Schullehrer-Seminar zu Addison, Illinois.* Undated brochure of information, published about 1900.

Lindemann, J. C. W. *Amerikanisch-Lutherische Schul-Praxis.* St. Louis: Concordia Publishing House, 1879.

Meyer, Carl S. *A Brief Historical Sketch of The Lutheran Church — Missouri Synod.* St. Louis: Concordia Publishing House, 1963.

Poellot, Daniel E. *A Century of Christian Education, 1849—1949.* St. Paul's Lutheran School, Addison, Ill. Publisher not given.

Repp, Arthur C., ed. *100 Years of Christian Education.* Fourth Yearbook of the Lutheran Education Association, 1947.

Scherer, Ross D. "The Evangelical Lutheran Orphan's Home (Addison, Illinois) 1873—1940." Unpublished master's thesis, University of Chicago, Chicago, Ill., 1947.

Schlesselman, Robert, ed. "Rejoice in the Lord." Golden-anniversary booklet of St. Paul's Evangelical Lutheran Church, Addison, Illinois.

Stellhorn, August C. *Schools of The Lutheran Church — Missouri Synod.* Saint Louis: Concordia Publishing House, 1963.

Weiss, Hildegard. "Excerpts for Concordia Teachers College Women's Auxiliary Rally," 1959. Unpublished.

Zagel, Hermann H. *Aus Frühlingstagen.* Erie, Pa.: The Erie Printing Company, 1923.

Others

Handbook of The Lutheran Church — Missouri Synod. 1963 edition.

Fuerbringer, Ludwig, Theodore Engelder, and Paul E. Kretzmann, eds. *The Concordia Cyclopedia.* St. Louis: Concordia Publishing House, 1927.

Lueker, Erwin L., ed. *Lutheran Cyclopedia.* St. Louis: Concordia Publishing House, 1954.

Appendices

Appendix A

FACULTY MEMBERS

Pre-Addison

	Year Installed	Accepted Another Call, Retired, or Resigned	Date of Death
Rev. Friedrich Lochner	1855	1857	Feb. 14, 1902
Rev. Philipp Fleischmann	1855	1864	Sept. 11, 1878
Rev. H. Ludwig Dulitz	1855	1857	Nov. 27, 1885

Addison and River Forest

	Year Installed	Accepted Another Call, Retired, or Resigned	Date of Death
C. August Selle	1861	1893	April 3, 1898
Johann C. W. Lindemann	1864		Jan. 15, 1879
1st President, 1864—79			
Karl Brauer	1866	1897	May 12, 1907
Herman Duemling	1870	1874	March 11, 1913
Clemens E. Haentzschel	1874		Oct. 21, 1890
T. Johannes Grosse	1875	1879 °	Feb. 14, 1919
Theodore Brohm	1879	1913	April 27, 1926
3d President, 1905—13			
Eugene A. W. Krauss	1880	1905	Oct. 9, 1924
2d President, 1880—1905			
Ernest Homann	1881	1911	Jan. 4, 1912
Johann L. Backhaus	1884	1915	March 11, 1919
Frederick Koenig	1891	1909	May 20, 1922
Frederick Lindemann	1893		Dec. 13, 1907
Frederick Rechlin	1893		Dec. 9, 1915
G. C. Albert Kaeppel	1897		Jan. 11, 1934
Albert H. Miller	1906	1943(—1947) †	July 30, 1959
Ferdinand H. Schmitt	1906 ‡	1946	Sept. 24, 1962
Edward W. A. Koehler	1909	1947(—1951) †	May 12, 1951
C. W. Gustav Eifrig	1909	1942	Nov. 1, 1949
Martin Lochner	1912		Feb. 6, 1945
William C. Kohn	1913	1939	March 13, 1943
4th President, 1913—38			
Ernst H. Engelbrecht	1915	1943(—1944) †	Feb. 28, 1944
Oscar F. Rusch	1916		Nov. 25, 1940
Henry C. Gaertner	1921	1943(—1951) †	March 7, 1952
Alfred F. Schmieding	1922	1958(—1963) †	May 4, 1963
Albert H. Beck	1923 ‡		May 30, 1962
Paul M. Bretscher	1923 ‡	1941	
Arthur E. Diesing	1923	1958	
Richard T. Rohlfing	1925 ‡		April 13, 1958
Theodore C. Appelt	1926 ‡		Jan. 15, 1961
Walter O. Kraeft	1926		March 30, 1960
Theodore J. C. Kuehnert	1927	1954(—) †	
Otto J. Beyers	1936 ‡	1937	
Wilfred F. Kruse	1938		

Albert V. Maurer	1939		
Arthur W. Klinck	1939	1953	Aug. 9, 1959
5th President, 1939—53			
Herbert H. Gross	1940		
Richard A. Lange	1941 ‡		
Walter R. Roehrs	1941	1944	
Edwin J. Wibracht	1941 ‡	1952	
Herman O. A. Keinath	1943		June 13, 1952
G. Herbert Reifschneider	1943		Sept. 10, 1944
Carl H. Scaer	1943		
Victor G. Hildner	1944		
Albert G. Huegli	1944 ‡	1961	
John W. Klotz	1945	1959	
Emil H. Deffner	1945 ‡	1962	
Walter E. Buszin	1946	1947	
Siegbert W. Becker	1947	1963	
Carl F. Halter	1948		
Paul G. Bunjes	1951		
John F. Choitz	1951	1958	
Walter A. Vahl	1951 ‡		
Paul A. Mundinger	1952 ‡		
Martin C. Pieper	1953 ‡		
Daniel E. Poellot	1953 ‡		
Neelak S. Tjernagel	1953		
Martin L. Koehneke	1954		
6th President, 1954—			
F. Samuel Janzow	1954		
Carl L. Waldschmidt	1954 ‡		
Victor C. Krause	1955 ‡		
Arvin W. Hahn	1957 ‡		
Waldemar W. Affeldt	1958 ‡		
Albert E. Glock	1959 ‡		
Ralph L. Reinke	1959 ‡		
Leslie R. Zeddies	1959 ‡		
Merle L. Radke	1960 ‡		
Marvin J. Dumler	1961 ‡		
Paul G. Grotelueschen	1961 ‡		
William H. Lehmann, Jr.	1961 ‡		
Wilbert H. Rosin	1961		
Ralph D. Gehrke	1962 ‡		
Lawrence R. Rast	1962 ‡	1964	
James O. Roberts	1962 ‡		
Thomas E. Gieschen	1963 ‡		
Richard W. Hillert	1963 ‡		
Eldor C. Sieving	1963 ‡		
Victor B. Streufert	1963 ‡		
Kenneth A. Domroese	1964 ‡		
Kenneth R. Schueler	1964 ‡		
Al H. Senske	1964 ‡		
Walter M. Wangerin	1964 ‡		

* Continued to serve part-time.

† After retirement continued to serve on modified service until year indicated in parentheses.

‡ Served prior to installation as professor (see next list).

Visiting Professors, Lecturers, Assistant Professors, Instructors, Part-Time Instructors, Graduate Assistants, Assistants, or Coaches

Wilhelm F. Hoffmann 1865—66
Rev. T. Johannes Grosse 1879—82
Rev. Theodore J. Brohm 1879—81
J. Merkel 1879—81
Ferdinand H. Schmitt 1905—06 °
A. Guettler 1909—10
W. Sassmannshausen 1910—12
H. B. Camann 1911—13
Alfons Kaeppel 1912—13
Albert H. Beck 1914—23 °
Theodore C. Appelt 1915—17 °
Paul M. Bretscher 1915—18 °
Rev. Herbert Fehner 1917—20
Rev. E. Jahn 1918—19
Rev. Herbert Moeller '1919—21
Rev. F. C. Rathert 1920—23
Richard T. Rohlfing 1921—23 °
Adolf Smukal 1921—22
Bernhard Bunjes 1922—25
Rev. H. C. Guebert 1922—23
H. Rauschelbach 1923—24
Rev. Paul Boester 1923—25
Rev. C. Abel 1924—26
Harold Pollex 1924—26
Emanuel Unrath 1924—26
Fred C. Schmitt 1925—28
Edgar Jaeger 1926—27
Luther Schuessler 1926—31
Arthur W. Gross 1927—37
G. Rast 1927—28
A. C. Koy 1929—34
H. F. Ellerman 1933—37
Otto Beyers 1935—36 °
William A. Hedtke 1937—40
Richard A. Lange 1936—41 °
Rev. O. A. Geiseman 1939—40
Edwin J. Wibracht 1938—41 °
Emil H. Deffner 1938—45 °
Ernst A. Flotow 1939—43
Herbert C. Albrecht 1940—42
Albert G. Huegli 1940—44 °
Marga Link 1941—
Emory Bauer 1941—43
Elmer F. Eggold 1942—45
Liberty Bergengren 1943—45
Ruth Eggold 1943—44
Rev. Enno O. Gahl 1943—44
Eugene Huebschmann 1943—46
Emma Menke 1943—64

Rev. E. H. Pittelko 1943—44; 1952—56
Rev. Paul Roeder 1943—45
Charlotte Beckman 1944—45
Edwin Eggers 1944—48
Norbert R. Engebrecht 1944—53
Elmer Jagow 1944—56
Edward Krafft 1944—45
Edward O. Lange 1944—47
Laura Mackensen 1944—59
James Engel 1945—46
Eugene W. Jobst, Jr. 1945—46
Verna Reich 1945—46
Robert Breihan 1946—47
Eugene H. Burger 1946—48
Don C. Dinkmeyer 1946—54
Clarence M. Drews 1946—
Rev. August H. Lange 1946—56
Alma Muller 1946—48
Martin C. Pieper 1946—53 °
Helen Schaper 1946—56
Helga Tjernagel 1946—48
Carl L. Waldschmidt 1946—54 °
Jane Waltz 1946—47
Richard Wegner 1946—47
Gladys Robertson Geisler 1947—48
Rev. Richard Luecke 1947—49
Matthew Lundquist 1947—54
Theodore Schmidt 1947—48
Theodore Beck 1948—49; 1951—53;
    1960—61
Edith Morrison 1948—
Rev. Robert L. Schroeter 1948—57
Lorraine Storz 1948—50
Edwin Trusheim 1948—50
Walter A. Vahl 1948—51 °
Kenneth Breimeier 1949—50
Margaret Hermes 1949—55
Edward A. Lange 1949—50
Margaret Luecke 1949—52
Carl Schalk 1949—50
Alfred Gras 1950—59
William J. Hassold 1950—51
Kenneth L. Heinitz 1950—51; 1957—
Evelyn Heidtke 1950—53; 1954—64
Victor C. Krause 1950—55 °
Rev. Richard C. Stuckmeyer 1950—54
Arvin W. Hahn 1951—57 °
Rev. Paul A. Mundinger 1951—52 °
Rev. Daniel E. Poellot 1951—53 °

A. Kurt Grams 1952—53
Carol Nagle 1952—55
Rev. E. H. Pittelko 1943—44; 1952—56
Rev. Delwin B. Schneider 1952—53
Fred A. Spurgat 1952—
Victor B. Streufert 1952—54;
  1957—63 *
Robert Greising 1953—55; 1962—63
Paul G. Grotelueschen 1953—61 *
Donald P. Meyer 1953—55
Harriet Meyer 1953—55; 1956—59
Erich Von Behren 1953—54
Leslie R. Zeddies 1953—59 *
Phillip Elbert 1954—55
Robert L. Conrad 1954—55
Milton W. Schmidt 1954—58
Reuben V. Stohs 1954—59
Herbert Jaekel 1955—56
Lewis Kuehm 1955—56
Cornell J. Kusmik 1955—
William H. Lehmann, Jr. 1955—61 *
Paul A. Meyer 1955—57
Lawrence R. Rast 1955—62 *
Francis L. Schubkegel 1955—57
Jerome T. Schwab 1955—56
Gerhardt C. Becker 1956—57
Paul B. Bouman 1956—57
Harold F. Brockberg 1956—
Ronald E. Freudenberg 1956—59
Werner Grams 1956—57
Rudolph W. Heinze 1956—58; 1964—
Julia Hennig 1956—58; 1962—
Rodney E. Millard 1956—58
Frederick H. Pralle 1956—63
Ralph L. Reinke 1956—59 *
James O. Roberts 1956—62 *
Donald D. Wall 1956—60
Andrew M. Weyermann 1956—58
Paul Bartels, Jr. 1957—58
Robert L. Busse 1957—
Thomas E. Gieschen 1957—63 *
Albert E. Glock 1957—59 *
Edna Mae Goshen 1957—58
Wayne Hahn 1957—59
Eunice Heyne 1957—
Ruth Ladewig 1957—60
Walter W. Martin 1957—
August Prahlow 1957—59
Merle L. Radke 1957—60 *
Arthur Simon 1957—59
Gordon O. Besch 1958—
Kenneth A. Domroese 1958—64 *

Marvin J. Dumler 1958—61 *
Roberta Esch 1958—62
Clayton A. Fischer 1958—59
Herbert M. Gotsch 1958—
James B. Ilten 1958—60
Beverly Lueking 1958—60
George Martinek 1958—61
Charles R. Smith 1958—59
Agnes Vetter 1958—61
David L. Wetzel 1958
Janet Adler 1959—60
Theodore Bundenthal 1959—62
Harvey Chandler 1959—60
Gerald A. Danzer 1959—61
William Galen 1959—60
Gloria Bonnin Hillert 1959—62; 1963
Richard W. Hillert 1959—63 *
Frances Becker Koenig 1959—64
Henry L. Lettermann 1959—
Rev. Stephan Mazak 1959—60
Martin J. Neeb, Jr. 1959—
George R. Nielsen 1959—
Walter E. Penk 1959—62
Audrey Ricketts 1959—60
Harold W. Rock 1959—
Kenneth R. Schueler 1959— *
Donald A. Spitz 1959—64
Walter M. Wangerin 1959—64 *
Carl W. Bollwinkel 1960—
Max R. Culver 1960—
Edwin K. Eckert 1960
Marion Hackbarth 1960—61
Wesley W. Isenberg 1960—
Carl H. Ivey 1960—
Natalie Jenne 1960—
Frederick D. Koenig 1960—61
Frederick L. Kolch 1960—62
Adolph H. Kramer 1960
Paul T. Kreiss 1960—
Henry R. Latzke 1960—
Joyce Nahrwold 1960—62
Lowell Nissen 1960—61
Allan Oesterreich 1960—62
Joyce Panke 1960—64
Theodora Poehler 1960—61
Andrew K. Prinz 1960—
Harold T. Rohlfing 1960—
Al H. Senske 1960—64 *
Marvin C. Wunderlich 1960—64
Arthur L. Cohrs 1961—
Lloyd C. Foerster 1961—
Ulric C. Foster 1961—

Ralph D. Gehrke 1961—62 *
Richard J. Gotsch 1961—64
Kenneth L. Heinitz 1950—51; 1957—
Nicolas K. Kiessling 1961—
Patricia Schad Leege 1961—64
Harlan D. McConnell 1961—
Judith Miessler 1961—63
Charles W. Ore 1961—
Karl A. Robert 1961—
Ray N. Scherer 1961—62
Roy V. Schoenborn 1961—
Kenneth E. Shewmaker 1961—64
Eldor C. Sieving 1961—63 *
Marvin H. Bartell 1962—
Charles R. Englund 1962—
Charles D. Froehlich 1962—
John L. Haubenstricker 1962—
Joan Isenberg 1962—63
John D. Jungemann 1962—
Robert R. Kirst 1962—
David C. Leege 1962—64
James A. Lichtenberger 1962—64
Elyse Machnek 1962—64
Roland W. Oesterreich 1962—
Walter E. Peterson 1962—
Arnola Reinitz 1962—
David E. Rhea 1962—64
Carol Rubow 1962—
Stephen A. Schmidt 1962—
Gertrude Schlueter 1962—63
David T. Stein 1962—
Susanne Swibold 1962—63
Roger W. Uitti 1962—
John D. Weinhold 1962—
Elmer A. Arnst 1963—
John E. Bohnert 1963—

Walter R. Bouman 1963—
James F. Cassens 1963—
Darlene Crampton Fahrenkrog 1963—
Edward J. Keuer 1963—
Ralph J. Kirchenberg 1963—
Lois Klatt 1963—
Ruth Lassanske 1963—
Wayne E. Lucht 1963—
Judith Meier 1963—
Frank B. Miller 1963—
Raymond M. Moehrlin 1963—
Elizabeth Oswald 1963—
Clara Putnik 1963—
Ernst H. Roemke 1963—
Miriam Roth 1963—
Robert Sorenson 1963—
Arnold D. Studtmann 1963—
Gail Voigt 1963—64
Richard W. Wetzel 1963—64
Diana Wolf 1963—
Mary L. Almjeld 1964—
Karin Anderson 1964—
Herbert J. Arkebauer 1964—
Conrad J. Aumann 1964—
Doris Breitenfeld 1964—
Clarence J. Dockweiler 1964—
Thomas O. Faszholz 1964—
Alfred J. Freitag 1964—
David W. Friedrichs 1964—
Charles W. Goan 1964—
Richard J. Heschke 1964—
Elaine F. Klein 1964—
Evangeline L. Rimbach 1964—
Carol E. Stellwagen 1964—
Iris J. Wiese 1964—
Wesley H. Wilkie 1964—

* Called to a professorship (see previous list).

Supervising Teachers at the Campus Training School

The following teachers have been engaged by the college to serve at the campus training school, Grace Lutheran School, River Forest, and at times have assisted in the instructional program of the college.

Herman J. Speckhard 1930—42
Irma Beck 1937—42
Morella Mensing 1942—
Elfrieda Miller 1942—
Marie Henricksen 1947—50
Gertrude Drews 1947—51
Elaine Guba 1951—52
Beatrice Kimbllin 1951—
Verna Rahdert 1951—

Eleanore Kressman 1952—53
Evelyn Kressman 1952—54
Doris Brauer 1953—54
Eunice Merz 1954—55
Loise Blase Lohman 1955—57
Nancy Dombros Saar 1956—59
Betty Oehmke 1960—62
Katie Berg 1962—64
Marjorie Raess 1964—

Appendix B

MEMBERS OF THE BOARD OF CONTROL

Rev. Adolph G. G. Francke 1864—79
Rev. Henry Wunder 1864—89
F. Krage 1864--72
E. H. W. Leeseberg 1864—96
F. Buchholz 1872—81
H. Oehlerking 1872—93
Rev. William Bartling 1875—80
(Teacher Henry Bartling 1875—96)
  (appointed treasurer by board)
Rev. T. Johannes Grosse 1880—93
T. C. Diener 1881—83
H. Meier 1884—1906
Rev. Henry H. Succop 1890—1903
Rev. August Reinke 1893—1900
Johann Harmening 1893—1908
A. Weber 1896—1908
Rev. Hermann Engelbrecht 1900—09
Rev. Theodore Kohn 1903—13
Paul Schulze 1906—48
F. Rosenwinkel 1908—10
Louis Leeseberg 1908—13
Rev. William C. Kohn 1909—13
L. Blecke 1910—13
Rev. Frederick H. Brunn 1913—27

Rev. Ernst Werfelmann 1913—29
C. H. Zuttermeister 1913—32
G. A. Fleischer 1913—14
William Thoms 1914—16
William Schlake 1916—40
Rev. Alex Ullrich 1927—36
Rev. Adolf W. Bartling 1929—44
Christ H. Garbers 1932—52
Rev. Ernest T. Lams 1936—45
F. O. Linstead 1940—52
Rev. Paul L. Kluender 1944—52
Rev. Arthur H. Werfelmann 1945—60
Walter Peckat 1947—53
Teacher Alwin R. Roschke 1947—54
Teacher Emil H. Ruprecht 1950—
Dr. Waldemar Link 1950—59
Rev. Erwin L. Paul 1951—60; 1962—
Edgar M. Elbert 1953—
Lawrence W. Forster 1953—
Teacher Walter H. Hartkopf 1955—63
Rev. Enno O. Gahl 1959—
Adolph H. Rittmueller 1959—
Rev. Theodore F. Nickel 1960—
Teacher Roland F. Eggerding 1963—

The following Presidents of the Synod were ex-officio members of the board:

Carl F. W. Walther 1864—78
Henry C. Schwan 1878—99
Francis Pieper 1899—1911

Frederick Pfotenhauer 1911—35
John W. Behnken 1935—62
Oliver R. Harms 1962—

Appendix C

100TH ACADEMIC YEAR OFFICERS

The Lutheran Church — Missouri Synod

The Rev. Oliver R. Harms, D. D., *President*
The Rev. John W. Behnken, D. D., *Honorary President*
The Rev. Roland P. Wiederaenders, D. D., *First Vice-President*
The Rev. Theodore F. Nickel, D. D., *Second Vice-President*
The Rev. George W. Wittmer, D. D., *Third Vice-President*
The Rev. Arthur C. Nitz, D. D., *Fourth Vice-President*
The Rev. Walter C. Birkner, D. D., *Secretary*
Milton Carpenter, *Treasurer*

Board for Higher Education

The Rev. Hugo G. Kleiner, LL. D., *Chairman* (died Dec. 14, 1963)
The Rev. Leonard W. Heidemann, B. D., M. S. (elected *Chairman* April 1964)
Edwin Meese, Jr.
The Rev. Herbert A. Mueller
Donald Rosenberg, M. Ed.
Martin E. Strieter, LL. D.
Louis A. Wolfanger, Ph. D.
Arthur M. Ahlschwede, M. A., Litt. D., *Executive Secretary*

Board of Control

The Rev. Erwin L. Paul, President of the Northern Illinois District of The Lutheran Church — Missouri Synod, *Chairman*
Lawrence W. Forster, B. A., *Vice-Chairman*
Walter H. Hartkopf, M. A., *Secretary*
Edgar M. Elbert, M. A., LL. D.
The Rev. Enno O. Gahl, B. A.
Adolph H. Rittmueller
Emil H. Ruprecht, M. A.

Administrative Council

The Rev. Martin L. Koehneke, M. Ed., LL. D., *President*
Carl L. Waldschmidt, M. Mus., Ph. D., *Academic Dean and Acting Director of the Graduate Division*
Carl F. Halter, B. S., M. Mus., *Dean of Students*
Wilfred F. Kruse, M. S., LL. D., *Registrar and Director of Admissions*
Waldemar W. Affeldt, Ph. D., *Dean of Administration*
Frederick A. Spurgat, B. S., M. B. A., *Business Manager*
Martin J. Neeb, Jr., B. D., M. A., *Director of Field Services*

The Faculty

Affeldt, Waldemar W., Ph. D., Associate Professor of Education and Psychology
Arnst, Elmer A., M. A., Visiting Assistant Professor of Education and Psychology
Bartell, Marvin H., M. S., Instructor in Science and Mathematics

Besch, Gordon O., Ed. M., Assistant Professor of Science and Mathematics
Bohnert, John E., M. S., Instructor in Geography
Bollwinkel, Carl W., M. S., Assistant Professor of Biology
Bouman, Walter R., Th. D., Assistant Professor of Religion
Brockberg, Harold F., M. S., Assistant Professor of Physical Education
Bunjes, Paul G., M. Mus., Professor of Music
Busse, Robert L., M. Mus., Assistant Professor of Music
Cohrs, Arthur L., M. Mus., Instructor in Music
Culver, Max R., B. D., Assistant Professor of Sociology
Domroese, Kenneth A., Ph. D., Assistant Professor of Biology
Drews, Clarence M., M. A., Assistant Professor of Geography
Dumler, Marvin J., Ed. D., Associate Professor of Education and Psychology
Englund, Charles R., M. A., Instructor in Science and Mathematics
Fahrenkrog, Darlene Crampton, B. A., Instructor in Art
Foerster, Lloyd C., M. Ed., Assistant Professor of Education and Psychology
Froehlich, Charles D., A. M., Assistant Professor of Religion and Humanities
Gehrke, Ralph D., Ph. D., Associate Professor of Religion
Gieschen, Thomas E., M. Mus., Associate Professor of Music
Glock, Albert E., B. D., Associate Professor of Religion
Gotsch, Herbert M., M. Mus., Assistant Professor of Music
Gotsch, Richard J., S. T. M., Instructor in Religion
Gross, Herbert H., Ph. D., Professor of Geography
Grotelueschen, Paul G., M. A., Associate Professor of Speech and English
Hahn, Arvin W., Ph. D., Associate Professor of Geography and History
Halter, Carl F., M. Mus., Professor of Music
Haubenstricker, John L., B. S., Instructor in Education and Psychology
Heinitz, Kenneth L., Ph. D., Assistant Professor of English
Henning, Julia A., M. Mus., Assistant Professor of Music
Heyne, Eunice R., M. S. W., Assistant Professor of Social Science
Hildner, Victor G., M. Mus., Associate Professor of Music
Hillert, Richard W., M. Mus., Associate Professor of Music
Isenberg, Wesley W., B. D., Instructor in Religion
Ivey, Carl H., M. A. Ed., Assistant Professor of Education and Psychology
Janzow, F. Samuel, M. A., Associate Professor of Religion and English
Jenne, Natalie R., M. A., Assistant Professor of Music
Jungemann, John D., M. Ed., Instructor in Education and Psychology
Keuer, Edward J., Ph. D., Assistant Professor of Education and Psychology
Kiessling, Nicholas K., M. A., Instructor in Language and Humanities
Kirchenberg, Ralph J., M. S., Assistant Professor of Science and Mathematics
Kirst, Robert R., M. A., Instructor in Language and Humanities
Klatt, Lois A., B. S., Instructor in Physical Education
Koehneke, Martin L., LL. D., Professor of Religion
Koenig, Frances M., M. S., Assistant Professor of Physical Education
Krause, Victor C., Ph. D., Associate Professor of Education and Psychology
Kreiss, Paul T., Ed. M., Assistant Professor of German
Kruse, Wilfred F., LL. D., Professor of Chemistry
Kusmik, Cornell J., M. S. L. S., Assistant Professor of Education
Lange, Richard A., M. A., Associate Professor of Mathematics and Physics
Lassanske, Ruth J., M. A., Instructor in Language and Humanities
Latzke, Henry R., M. S. L. S., Instructor in Education
Leege, David C., B. A., Instructor in Social Science
Leege, Patricia A., M. Mus., Instructor in Music

Lehmann, William H., Jr., M. A., Associate Professor of Philosophy
Lettermann, Henry L., M. A., Assistant Professor of English
Lichtenberger, James A., B. S., Instructor in Physical Education
Link, Marga B., B. Mus., Instructor in Music
Lucht, Wayne E., Ph. D., Assistant Professor of Education and Psychology
Machnek, Elyse J., M. Mus., Instructor in Music
Martin, Walter W., M. A., Assistant Professor of Art
Maurer, Albert V., Ph. D., Professor of Education and Psychology
McConnell, Harlan D., M. Mus., Instructor in Music
Meier, Judith C., B. S., Graduate Assistant in Social Science
Menke, Emma, B. Mus., Assistant Professor of Music
Miller, Frank B., Ph. D., Visiting Professor of Education and Psychology
Moehrlin, Raymond M., M. S., Instructor in Science and Mathematics
Morrison, Edith M., B. A., Assistant Professor of German
Mundinger, Paul A., M. A., Associate Professor of Religion and History
Neeb, Martin J., Jr., Assistant Professor of Speech
Nielsen, George R., M. A., Assistant Professor of Social Science
Oesterreich, Roland W., M. A., Instructor in Language and Humanities
Ore, Charles W., M. Mus., Instructor in Music
Oswald, Elizabeth A., M. Mus., Instructor in Music
Panke, Joyce D., B. S., Instructor in Music
Peterson, Walter E., A. M., Assistant Professor of Physics
Pieper, Martin C., M. A., Associate Professor of Mathematics and Education
Poellot, Daniel E., B. D., Associate Professor of Religion
Prinz, Andrew K., Ph. D., Assistant Professor of Social Science
Radke, Merle L., M. A., Associate Professor of English
Rast, Lawrence R., M. Mus., Associate Professor of Music
Reinke, Ralph L., M. S., Associate Professor of Education and Psychology
Rhea, David E., B. A., Instructor in Social Science
Robert, Karl A., M. A., Assistant Professor of Social Science
Roberts, James O., Ph. D., Associate Professor of Education and Psychology
Rock, Harold W., M. S., Assistant Professor of Biology
Roemke, Ernst H., M. A., Assistant Professor of Education and Psychology
Rohlfing, Harold T., M. Mus., Instructor in Music
Rosin, Wilbert H., Ph. D., Associate Professor of Social Science
Roth, Miriam C., M. A., Instructor in Language and Humanities
Rubow, Carol L., M. A. Ed., Instructor in Education and Psychology
Scaer, Carl H., M. A., Associate Professor of English
Schmidt, Stephen A., M. A., Instructor in Education and Psychology
Schoenborn, Roy V., M. A., Assistant Professor of Art
Schueler, Kenneth R., B. A., Associate Professor of Religion
Senske, Albert H., Ed. D., Associate Professor of Education
Shewmaker, Kenneth E., M. A., Instructor in Social Science
Sieving, Eldor C., M. A., Associate Professor of Education and Psychology
Spitz, Donald A., M. Ed., Assistant Professor of Physical Education
Spurgat, Frederick A., M. B. A., Assistant Professor of Economics
Stein, David T., M. A., Instructor in Language and Humanities
Streufert, Victor B., M. A., Associate Professor of Sociology
Studtmann, Arnold D., B. A., Instructor in Science and Mathematics
Tjernagel, Neelak S., Ph. D., Professor of History and Religion
Uitti, Roger W., B. D., Instructor in Religion
Vahl, Walter A., M. A., Associate Professor of History and Political Science
Voigt, Gail L., B. A., Instructor in Music

Waldschmidt, Carl L., Ph. D., Professor of Music
Wangerin, Walter M., Ph. D., Professor of Religion and Education
Weinhold, John D., M. A., Instructor in Science and Mathematics
Wetzel, Richard W., B. D., Instructor in Psychology
Wolf, Diana J., M. S., Instructor in Art
Wunderlich, Marvin C., B. S., Instructor in Mathematics
Zeddies, Leslie R., Ph. D., Associate Professor of Music

Part-Time Faculty

Cassens, James F., B. D., Instructor in Psychology
Hillert, Gloria R., M. A., Assistant Professor in Biology
Miller, Elfrieda H., M. A., Assistant Professor of Education and Psychology
Putnik, Clara G., Doc. Sc., Visiting Assistant Professor of German

Emeriti

Deffner, Emil H., A. M., Associate Professor of Art
Diesing, Arthur E., M. A., Associate Professor of English and Humanities
Kuehnert, Theodore J. C., Litt. D., Professor of Education and Social Science
Mackensen, Laura, LL. D., Dean of Women

Appendix D

ENROLLMENTS, 1864—1964

The enrollments for 1864—1936 are men only, high school and college departments combined in the total.

1864—65	55	1888—89	203	1912—13	168
1865—66	58	1889—90	184	1913—14	188
1866—67	80	1890—91	202	1914—15	200
1867—68	94	1891—92	210	1915—16	233
1868—69	98	1892—93	223	1916—17	237
1869—70	94	1893—94	251	1917—18	208
1870—71	81	1894—95	197	1918—19	223
1871—72	75	1895—96	188	1919—20	213
1872—73	86	1896—97	180	1920—21	230
1873—74	99	1897—98	175	1921—22	315
1874—75	114	1898—99	176	1922—23	327
1875—76	136	1899—1900	183	1923—24	332
1876—77	118	1900—01	182	1924—25	416
1877—78	119	1901—02	195	1925—26	404
1878—79	122	1902—03	213	1926—27	382
1879—80	124	1903—04	222	1927—28	387
1880—81	115	1904—05	226	1928—29	376
1881—82	131	1905—06	225	1929—30	346
1882—83	124	1906—07	195	1930—31	401
1883—84	161	1907—08	201	1931—32	377
1884—85	200	1908—09	194	1932—33	324
1885—86	239	1909—10	175	1933—34	284
1886—87	207	1910—11	174	1934—35	275
1887—88	209	1911—12	171	1935—36	287

	High School			College			Special Students			Graduate Students			
	Boys	Girls	Total	Men	Women	Total	Men	Women	Total	Men	Women	Total	Grand Total
1936—37	162	2	164	127		127							291
1937—38	151		151	134		134							285
1938—39	161	15	176	136	23	159							335
1939—40	142	27	169	173	45	218							387
1940—41	150	46	196	148	53	201							397
1941—42	147	52	199	115	52	167							366
1942—43	146	58	204	119	59	178							382
1943—44	164	79	243	116	70	186							429
1944—45	147	87	234	97	93	190							424
1945—46	146	88	234	124	107	231							465
1946—47	115	76	191	164	112	276							467
1947—48	61	53	114	209	142	351							465
1948—49	34	44	78	223	178	401							479
1949—50	13	17	30	265	226	491							521

Appendix

	High School			College			Special Students			Graduate			Grand Total
	Boys	Girls	Total	Men	Women	Total	Men	Women	Total	Men	Women	Total	
1950—51	(High School			319	240	559							559
1951—52	discontinued)			337	220	557							557
1952—53				328	229	557							557
1953—54				341	280	621							621
1954—55				308	330	638							638
1955—56				300	364	664							664
1956—57				317	406	723							723
1957—58				320	474	794	1		1				795
1958—59				376	453	829	1	1	2				831
1959—60				362	488	850	2	9	11	16	2	18	879
1960—61				380	561	941	1	9	10	11	3	14	965
1961—62				410	617	1,027	4	7	11	19	4	23	1,061
1962—63				433	670	1,103	11	19	30	20	1	21	1,154
1963—64				429	680	1,109	6	17	23	20	6	26	1,158

SUMMER SCHOOL ENROLLMENTS

		College			Graduate School			Total Enrollment
		Men	Women	Total	Men	Women	Total	
1932	1 week	155	48	203				
1933	3 weeks	60	53	113				
1934	” ”	47	15	62				
1935	” ”	38	13	51 +	98 in institutes			
1936	5 ”	81	21	102 +	162 ” ”			
1937	” ”	88	24	112 +	96 ” ”			
1938	” ”	101	41	142 +	62 ” ”			
1939	” ”	104	23	127 +	34 ” ”			
1940	” ”	111	34	145 +	39 ” ”			
1941	” ”			155				
1942	” ”	88	38	126				
1943	11 weeks *	171	55	226				
1944	” ”			304				
1945	” ”			388				
1946	5 weeks	144	125	269				
1947	” ”	160	190	350				
1948	” ”	127	176	303				
1949	7 weeks	161	250	411				
1950	” ”	189	292	481				
1951	” ”	191	253	444				
1952	” ”	200	268	468				
1953	” ”	161	275	436				
1954	” ”	203	299	502				
1955	” ”	240	368	608				
1956	” ”	243	381	624				
1957	” ”	223	356	579				
1958	” ”	177	427	604	81	12	93	697
1959	10 weeks	204	464	668	110	17	127	795
1960	” ”	214	387	601	100	12	112	713
1961	” ”	186	378	564	118	22	140	704
1962	” ”	207	325	532	135	26	161	693
1963	” ”	211	358	569	127	37	164	733
1964	” ”	173	327	500	136	49	185	685

Appendix E

MAJOR EVENTS OF THE CENTENNIAL YEAR

Centennial Services of Worship and Academic Events

Epiphany Festival Service, January 6, 1964
    Preacher: Oliver R. Harms, D. D., LL. D.
        President, The Lutheran Church — Missouri Synod

Service of Dedication and Prayer, April 24, 1964
Distribution of Calls and Assignments
    Preacher: Martin L. Koehneke, M. Ed., LL. D.
        President, Concordia Teachers College

Centennial Baccalaureate Service, May 29, 1964
    Preacher: Erwin L. Paul, Chairman of the Board of Control of the College
        President of the Northern Illinois District,
        The Lutheran Church — Missouri Synod

Centennial Commencement, May 29, 1964
    Speaker: O. P. Kretzmann, D. D., LL. D.
        President, Valparaiso University

Summer Commencement, August 20, 1964
    Speaker: Arthur M. Ahlschwede, M. A., Litt. D.
        Executive Secretary, Board for Higher Education,
        The Lutheran Church — Missouri Synod

Opening Service of the 101st Academic Year, September 13, 1964
    Preacher: Martin L. Koehneke, M. Ed., LL. D.
        President, Concordia Teachers College

Dedication of Fine Arts I and Gymnasium Additions, October 11, 1964
    Preacher: John W. Behnken, D. D., LL. D.
        Honorary President, The Lutheran Church — Missouri Synod

Synodical Centennial Sunday, October 11, 1964

Founder's Day Convocation, October 12, 1964
    Speaker: Arthur L. Miller, Ph. D.
        Executive Secretary, Board of Parish Education,
        The Lutheran Church — Missouri Synod

Honors Convocation, November 5, 1964
    Speaker: Walter F. Wolbrecht, D. D., LL. D.
        Executive Director, The Lutheran Church — Missouri Synod

Closing Centennial Service, December 13, 1964
    Preacher: Martin L. Koehneke, M. Ed., LL. D.
        President, Concordia Teachers College

Centennial Cultural Events
LECTURE SERIES

The guest of the Division of Science and Mathematics:
FRANCIS O. SCHMITT, Ph. D.
Institute Professor, Massachusetts Institute of Technology
January 17, 1964

The guest of the Division of Language and Humanities:
JOHN CIARDI
Poetry Editor, *Saturday Review;* Visiting Professor, Tufts University
February 24, 1964

The guest of the Division of Education and Psychology:
ARTHUR T. JERSILD, Ph. D.
Professor, Teachers College, Columbia University
April 7, 1964

The guest of the Division of Religion:
CONRAD BERGENDOFF, Ph. D.
Executive Secretary, Board of Theological Education,
Lutheran Church in America; Former President of
Augustana College and Seminary
May 20 and 21, 1964

The guest of the Division of Music:
HOWARD HANSON, Ph. D.
Director of the Eastman School of Music, University of Rochester
October 19 and 20, 1964

The guests of the Division of Social Science:
ALBERT HUEGLI, Ph. D.
Vice-President of Academic Affairs, Valparaiso University

JAMES HASTINGS NICHOLS, Ph. D.
Professor, Princeton University
November 11 and 12, 1964

MUSICAL EVENTS

Benefit Concerts
The College Chorus and the Chicago Symphony Orchestra
Carl L. Waldschmidt, Ph. D., Director

The Passion of Our Lord According to St. Matthew
Orchestra Hall, Chicago, March 17, 1964

The Concordia Senior Choir
Thomas E. Gieschen, Director

Concert Tour in Michigan, New York, Connecticut, Maryland,
and Pennsylvania, March 31—April 6, 1964

The Concordia Junior Choir
Charles W. Ore, Director
Benefit concerts in 1964 in congregations cooperating with the
college in its Student Teaching Program

Other Events
Organ Recital, DAVID CRAIGHEAD
Eastman School of Music
January 21, 1964

Band Concert
Harold T. Rohlfing, Director
March 5, 1964, and May 3, 1964

DON COSSACK CHORUS AND DANCERS
March 7, 1964

Spring Concert: Concordia Senior Choir
April 12, 1964

Spring Concert: Concordia Junior Choir
April 26, 1964

Lecture Recital: Clavichord, Harpsichord, Piano
NEWMAN POWELL, Professor, Valparaiso University
May 12, 1964

Polychoral Festival: College Choirs
December 6, 1964

Advent Concert: College Chorus and Orchestra
The Messiah
December 6, 1964

DRAMATIC PRODUCTIONS

"The Enchanted"

Concordia Players
Roland W. Oesterreich, Director
February 1 and 2, 1964

"The Music Man"

David T. Stein, Director; Herbert M. Gotsch, Musical Director
May 9 and 10, 1964

"A Sleep of Prisoners"

Concordia Players
William H. Lehmann, Jr., Director
November 7 and 8, 1964

ART EXHIBITS

Paintings and Graphics from the collection of
JOSEPH RANDALL SHAPIRO, Oak Park, Illinois
February 2—21, 1964

Paintings by
SIEGFRIED REINHARDT, Kirkwood, Missouri
November and December 1964

Centennial Publications

COLLEGE WITH A CAUSE
A 304-page history of Concordia Teachers College, by Alfred J. Freitag, Superintendent of Walter A. Maier Memorial Lutheran High School, Los Angeles, California

CENTENNIAL THEOLOGICAL ESSAYS
Essays delivered by members of the Concordia Teachers College theological faculty at District conventions

CENTENNIAL EDUCATIONAL ESSAYS
Essays delivered by members of the Concordia Teachers College Faculty at District teachers conferences

MY SONS AND DAUGHTERS IN CHRIST
The brief addresses to graduates delivered by the President of the college in the past decade

CHANGELESS CHANGE
A 20-year report on Concordia Teachers College, embracing the decade of 1954—64 in retrospect, and a presentation of the 10-year program of the college for 1964—74

MOTIF
An on-campus journal designed to stimulate creative writing and creative activity in the arts, begun in 1960

THE PILLARS
The college yearbook enlarged in commemoration of the centennial

Centennial Gifts to the Church
"COLLEGE WITH A CAUSE"
A 16mm. color and sound recruitment film
June 1, 1964

"ALPHA AND OMEGA"
A 16mm. color and sound film on the process of Christian education
Christmas 1964

THE CENTENNIAL CHILDREN'S ALBUM
Designed to lead the lambs of Christ to the praise of their Creator, Redeemer, and Sanctifier
October 11, 1964

THE CENTENNIAL MUSIC ALBUM
Featuring choirs and artists on the college faculty
Homecoming 1964

CORRESPONDENCE DIVISION OFFERINGS
Designed to substantially enlarge its offerings
New catalog — February 15, 1964

SUNDAY SCHOOL TEACHER TRAINING BY CORRESPONDENCE
Designed to translate the present synodical Sunday School Teacher Training Course into a correspondence program
Initiation date: October 12, 1964

COLLEGE WITH A CAUSE
A history of the college sent to the libraries of all colleges and universities in the United States
Homecoming 1964

Centennial Summer Session
Summer school classes taught by professors of the college
June 15—August 21, 1964

Centennial Institutes
The Renaissance of the Organ and Its Literature, July 6—10
Paul G. Bunjes, Herbert M. Gotsch

Administration of District Parish Education, July 13—17
Edward J. Keuer, Donald A. Rosenberg

Sets, Operations, and Patterns, July 20—24
Richard A. Lange

Christian Education in the Inner City, July 20—24
Victor C. Krause, Victor B. Streufert

Parish Administration for Pastors and Principals, August 3—7
Waldemar W. Affeldt, Martin L. Koehneke

Lay Institute in Theology, August 3—7
Kenneth L. Heinitz, Kenneth R. Schueler, Walter M. Wangerin

Church Music Composition, August 10—14
Paul G. Bunjes, Richard W. Hillert, and others

Supervision of Student Teachers, August 10—14
A. H. Senske

Administration of Secondary Education, August 17—22
Paul W. Lange and others

Centennial Convention Essays and Essayists

SYNODICAL DISTRICT CONVENTIONS

Members of the theological faculty of the college presented the traditional theological essays at the majority of the District conventions during 1964.

DISTRICT TEACHERS CONFERENCES

Members of the faculty presented an essay at almost all annual District teachers conferences during 1964.

Centennial Homecoming Celebration

Every alumnus or alumna was asked to participate in the Homecoming celebration by their presence, writing letters to classmates, telephoning classmates on the night of October 17, and by contributing $100 or multiples thereof towards the Alumni Thankoffering.
October 16 and 17, 1964

Centennial Thankofferings

FOR SYNODICAL PURPOSES

The children of the church, especially in the Lutheran elementary schools, were asked to have a Service of Thanksgiving during the Centennial Year, as well as the young people attending Lutheran high schools, their offerings designated for the "Faith Forward" venture of the synod at Ebenezer Lutheran School in the inner city of Chicago, Illinois, and in support of the schools of the Southern District, respectively.

A traditional door collection for the Synodical Centennial Sunday, October 11, 1964, for scholarships and educational grants.

FOR CONCORDIA TEACHERS COLLEGE, RIVER FOREST, ILLINOIS

Alumni contributions of $100 for projects designated by the college.

Pastors and teachers conferences during 1964 were asked to designate offerings for scholarships and educational grants to students studying for the teaching ministry, as well as by District conventions and off-campus concerts of choirs and individual artists of the college.

THANKOFFERING OF THE NORTHERN ILLINOIS DISTRICT,
THE LUTHERAN CHURCH — MISSOURI SYNOD

In 1958 the Northern Illinois District resolved to make a thankoffering to God for the blessings accruing to the District from having the college in its midst. The goal of $875,000 for the erection of a chapel-auditorium culminated on March 8, 1964, with plans set for ground-breaking for The Memorial Chapel of Our Lord on Centennial Sunday, October 11, 1964.

Centennial Community Services

CONCORDIA CENTENNIAL TREES

One thousand rare and decorative dwarf red chestnut trees were to be planted in the Village of River Forest in the spring of 1964 upon favorable acceptance of the offer by the residents of the village.

FIFTH ANNUAL CHRISTMAS CIVIC CLUB DINNER

The college hosted the civic leaders of the community at a dinner and an evening of music provided by the choral and instrumental organizations of the college, December 5, 1964.

HISTORY OF THE COLLEGE

The history of the college was sent to the libraries of colleges and universities throughout the United States.

FEATURE ARTICLES

Feature articles and releases were made available to the various local and national communications media.

SUMMER SESSION

The educational opportunities of the centennial summer session were offered to the Chicagoland community.

Index